FASHION UNRAVELED

Jennifer Lynne Matthews

Publication by Los Angeles Fashion Resource

How to Start and Manage Your Own Fashion Design Business

Second Edition

Cover Design by Helen Munch-Ellingson

Book Design by Designarchy

Services for our readers:

Colleges, fashion schools, wholesale purchasing:
The Los Angeles Fashion Resource offers special rates
for universities, fashion schools and wholesale purchasing.

Updates:
Information contained in this book was current at the time
of publishing. For updates, check our website.

Contact us:
Los Angeles Fashion Resource
info@lafashionresource.com

Second printing February 2011

Publication by Los Angeles Fashion Resource

ISBN-10: 0983132801

ISBN-13: 978-0-9831328-0-6

Library of Congress Control Number: 2010916682

Acknowledgments

Special thanks to everyone who has supported me through my business and this book.

Misty Rose, I couldn't have gotten past the original book outline without your help.

Ashley Burke, you are an excellent editor even though you griped through it, thanks sissy.

Greg Matthews, my favorite accountant and father, your advice and guidance through the publishing world is grateful.

Kathy Matthews, I will always ask for your advice and listen to it.

David Fairbanks, my soul mate and the love of my life, you have been such an amazing influence in my life, thanks for being a part of it.

Tessa Poppe, my bff and partner-in-crime, your entrepreneurial drive keeps me going.

Irene Hernandez-Feiks, your encouragement and support has been a driving force in my business endeavors.

Andrea Baker, my friend and colleague, thanks for being a part of my book and letting me interview you over and over and over again.

Thanks to all my contributors: Timothy James Andrews, Colleen Quen, "M", Mallory Whitfield, Candice Gwinn, Simplicio Michael Luis and Lorraine Sanders.

Thanks to my illustrators: Krystle de los Santos, Val Chang and Kristen Blackmore.

And last but not least, my students at FIDM who are my inspiration.

Contents

Preface

I opted to write the second edition of Fashion Unraveled because times are changing, and changing fast. The first edition was written before the economic crash of 2008 and was released in early 2009. Since then, the industry has changed drastically, leading to a rise in entrepreneurs. The second edition covers more material, including additional business building forms and a book-wide case study. The case study follows a small business from its initial planning phase through to its production development. Each form in the book is followed by this case study.

This edition is not just an update, but a complete rewrite. One may find owning both editions to be helpful in building their business. Many chapters have changed and the order has been rearranged, but my message remains constant. I want you to have a business that thrives. The first edition will remain available for purchase.

This was once a book of 25 chapters, but I chose to break down the chapters into more specific sections for ease of use and reading. Designed for the creative mind (a.k.a. individuals that might be prone to having a short attention span), I limited the size of text areas and added space for your own notes, ideas and research.

I understand that every business is not the same, so I have elaborated in some areas and provided links for further research on particular subjects. As for starting any business, I highly recommend reading everything you can get your hands on during the research stage of your business. There are some additional texts listed throughout this book as recommended reading. I also recommended reading books on small business management and marketing strategies.

Many of the sections in this book include forms to assist you in your business venture. The forms are also available as a PDF forms-only book (which is downloadable) on the Fashion Unraveled website (www.fashionunraveled.com). To assist in your business development, fill out each form as thoroughly as possible before proceeding to the next chapter. If you must stop and conduct additional research, please take the time and do so. Your research will help you through the process of building your business concept.

Throughout this book, I offer advice based on my personal experience. It is not to be construed as legal advice by any means. It is best to consult a lawyer for any legal issues concerning your business.

My Story

My story starts in 1976. At my birth, the doctor exclaimed "this little girl will one day be a fashion designer." Ok, that didn't happen, but I did know from a very early age that I was going to make clothes for a living. My grandmother, Nana, looked after my sister and I after school in our formative years. An artist at heart, she helped us discover the creativity within ourselves. Each day of the week was designated for different crafts: pottery and sculpture, sewing and crocheting, painting and cooking. I learned to love the sewing aspect and my sister grew to love the painting. Needless to say, we both went into the arts.

Initially, I made clothes for myself and friends, starting around the age of 12 with simple tops, hats & scrunchies. When I decided to go away to college, I chose Florida State University (for an in-state school) and majored in fashion design. I quickly outgrew their program. Craving more knowledge, I moved upwards towards New York. I transferred to New York City's Fashion Institute of Technology, specialized in intimate apparel and finally graduated in 1999. After a very brief stint working for the most wretched designer in NYC, (preceded by a very lengthy process of finding that job) I decided I was not meant to work for anyone but myself.

I moved back to Florida in 2000 and went back to school for graphics, web design and even a little programming. My new career path lasted only a year before I was itching to design clothes again. In 2002, I moved to San Francisco with the ambition to start my own fashion design business. I read every book out there on the subject, met with advisors and consultants, hired a pattern maker to review my patterns, and answered every single ad on Craigslist for designers and got my name (now chosen as Porcelynne) out there.

Where did this get me? 2004 and $20,000+ in the hole. This following a series of financial mistakes due to my lack of planning and advisors telling me I was ready to launch my business. I had invested in a beautiful silk charmeuse and a French lace (that I wanted so badly), only to discover that my customer was so off target, I didn't sell a single thing. No book told me, nor did any of the fashion consultants warn me of the complexities of what I was getting ready to dive into.

One year later, I had to step away from my business and reevaluate what I was doing. Unfortunately, I had mounted enough debt to put a down payment on a house. I regrouped, started a restaurant job, and put every extra cent I had into building up my business again, but with a new perspective.

I had re-launched my business from scratch. The money that I had saved to start my business back in 2002, was long gone. I re-launched my business without capital and insisted on doing all my own production to help save on expenses. However, this resulted in back pain and additional stress.

Things started to turn around. A few years went by, I had my designs in several stores, had taken my production to a factory, and then a new opportunity crossed my path. Without any planning, I decided over the course of a Christmas cocktail party and a bottle of wine to open up my own boutique. What better place to showcase my designs than my own storefront. It was great to have all my designs in the front window, but I was not prepared for the 80-90 hour work weeks. Too much of my focus was on keeping the store open and not on my clothing line.

Two years later, I closed the shop's doors for good. The store had evolved into an independent designer cooperative boutique where a dozen designers took turns working and sharing store responsibilities. Despite this, I was doing nothing for my clothing line, my sanity, or my bank account. I had maxed out my credit cards just to keep the doors open. Once I closed the store, I was able to see that opening it in the first place was not the right move for what I really wanted to accomplish.

After all this, here's the funny part. Once I closed the store and took my business online, I actually started selling more than I ever did before. I now spend 5-10 hours a week on my business and am making a profit, three times more than when I worked 90 hour weeks. 10 years later and I am now where I want to be.

I am now an educator, a mentor, a designer and a successful business woman. My hope is that this book will help you work through your own business planning, while avoiding the mistakes that I made.

- Jennifer Lynne Matthews

Designer, Porcelynne Lingerie

www.porcelynne.com

INTRODUCTION TO THE INDUSTRY AND BUSINESS OWNERSHIP

Chapter 1
Introduction to the Fashion Industry

In the mid 1800's, an Englishman by the name of Charles Frederick Worth became the first recognized fashion designer. Worth started his career working in English textile houses, although he later moved to Paris and took work at a fashion accessories boutique.

While working there, he met his bride, a model for the store's accessories. He designed dresses for her to wear while modeling the store's merchandise and attention to his clothing immediately followed. Worth proposed a business partnership with the accessories designers, but they did not wish to expand their business to include clothing. Dressmaking was not seen as a glamorous profession and they didn't want to scar their reputation by adding such a venture to their successful business.

Worth knew he had something, given all the attention he received for his wife's outfits. He sought out an investor and opened up a dress shop. This was unique at the time. Most women would go to a dressmaker and have their desires created in a fabric they hand picked. The idea of purchasing a ready made garment "off the rack" was unheard of.

He created 4 collections each year and showed them off in a seasonal fashion show. His dress shop later became described as an atelier. Women traveled to his shop and had his collection modeled for them. They choose a design to fit their style and had it tailored to fit their bodies.

Worth was meticulous about fit and had a love for exquisite fabrics (due to his earlier career).

Worth marketed his designs to royalty and soon after his creations were seen on the wealthy, he became a highly demanded designer. Worth is credited as being the first to sew a designer label into a garment.

In Paris, he was considered a couturier, however today, we recognize him as the father of what we now know as Haute Couture. Since Worth, the profession has expanded beyond the local tailor and covers the gamut of small local designers to large fashion producers.

Education in Fashion

Education (in the United States) in the area of fashion design began in 1904 at Parsons School of Design in New York. It was founded as a creative and artistic extension of the industrial revolution, joining such ranks as graphic designers and illustrators. It is reported that the first school to teach fashion design internationally was actually in 1841 at ESMOD International. The number of schools that offer fashion design programs in the United States is just over 100 (117 on my last count) out of the estimated 200 fashion design programs worldwide.

Fashion design has become a sought after profession thanks to the popularity of shows such as Project Runway, Launch My Line, The Fashion Show and Guide to Style. The mother of these show, Project Runway, initially aired in 2004 and has created a tidal wave of new aspiring designers into the schools and ultimately in the industry workforce.

The urgency for graduates to work for big designers has decreased in recent years. The crumbling economy has given these aspiring students a different job market. Ten years ago, students were told that there was only 1 job for every 10 graduates. Today, those numbers are closer to 1 for every 20. This is a disappointing number for our graduates, but these numbers aren't industry specific. A down economy forces more and more people to go back to school, and the more graduates we have, the higher the demand is for these jobs.

Schools are slowly adapting to the idea of a tight job market and have begun adopting entrepreneurship programs to help ensure their graduates' success. Fashion Unraveled is designed to work with these entrepreneurship programs and is already being used in a dozen educational programs worldwide.

Entrepreneurs in Fashion

The most common misconception about the fashion industry is that is it glamorous and it will make you famous. You can become famous if you get lucky, but in reality most designers and design businesses live well beneath the window of fame and exist in local industry. As for being glamorous, if you enjoy working long hours with a high level of stress, you are in luck! That is what you might expect, unless you have a trust fund and can hire a plethora of minions to answer to your every beckoned call.

Many designers that intend to start their own business have not weighed all the work involved and do not have a background in business. Many do not know how to plan for the future, and very few know anything about running a business. This lack of planning and education is the reason so many design businesses fail. According to the U.S. Small Business Office of Advocacy, 3 out of 10 small businesses fail in the first 2 years and only about 5 of those 10 survive after 5 years. These statistics have changed significantly. Not even 5 years ago, the statistics were that 95% of small businesses fail in the first 5 years. This shows that we are learning how to run a business better than our predecessors had.

Here's a reality check. You are about to become a business owner. You will be spending more than 90% of your time running your business and less than 10% of your time designing (and in many cases that percentage is closer to 1% or 2%). After reading this book, hopefully, the 90% will look just a little bit less intimidating.

The Design Process

In this age of technology, it is common to forget that the process of creating a product—in the fashion industry or any other—takes much longer than just a click of a button. On average, an entrepreneurial designer takes one to two years to go from the initial design concept to a completed product ready for sales and production. (Although this is true, there are opportunities such as Etsy.com and Artfire.com that provide the ability to get a product into the marketplace much faster. Even though programs like these are available, many crafters, hobbyists and designers place their product into the marketplace before properly pricing their merchandise for profit.)

The first step for any creative business is researching the market and creating a product that caters to that market. Many designers choose to design their collections within the trends for each season. One reason for this, the retail giants advertise the trends they sell, which causes shoppers to desire those trends. Designing to those trends brings customers closer to the purchase.

In planning collections, how would one know the trends for 1 to 2 years away? Based on the current trends, designers can make predictions of what the trends will evolve into; or use trend reporting services such as Doneger, Perlers or Promostyl. These services are often too costly for designer entrepreneurs to acquire, but online subscriptions to sites such as Worth Global Style Network (WGSN) are well used in this manner. Occasionally, it is possible to attend a webinar or presentation from one of the trend forecasters (although usually to help solicit business).

The second step is sourcing, or finding resources for the fabrics and trims that you will be using for construction. This begins the development of your collection. Whether you develop patterns and samples on your own, or work with a technical designer; you must create prototypes for the entire collection and test them for fit and design. The samples usually go through several changes before the final products are chosen. Many designs are changed and sometimes even canceled before they hit the production room floor. (This is covered in detail in the section on production, starting at Chapter 8.)

The samples that were created are then marketed to retail buyers. They can be exhibited at trade shows, shown through showrooms and independent reps, or directly marketed to a store. In traditional selling, retailers place their orders up to six months prior to the actual season when they plan to sell the collection. These orders specify the quantity of the product you will produce and when the retailer expects delivery. (This is covered in the section on sales, beginning on Chapter 20.)

Chapter 2
Entrepreneurship

What do you expect by becoming a small business owner? Why is it that you want to start your own business? Is it the money? The hours? Is it due to unemployment? Is it a life long dream of yours? Or is it because the jerk that works across the hall from you steals your lunch and hums tunes from Disney films all day?

There are many reasons to decide to be your own boss, but it is important to be realistic about your expectations. Take a minute to answer these questions:

- How much money do you expect to earn?

- When do you expect to make a profit?

- Will you be seeking investors or a loan?

- How much of an investment do you plan on contributing to your business in order to get it started?

- Do you plan on keeping your job while you get your business started?

- What type of business owner are you?

Notes:

Notes:

How much money do you expect to earn?

You may have high hopes of making 6 figures in your first year of business, but where will that money coming from? In reality, most start-up businesses don't see a profit until their second year and often not until even their third. If you are seeking a loan or an investor, you must show realistic financials with your business plan, including your salary. If you plan to obtain a $100,000 loan, consider how much of this will become your salary. We will discuss this further in Chapter 36.

When do you expect to make a profit?

Making a profit in your first year is not very realistic if you are starting from scratch. In rare cases if you have already developed your product and lined up production, you may turn a profit in your first year, but you will have to work very hard to make this happen.

Will you be seeking investors or a loan?

You must have a sound business and financial plan written in order to attract investors and convince them you are a good investment. They will not invest unless they will make a profit. Banks are the same. This too is discussed later in the book. We have developed an online software tool available at www. fashionunraveled.com to assist in the development of your business and financial plans.

How much of an investment do you plan on contributing to your business in order to get it started?

You must make a significant financial contribution if you plan on seeking a loan from a bank or investor. Typically 10% of the requested amount for a loan is required, although some banks may require 20%. Starting your business with nothing in the bank can be very challenging, but with careful budgeting it is possible. You will need to do careful and successful marketing and watch every dollar you spend. Try to give your business a monetary contribution from each paycheck until you have enough for the expenses you estimated in your business plan.

Do you plan on keeping your job while you get your business started?

If you don't have an investor for your business, leaving your job should be carefully weighed. Even if you have set money aside for your business, giving up your job could be risky. What if your business doesn't see a profit until sometime in the 3rd year? It will be important to create a living budget, including rent or mortgage, food and daily regular expenses (gas, utilities, coffee) before handing in your letter of resignation.

What type of business owner are you?

Before you start thinking about how you will get your product out into the world, you need to figure out what your strengths are. Are you a fabulous technical designer, but don't know squat about selling and bookkeeping?

Take a few minutes to bullet point what you know a lot about, what you know little about, and what you don't know at all. Even though you may not be strong in all areas, it doesn't mean you don't have what it takes to start your business. Learning how to delegate and contract out work is crucial. As smart and determined as you are, you cannot do everything yourself. Knowing up front what you need help with, is essential in building a successful business venture.

Notes:

Notes:

How do you know when to delegate and share responsibilities? The decision will vary depending on your specific circumstances. Everyone's experience with delegating work is different. I didn't learn how to do so until my third year in business, but I can assure you I wish I had done it sooner.

Entrepreneurship

Why do you want to start your own business?

How much money do you expect to earn?

When do you expect to make a profit?

Will you be seeking investors or a loan? Have you researched who to approach?

How much of an investment do you plan to contribute to your business to get started?

Do you plan on keeping your job while you get your business started?

State whether these personal traits are a strength or weakness and explain your answers.

Artistic expression through art and illustration	❑ Strength	❑ Weakness
Pattern drafting or draping	❑ Strength	❑ Weakness
Selling	❑ Strength	❑ Weakness
Researching	❑ Strength	❑ Weakness
Financial Planning/Management	❑ Strength	❑ Weakness
Marketing	❑ Strength	❑ Weakness

Case Study: Entrepreneurship

Why do you want to start your own business?
I wanted to start a business that could sustain my family and simultaneously be scalable. I also wanted a way to exercise my creativity in a daily and meaningful way.

How much money do you expect to earn?
I actually don't "EXPECT" to earn anything. I would like to sell enough to make about $50,000 a year.

When do you expect to make a profit?
To make a profit that will pay for my costs AND give me a salary, I would say my 3rd season. That gives me enough time to learn my customers and respond to them.

Will you be seeking investors or a loan? Have you researched who to approach?
I am definitely not into a loan on a business whose industry is so fallible and turbulent. I wouldn't mind investors if they could hang for about 5 years

How much of an investment do you plan to contribute to your business to get started?
I already have invested $30,000 into it. So far I have received a great education from that money I plan on self financing the next $10,000 which will contribute to launching my Fall 2011 line.

Do you plan on keeping your job while you get your business started?
I am already self employed and do contract sewing for other designers as well as sell my line of hand bags. I won't be able to focus exclusively on my clothing line until it can pay its own bills

State whether these personal traits are a strength or weakness and explain your answers.

Artistic expression through art and illustration ✔ Strength ☐ Weakness

Pattern drafting or draping ☐ Strength ✔ Weakness
Not too strong, I can't draft from scratch

Selling ✔ Strength ☐ Weakness
I'm good at it, I just don't want to be doing it in the long run. It can be delegated

Researching ☐ Strength ✔ Weakness
I don't like doing it

Financial Planning/Management ✔ Strength ☐ Weakness

Marketing ✔ Strength ☐ Weakness

Web Design/Technology ☐ Strength ✔ Weakness
I'm so-so at it. I'm good at graphic design, just not web design.

Time Management

As an educator, I often hear my students say that they will sleep when they graduate. This type of attitude can lead to bad habits in the work place.

All my students have the same work load, yet some always scramble to get projects finished at the last minute and often end up turning in mediocre work. As an entrepreneur, you can often find yourself falling into this routine if you don't have a good time management system established.

Why does a student that sleeps 6-8 hours a night and works a full time job, give me more refined work than the student that sleeps 1-2 hours a night and maybe works part-time? She is not a better student, but she knows how to manage her time. Sleep is important to your mental and physical health and if you don't get enough, it can affect your work.

The work load I give my students is about 10 times lighter than the workload I give myself in my business. I manage just fine, but it took years of struggling with managing my time to finally find my groove.

One way that has helped me, is that I have become a purveyor of lists. A list for every day. I love the satisfaction of crossing things off, feeling I have really accomplished things. Personally, digital calendars & digital lists are ineffective for me; I prefer a standard old day planner and couldn't do without it. Please note that your management style may vary vastly from the way I work. You will need to develop a strategy that works for you.

We all wish we could have personal assistants following us

Notes:

Notes:

around and taking notes for us, but in reality, starting up a business, it will most likely just be you. Everyone has their own way of managing time, there is no one right way to do it. Here is an experiment. Pretend you were just hired as an assistant by an incredible designer to help get her organized. How would you do it? Where would you start?

Avoiding Burnout

What do I mean by avoiding burnout? It is easy to forget about yourself when running a business (or raising children). When starting, it can be really exciting, so exciting, in fact, that you may only want to work on your business and nothing else. But, if you are working a 40 hour week at a job, PLUS working on your business another 40 hours a week, how long will you last before you completely lose your mind, your partner or your friends?

It's important that you keep a balance in your life and your business. One of the hardest things to do is to find time for yourself. This should be considered with your time management plan.

Like any task, you can only work on it for so long before your eyes start to cross and you need a break. Smokers have it all figured out, don't they? When they need a break, they leave what they are doing for a 15 minute smoke break. You don't have to be a smoker to take breaks. It's required by law that you receive a 15 minute break for every 2 hours of work.

When it comes to your own business, you need breaks too. If you give yourself a break to take a walk or go outside, you can clear your head and sometimes even solve a problem you might have been wasting time on.

I personally take a walk or go on a hike at least four days a week to clear my head and think about my business issues. Walking with a partner is even better, think of it as free therapy. It's even better than great if you walk with another business owner, you can gain so much from talking to others.

I get a massage every other week, a pedicure once a month, a designated weekly pajama day and a short vacation every 3 months. Since I started this routine, my stress has lessened, my ulcers have disappeared and my profits have doubled. The less you are staring at your email and bank account, the more they seem to fill up.

You may notice that when one thing goes wrong, everything seems to go wrong. Thinking positively about your business will help your mindset, whether you believe the universe is revolving around you, or you just believe in positive energy, just make sure you take mental and physical health breaks. Oh- and this means scheduling times to eat and an occasional glass of wine.

Notes:

Time Management

How do you manage your time?

What do you do to relax?

How often do you take time for yourself?

Do you get any physical exercise?

If you do exercise, how often and how will that change when you start your business?

Case Study: Time Management

How do you manage your time?

That's funny. Actually, I do a pretty good job of time management now that I have had some practice (and 2 children, a husband, part time job at my son's school and a plethora of other activities). I don't watch TV during the day and I don't multi task. I make a daily plan and stick pretty closely to it. I allow myself to adjust with the day.

What do you do to relax?

I am actually pretty low profile. I hang out at home and watch movies with my family or I get together with my friends (which is rare). Mostly I talk on the phone to connect or Facebook. It sounds kind of sad, but drinking at home means you don't have to find a ride later (lol).

How often do you take time for yourself?

I don't really. I would like to change that. Motherhood + workaholic = no shower for 3 days sometimes, let alone a haircut and massage! It's a good thing I don't have coworkers.

Do you get any physical exercise?

Yes, I have lately. I have found that getting in a mile or so walk daily with the kids is awesome. I should have done it a lot sooner.

If you do exercise, how often and how will that change when you start your business?

Hopefully I can just keep up what I started!

DEVELOPING YOUR LINE

Chapter 3
Define Your Market

What is your market and how do you define it? Simply put, you need to determine the **price point** at which your product will sell.

Your fabric choices, the garment construction details, and the quality of sewing are major factors in determining which design market your work falls into. You most likely have an idea of where you want to sell your product, now you need to determine if that location meets your market.

The two prime design classifications are Couture and Ready-to-Wear. Ready-to-wear is a wide classification and can be broken down into several markets.

Couture

Couture describes fine tailoring and custom made-to-order garments. Many of the design details are done by hand. Fabrics are of exquisite nature and some even contain hand-made laces. These garments are not found in department stores, but in **ateliers**. Design businesses such as Juicy Couture are NOT a couture business and use the term rather loosely and inappropriately.

Price Point: *The price range which determines the various markets from low end to high end, including budget, moderate, bridge, or designer.*

Atelier: *Traditionally, a Parisian studio and workroom*

Notes:

To be called haute couture, is a privilege and an honor, as it is protected by French law. One must be selected by the Chambre de Commerce et d'Industrie de Paris to receive this honor. Their criterion are strict and include having an atelier in Paris that employs at least fifteen people full-time, design made-to-order items for private clients, with one or more fittings and must present a collection to the Paris press twice a year; comprising at least thirty-five designs for both daytime and evening wear. The Chambre established these rules in 1945 and have less than a dozen current members by definition.

Ready-to-Wear
Ready-to-Wear describes any garments that are manufactured in quantity. This can also be referred to as "off the rack."

Designer describes well known brands such as Gucci, Chanel and Louis Vuitton. Their price point is high and can range into the thousands for one garment. Customers are often wealthy and have disposable income. Fabrics are of a high quality and are costly. These designer brands can be found in high end boutiques or brand-name department stores such as Barneys, Saks, and Nordstrom's.

Bridge or Contemporary describes a market catering to a larger customer base than Designer. Price points are lower than designer and can range in the hundreds for one piece. The fabrics are generally of high quality. Many brands launched by celebrities such as Ed Hardy are considered to be contemporary. These designer brands can be found in department stores such as Neiman Marcus, Bergdorf Goodman, and specialty boutiques.

Moderate describes a much wider customer base and comprises much of the clothing market. Many independent designers fall in the moderate design market, along with Tommy Hilfiger and Jones of New York. The price points are moderate and fabrics are of medium quality. Designs of this sort can be found in shopping malls and smaller independent boutiques.

Budget describes an inexpensive market which can be found at large chain stores such as Forever 21 and the fast fashion giants such as H&M and Zara. Budget designs are also sold at mall chains such as Abercrombie & Fitch. Price points are usually under $100 per garment. Fabrics are cheap, and garments are generally poorly made. These garments are sometimes referred to as disposable clothing.

Mass Market describes off-price clothing, seconds, and closeouts. These designs can be found at stores such as Marshall's, TJ Maxx, and Ross. Merchandise is sometimes flawed or last season and is priced to move quickly. The price range is generally around or under $20 per piece.

Each of these markets can be further broken down into separate classifications. Here is an abridged list for example purposes. Please note that this can vary from market to market.

> **Womens:** Juniors, Misses, Petites, Plus Size, Maternity, Intimate Apparel, Active wear, Outerwear, Evening wear
> **Mens:** Big & Tall, Outerwear, Casuals, Tees, Suits
> **Children:** Infant, Toddler, Girls, Boys, Toys
> **Accessories**: Bags, Shoes, Hats, Scarves, Gloves

Notes:

Notes:

Private Label

Private Label brands are manufactured designs commissioned by stores who want to sell under their own brand name. The price points and actual markets can vary vastly. This has become a popular option for smaller design businesses as they have smaller collections and can offer exclusive designs to a store or boutique. Many department stores carry private label designs and so do stores such as Urban Outfitters and Anthropology.

Market Classification

Do you see your product selling in a particular geographical area?
(locally, nationally, internationally, or a specific city)

What sales outlets do you see your product selling well in?
(i.e. department stores, boutiques, online, etc)

What specific stores do you see your product selling in?

What prices do you expect your items to retail for?

What design market does that place you in and why?

❑ Couture ❑ Designer ❑ Contemporary ❑ Moderate ❑ Budget

What area in this design market are you targeting? Be specific (e.g. juniors, plus size, etc.)

❑ Women ❑ Men ❑ Children ❑ Accessories

What types of items do you hope to create (pants, dresses, etc)?

What types of fabrics do you plan on using?

Case Study: Market Classification

Do you see your product selling in a particular geographical area?

(locally, nationally, internationally, or a specific city)

I know there are differences in aesthetic between the east coast and west coast. While I don't want to try to serve every taste, I feel my line would sell well in most geographies.

What sales outlets do you see your product selling well in?

(i.e. department stores, boutiques, online, etc)

Independent boutiques, online and my own retail establishment

What specific stores do you see your product selling in?

Origin Design Lab & Beautiful People Boutique. A for additional accounts, I haven't done all my research yet. Once I determine my competition, it should be easier for me to narrow it down.

What prices do you expect your items to retail for?

I expect they will fall into the boutique price range $35-$200. I have not done all my costing and solidified my fabric sources, so this may not be that accurate, but this is where I want them to be.

What design market does that place you in and why?

❑ Couture   ❑ Designer   ✔ Contemporary   ❑ Moderate   ❑ Budget

What area in this design market are you targeting? Be specific (e.g. juniors, plus size, etc.)

✔ Women   ❑ Men   ❑ Children   ❑ Accessories

Missy

What types of items do you hope to create (pants, dresses, etc)?

I plan to design a set of basics (skirt, dress, pants and top) for my collection which will be a part of my collection indefinitely with a few modifications each season. I will also add in creative pieces to mix and match with each of these basics.

What types of fabrics do you plan on using?

Hemp silk charmeuse, linen, some wool, eco fabrics, and I'd like to experiment with using bamboo because of the handle of it.

Market Research

Once you have developed where your product fits in the market, you need to conduct research on the market itself. Researching your market will lead you to discovering who your competition is as well as your customer. This is important in your business planning and will give you an idea if your market is profitable. How much of the industry does your market make up? If you are knowledgeable of this, investors will be more confident in you and your business plan.

In the first edition of this book I defined the market research for the lingerie industry. This information was rather brief, but states the expected growth in the industry based on prior years' trends.

> According to "The USA Intimate Apparel Market Research Report" published in January 2008 by Infomat, Inc., "Intimate apparel is now a $9.6 billion dollar industry, up nearly 4% from previous years. Total apparel sales have reached up to $181 billion with intimates and sleepwear helping to fuel growth." As stated in this report, this growth is expected to continue and increase up to 10% by 2012. Sales numbers are not specified to one particular market and cover all areas from budget to designer.

I relied on an industry report for my research. You can also research the past few years of the industry and make educated assumptions as to what will trend in the future. Review the total revenue, units sold, employment statistics and growth rates. This information can usually be obtained with the help of your local librarian.

Notes:

Notes:

Something I did not include in my research was how much the average wages were for professionals in this industry. Including this information will help you set your own salary and will help investors evaluate the wages you plan on paying yourself and your employees. The discussion on salaries and wages appears in a later chapter, but it is a good idea to have an idea of what professionals are being paid for your intended role.

In the past few years, we were witness to how the world reacts to unstable economic conditions. Evaluate such possible conditions and how they may affect your business. When oil prices rose, what happened? Manufacturing slowed internationally and returned stateside. When jobs were being lost, what did we see as a result? New businesses began to form. Look at what could go wrong in our economy and speculate how your business can cope with it.

In your research, you should also consider the fashion industry's seasonality. During the holiday shopping season, did you know that most people spend around 75% of their entire spending cash for the year? When might it be slow and why? Sale season is usually around March and then again around July. Retail merchandise orders may be slow during these times, but wholesale orders may be high due to buyer planning and trade shows.

Knowing when your busy months might be will help you account and budget for the slow ones. Remember, you will incur the expenses of your fall collection in late spring, when income may not be very high.

Market Research

How much money does a customer in your target market spend on your market each year?

What is the average pay for the roles in your business for the most current year?

How would you classify your business in your market research?

How much revenue does your industry produce?

What percentage of the industry is made up on your market?

List the growth statistics for your market?

Factor	5 Years Ago	2 Years Ago	Last Year	This Year	Next 2 Years
Industry Growth					

How would you describe the seasonality for your specific market in the industry?

List any other market research you wish to include?

Case Study: Market Research

How much money does a customer in your target market spend on your market each year?

Approximately $3000 to $5000 annually

What is the average pay for the roles in your business for the most current year?

The average pay for fashion designers is $44,833 – info from salary.com

The average pay for entrepreneurs is $111,000 – info from entrepreneur.com

How would you classify your business in your market research?

Women's Apparel Manufacturing

How much revenue does your industry produce?

$9,199,000,000 – info from IBISWorld

What percentage of the industry is made up on your market?

60% of the industry – info from marketresearch.com

List the growth statistics for your market?

Factor	5 Years Ago	2 Years Ago	Last Year	This Year	Next 2 Years
Industry Growth		3.22%	2.87%	3.24%	11.7%

How would you describe the seasonality for your specific market in the industry?

The busiest season for my market would be fall, followed by holiday, spring and summer.

List any other market research you wish to include?

Chapter 4
Define Your Customer

One of the first questions you should ask yourself is: Who is your customer? If your answer is "everyone," you have not done enough research. Hopefully, by the end of this chapter, you will begin to develop a better idea of who that person is.

Understanding your customer is just as important as developing your product. If you can not define a customer, you cannot focus your marketing, create your patterns and fit, develop your color palette, or figure out where to sell your merchandise. Everything factors into your customer.

Your customer may change during the development of your line, but this is not something to get hung up on. Learning to adapt is a key trait to being a successful business owner. There will be times when you are in love with one of your designs, but if the price is too high for your customer, you learn to adapt. Once your business grows large enough, you can develop tiers of designs to cater to other markets. An example of a designer who does this is Donna Karan. Donna Karan the brand is a Contemporary line, but DKNY is a Moderate line.

Notes:

Notes:

At this stage in your business development, you are most likely unaware of what it will cost to produce your collection. This uncertainty can teeter you between different markets and the price points it might fall into. This alone is the primary reason why your customer might change. Keep an open mind throughout your development that nothing is set in stone and every aspect of your business is meant to evolve.

An exercise I conduct in school involves creating a customer profile board. This can be very handy when developing who you have in mind as your customer. Try compiling images of who you imagine your customer is, what they buy, what they wear, what car they drive, vacation spots they frequent, and anything that describes your ideal buyer. This type of collage is a visual way of showing yourself, and other professionals you work with, who your customer is. This will be helpful when beginning the branding and marketing process.

If you are having difficulties discovering your customer, look towards similar businesses; ones who can be your competition and research who their customer is.

Once you have an idea of your customer, you can use the provided form to help define that target customer. This form will help you specify that one perfect customer. One thought that may occur to you is, "I want several different types of people to wear my clothes, not just one specific profile!" Your actual customer may not fit cleanly into the description of your target customer, but creating your perfect target customer will focus the direction of your business.

In my business, I define my target customer as a working woman between the ages of 25 and 40 who earns $45,000 per year. My customers, however, range from 16 to 60 years old and have consisted of students as well as women earning over $200,000.

Notes:

Customer Profile

Create your ideal customer. This will not limit who your customer is, but will help you narrow your focus.

Age: _____

Sex: ❑ Female   ❑ Male

Marital Status: ❑ Single   ❑ Married   ❑ Separated   ❑ Divorced   ❑ Widowed

Occupation: _____

Annual Income: _____

Geographic Location: _____

Buying Habits:

_____

_____

Lifestyle:

_____

_____

Leisure Activities:

_____

_____

Vacation Destinations:

_____

_____

Favorite Designers:

_____

_____

Favorite Stores:

_____

_____

Case Study: Customer Profile

Create your ideal customer. This will not limit who your customer is, but will help you narrow your focus.

Age: _Late 20's to Late 40's_

Sex: ✔ **Female**   ☐ **Male**

Marital Status: ☐ **Single**   ✔ **Married**   ☐ **Separated**   ☐ **Divorced**   ☐ **Widowed**

Occupation: _____

Annual Income: _$50,000 - $60,000 a year_

Geographic Location: _West Coast_

Buying Habits:
She spends money relating to fitness & health; gym memberships, athletic gear, health food. She typically spends much of her money on her home and her children

Lifestyle:
She had a bit of disposable income. Cost of living for the household would be around $45,000 and a combined income of about $100,000.

Leisure Activities:
She typically participates in fitness, community volunteering & activities with her family

Vacation Destinations:
Costa Rica; low cost but high culture vacations

Favorite Designers:
Eileen Fischer, she support independent handmade work.

Favorite Stores:
She shops local boutiques and not at department stores. She supports the local arts and makers.

Notes:

Not knowing who your customer is could set you up for a financial mistake. Make sure you revisit your customer profile throughout your business development progress and make updates when needed.

Competition

You've researched your customer and your market; now consider your competition. To put it bluntly, who would you like to take customers away from? Use the worksheet at the end of this section to evaluate your closest competition. These should be companies that you see selling in your market and at a similar price point. These companies may sell next to yours in a boutique.

Questions to consider: Is there room for your product in the market? Is your product different from what's already out there? Do you have a niche?

Write a list of things that make you stand out. Is it your business practices? Your fabric choices? The fit of your garments? What is your competitive advantage?

If you find yourself falling short of your customer, what kind of strategy could give you the advantage? Can you find a more efficient way to run your business? Is there a way your prices can undercut your competition?

What if you are saying to yourself, "I don't know who my competition is?" Take a walk around your local shopping districts. If you don't see your merchandise fitting into any of those stores, venture further. Take a field trip to the closest metropolitan area. Check out different neighborhoods and what sells in those areas. Once you find a neighborhood you would fit into, make note of what designers are being sold in those stores. This is your competition.

But what if......There are many excuses you can make to avoid finding out who your competition is, whether you live in a small town, you are a stay at home mom, or you just can't find the time. However, knowing your competition is crucial in creating a marketable product. Aim for three businesses that are comparable to your line. This too may alter your target customer and market you originally defined. Take stock in what their websites look like, whether they have an online store and what their prices and materials happen to be.

Go one step further and "follow" them on twitter, email lists and all other social networks. Take note of who their retailers are, maybe those could be yours too! A great web-based tool to research your competition is Compete.com (once you know who they are).

In summary: Do your $@!!$! research! You'll thank yourself later, I guarantee it.

Notes:

Competition

What makes your designs stand out from the rest?

On this form, describe the qualities of your business and 3 of your competitors. Check whether the item in question is a strength or a weakness of your business

	Your Company	Strength or Weakness	Competitor Name:	Competitor Name:	Competitor Name:
Brief Design Description					
General Observation					
Products					
Fabrics					
Price					
Quality					
Selection and Sizing					
Fit Reliability					
Location					
Sales Methods					
Advertising					
Press					

Case Study: Competition

What makes your designs stand out from the rest?

I want my pieces to be must-haves for a closet. They are the classic shapes that never go out of style and are timeless. They are built to last season after season.

On this form, describe the qualities of your business and 3 of your competitors. Check whether the item in question is a strength or a weakness of your business

	Andrea's Business	Strength or Weakness	Stewart & Brown	Marrika Nakk	Isda & Co.
Brief Design Description	Contemporary tailored and romantic wear	S	Contemporary high end casual	Contemporary romantic western wear	Contemporary office clothing
General Observation			Creates several different lines	Business longevity, around since 1980's	Closest competitor, a little dated
Products	Dresses, Pants, Tops & Skirts	S	Sweaters, pants, dresses, knits	Skirts, dresses, jackets, tops	Tops, some skirts and dresses
Fabrics	Hemp silk, silk organza, bamboo	S	Eco fabrics: hemp, organic cotton	Silk rayon velvet, stretch lace	Silks, cashmeres, linen, high-end fabrics
Price	Skirts 60-150, Pants 80-125, Tops and dresses 85-350	S	Tops, skirts & pants 100-150, dresses 150-300, tshirts 60-80	Skirts 150, jackets 700	Pants, dresses & jackets 100-150, tops 50-150
Quality	High Quality	S	High Quality	High Quality	High Quality
Selection and Sizing	Small 7-10 pieces, 2 colorways	W	Large 100 pieces, knits xs-l, woven 2-10	Moderate 20 pieces, S-XL	Moderate to large, 50 pieces, XS-XL
Fit Reliability	size 6-8 average size, sample size 8, mothers, hips	S	Narrow fit, not fit for curvy ladies	Better fit, curvy but not for short or petite	Best fit ever for curvy
Location	N. California	S	N. California	S. California	N. California
Sales Methods	Wholesale, online-etsy	S	Wholesale, online	Wholesale, custom made	Wholesale, online
Advertising	Trade shows, email list	S	Trade shows, Blog, Email list	Trade shows, print ads	Trade shows, email list, blog
Press		W	Celebrity placement, lots of press	Editorial press in western magazines	Limited local news

Chapter 5
Branding and Identity

What is a brand and how do you create it? In a nutshell, a brand is anything and everything that separates your business from the rest. Your brand creates an identity and explains who you are, what you do and why you do it. You may believe a brand is just a logo, but it is much more.

Creating an identity is every bit as important as creating your product, developing a customer and market and determining your competition. Branding links each of these areas together. It involves keeping consistent values in every aspect of your business. Always representing your business in the same manner creates recognition and customer loyalty. Approaching your business with a branding strategy before you start your product development might be a wise decision.

Branding starts with your mission statement and will be the backbone of your business. Your mission statement is the statement that defines you and your business and is used in your business plan. What are your company's values? Are you going to be an advocate against sweatshops? Are you only going to work with American grown cotton? Are a portion of your sales going to a charity? Are you going to create innovative

Notes:

Notes:

products for a specific market? What is your message?

Your mission statement must also include what your product is and what need it is filling. Jot down some ideas and come back to this after you've read the rest of the book. Your mission statement should only be a few sentences in length and will be a summary of your responses to these questions:

- Does your customer need this product?

- Why is your product better than the competitor?

In addition to your mission statement, consider what your vision is for your business and where you see it going. Do you envision your business taking off and your designs being the fore-runner for the red carpet? Or do you see your business becoming a legacy and a bread winner for your family, passing it down the family line for generations? Briefly explain how you see your business growing.

Once you have developed your mission statement and vision, proceed directly to go, collect $200, and now start working on your name and logo. Your own name should be first on your list, but you can also choose a word or phrase that is representative of you and/or your product. Choose a variety of names that you like and pre-screen them with family and friends. Before deciding on your name, google it and make sure you aren't using a competitor's name.

Fictitious Business Name:
A name under which you operate your business that is not the same as your given name. It is commonly referred to as a DBA (doing business as)

Once you've determined you are not using a competitor's name, you need to check that a local dry cleaner isn't going by that name either. You can search the ***fictitious business name*** database for your district (city, county or state). Most cities and states require this when registering a business, so check with your local statutes whether this pertains to you. I will explain how to register a fictitious business name in Chapter 24 (this may not apply if you form your business as a corporation or an LLC).

Once you settle on a name, buy the domain name ASAP. You don't want to lose it to someone with the same idea. Focus on a .com, and as a last resort use a .net or another ending. You may even opt to change or modify your name depending on domain availability. You can use GoDaddy.com to check domain availability.

Your next step is to design a logo representative of your chosen name. A logo is a unique and characteristic font and/ or image in which your name should always be rendered. If you have a background in graphic design, you can try to tackle this, but otherwise, leave it to an expert. What you think looks fabulous may not appear that way to a buyer or to the media. You want to convey a level of status and professionalism in your logo design. To do this properly, you may need to invest a few hundred dollars in an experienced graphic designer. It will be money well spent. Your logo will be your face to the world— so do it professionally. You may also wish to develop a short catch phrase to use in conjunction with your logo.

If you are hiring a graphic designer, have them design an image logo to accompany the full logo. This is usually part of the logo, but may be used as a stand-alone on your clothing labels, business cards, or your website. It will represent your name if the full logo isn't suitable for that particular placement. This isn't always needed, but it's recommended, especially if the

Notes:

Notes:

name is not short. Branding images you may be familiar with are Nike's swoosh logo, Levi's pocket red tab, and Joe Boxer's smiley face.

Last but not least is the choice of color. Consider colors that speak to the nature of your business. If you are not sure what these might be, start by researching the meanings of certain colors and the type of emotions they generate. Psychology is a major part of our industry and perception with color should also be considered. (If I were to elaborate on psychology in the fashion industry, this book would become twice the size.)

Here is a brief outline describing colors and their meanings.

- Red – This color is bold and draws attention. It shows off your confidence and passion.

- Orange – Orange is a color of unity and harmony.

- Yellow – Brighter yellow symbolizes cheer. Mellow yellows convey stability.

- Green - Represents growth, development, and motivation.

- Blue – Blue is associated with introspection and tranquility.

- Purple –This color is associated with creativity and spirituality.

- Pink – Pink is soothing and nurturing.

- Gray – Gray invokes balance and safety.

- Brown –This color represents grounding and security.

- Black – Black exudes mystery, authority, depth, and strength.

- White – White is the color of trust.

Branding and Identity

What company names are you considering and why?

What is your company's story? How did it evolve?

What is your vision for your company?

Branding and Identity - continued

What are your company's values and what do you promise with your product?

What kind of customer will identify with your brand?

What makes your company and product stand out?

What is the purpose of your product?

What is your design philosophy?

What is your company's mission statement?

Case Study: Branding and Identity

What company names are you considering and why?

Coco Martini - My alter ego, A.C. Baker Apparel - current business name, Andrea Baker - my full name

What is your company's story? How did it evolve?

It evolved through tears, literally. I worked in a boutique years ago, had more fun than ever before working. I was good at selling but got laid off after getting pregnant with my first son. I gained 75 pounds in the pregnancy and couldn't drop it after the birth of my first son. I was frustrated, I had no money and nothing fit. I had gone to school for art, so I started sketching ideas of things that I could wear, one page became pages. I took the sketches to a local clothier to see if they could make my designs because I didn't even know how to sew. She said if she maid them, they would be thousands of dollars to produce. She recommended that I start my own line and referred me to local contractors and manufacturers. I didn't know anything about the industry at this time, but started asking everyone questions. I wanted to learn the industry. My husband received 150 grand from an inheritance and I used 20 grand to start my business. I realized all too late that the people I had been asking questions to were full of bad advice. In actuality, I needed 20 for development alone and another 30 for production. I took the collection to market and failed, I was put in the wrong section and hired a "friend" to be a sales rep, which was a bad idea. All of the money had been used up so I had to step back and reevaluate everything. I learned how to sew, started making handbags, learned pattern making and 5 years later, I'm ready for a relaunch.

What is your vision for your company?

I want to keep my business modest, with my feet planted in reality. I want a sustainable company that is successful, is known for creating garments with great construction and great fabrics. I don't need to be a mega power. My goal is to release 2 collections or more a year. I want to create great work that is interesting and have a product that means something to me. I don't want to sell my company when it gets large, I want longevity and my kids to one day run my business. I expect to have employees besides myself. I want to be self sustainable. I NEVER want to work for another person again. I want to be the captain of my own boat. I want my children to learn amazing work ethics. When you make a thing that people use, it adds a dimension to the relations in your life – making a thing is a cool thing to do.

Case Study: Branding and Identity - continued

What are your company's values and what do you promise with your product?

I want everything to be American made. I believe in supporting my neighbor's business over producing at a fraction of the cost. Fair trade is effing bull. I believe a thing is fair traded if all parts of the trade is in your country. I don't believe in cutting out American workers, even if you do get cost breaks. Sustainability is local labor is important to me. I will produce in California, my home state and my residence. This is the cornerstone of my business

What kind of customer will identify with your brand?

Mothers, yoga mamas, west coast mentality, consumers with an etsy aesthetic, and those who focus back on the maker

What makes your company and product stand out?

Commitment to quality and sustainability, the style and fit speak directly to my customer's needs and lifestyle

What is the purpose of your product?

My designs will live in their closets for years. It helps my customer define their own lifestyle in their own unique way

What is your design philosophy?

Create subtlety, elegance and simplicity without being boring. These are pieces consumers want to wear all the time.

What is your company's mission statement?

A.C. Baker Apparel creates great designs and items that last for years. These designs exemplify the wearer not the trend. They are relational in nature; clothing made in the USA, using domestic labor and creates stability and community. I embrace Slow Fashion.

Chapter 6
Develop a Collection

You've defined yourself, your brand, your market and your customer. It is now the fun time to develop your collection.

Starting with a design philosophy should be first. The design philosophy is an extension of your branding/mission statement. It pertains to the overall focus of your work. Whether it is to have hand stitched tags on every garment or create fashion as forms of art. A design philosophy helps guide you in your overall look. In a smaller community, having a specific look will go far in brand recognition.

Staying true to your vision is the first key to success. The second is to not launch a product line with too many items. If you are taking on this business yourself, setting limits of 3-5 **silhouettes** in 2-4 fabrics is a good place to start for your first collection. Remember that even in these 8-12 pieces you will need to produce a full size range. This can easily add up to over 30 pieces you have to produce.

Have you thought about what sparks your creativity and inspires you as a designer? Are you inspired by fabrics or

Notes:

Silhouette: *The shape of the garment*

Notes:

colors? Is it your tactile or your visual sense that guides you? Regardless of where you pull your inspiration from, there comes a moment in every designer's process when you hit a creative wall. This is why it is so important to stay focused with your values.

For each collection, create a mood board. This mood board can be constructed in the same manner as your customer profile but will act as a prompt for your inspiration. In your collection development, don't limit yourself in your designing. Expect to design five times the number that you will actually take to production. You will gradually cut designs from your collection. Narrowing down your collection is part of the design process and can be done in several different and creative ways.

Try conducting small focus groups with friends or (even better) your target customers. Hiring a firm to conduct a focus group is an option, but highly expensive. An alternative is to use online postings to find your target customers, such as Craigslist.org. Post an ad pinpointing a specific customer and offer incentives for participation in your focus group. Free merchandise or gift cards are great ways to lure participants. If you have developed an email marketing list and have an online store, you could offer discounts to customers who fill out an online survey. SurveyMonkey.com is a free online survey tool (free up to 20 questions).

Many larger businesses use trending services to help with their collection development. These trending services predict which colors will be used several seasons down the road. They also dictate popular silhouettes for the season as well as the textiles that may be used. Have you ever noticed that items you purchase on sale from last season never match anything? Color schemes are developed through the trending services and all colors in one season are meant to be interchanged with each other, regardless of the designer. Items from season to season are not meant to match. Do you recall that conversation "The Devil Wears Prada" regarding the blue sweater? That was no exaggeration.

There are trend forecasting books available for around the thousand dollar mark or magazine subscriptions for around $400. Another possibility is to consult with services such as Peclers, Promostyl, Trend Union or WGSN, which isn't any more affordable than the predictive books.

Many independent designers choose not to follow these trend reporting services, however, for several reasons other than the large price tag. One, we consider ourselves unique, do not wish to follow trends, and want our products to stand out. Two, we purchase our fabrics from what is available, from textile companies that have already followed the trending services for colors. Three, we are closer to the manufacturing process than the larger companies, so we can react to trends already on the market and cater to them as opposed to planning out our collections years in advance (fast fashion at play – a discussion saved for later in this book).

Development Schedule

There are four main seasons in fashion: fall, holiday, spring, and summer. You may sometimes see additional "seasons" such as resort, pre-spring, or pre-fall. These are usually set up for *in-between deliveries* and are commonly used in fast fashion. When you are first starting out, don't try to design for all four seasons—you will drive yourself mad and possibly go broke in the process.

Notes:

Delivery: The window of tie that retailers accept shipments

In-Between Deliveries: The time in between major seasons during which retailer wish to receive shipments of goods

You might want to focus on one collection in your first year of business. This collection will most likely be a test as to whether you have nailed your market and customer. There is no sense in wasting your hard earned money on more than one collection if there is the slight chance you could be targeting the wrong market.

Planning your collection is done far in advance, sometimes up to a year. There are markets or trade shows that coincide with each of the major seasons. These markets are held approximately 4-6 months prior to the season of release or delivery. Here are a couple charts that give you an idea of the differences between the traditional seasons, fast fashion seasons and the recommended indie designer schedule.

In ideal season planning, you would be designing a collection for 1 year from today. If it were September now, you would be planning your fall collection for next year and taking your designs to Market in February or March. This ideal situation rarely happens, and designers end up creating a collection 1-2 months before taking them to market (in this example, if you were planning a fall collection, you might not be designing until January or February).

This table represents 4 seasons in the production schedule: Fall, Holiday, Spring and Summer. During each stage of a collection, design firms could be working on all 4 collections simultaneously.

Months:	Jan	Feb	Mar	Apr	May	Jun	Jul	Aug	Sep	Oct	Nov	Dec
Designing	F	F		H	H		SP	SP		SU	SU	
Patterns& Samples	F	F		H	H		SP	SP		SU	SU	
Sales		F	F		H	H		SP	SP		SU	SU
Production	SU	SU	SU	F	F	F	H	H	H	SP	SP	SP
Ship	SP	SP		SU	SU		F	F		H	H	

Designer Profile: Timothy James Andrews

Timothy James Andrews resides in east London. His textile based designs have been described as 'a rainbow attack of patterns and textures'. His designs are 'playful and fun, with bold, cartoon-like colour palettes', 'an exploration of colour and form, and is eager to break conventions'.

What is your design philosophy?

Colour and pattern, colour and pattern and even more colour and pattern. I want to make unique pieces that are truly loved. I don't expect people to wear a full outfit comprising of just my designs so I want to make each item I create truly special.

What general process do you go through when developing a collection?

I like to work with one simple idea to start with. It can be a movie, a painting, a performer, anything. From this I build a list of techniques and ideas I want to try and explore relating to this point. These ideas naturally grow, evolve and change into its own unique concept. Within the collection I try to develop an individualistic technique, as my own personal experiment.

Do you have a customer in mind when designing your collections?

I've always had the firm belief that if you design something you love, somebody else will love it too. The world is a big place filled with forward thinking people that follow the happenings of fashion. I started making clothes because I wanting to make a variety of fun pieces. I never thought about them being sold in shops but people from all around the world went mad for them.

How many pieces do you create for one collection?

I make a small collection of looks, but within each look there will usually be a few different pieces. In my first collection, 'some wear over the rainbow', the collection was only 8 looks, but overall I had nearly 40 separate pieces not including accessories. I love layering and miss matching. Putting together clashing patterns, colours and textures. The overall look is quite over the top but each piece has had a lot of time and effort put into it.

Do you consider your work wearable art or costume?

I like to think my work is a big mixing pot of art/costume/fashion. Some of the prints within my collections I now have framed and are hanging on my living room wall. I think the prints particularly are worthy of being a piece of art. Some of the pieces in the collection I make especially to be over the top, an idea pushed to its limit. These probably can be described as costume but have been popular with stylists, singers and performers so I feel have a place within fashion.

My knitted pieces are usually the most extreme. Being a less established designer it is difficult for me to get small production numbers made by knitwear factories. Even if I make simpler knitted pieces I cant produce them and nobody can buy them therefore I use the knitted pieces to be a bit of a show case for my more extreme ideas.

Where can someone find your collection if they wanted to be wearing a Timothy James Andrews?

At the moment, my primary stockist is Kokontozai in London and Paris.

What are some of your goals in the growth of your line?

At the moment I am really enjoying the designing and making process with small production runs. I think there is something special about creating a unique look; this seems to have been lost in modern day fashion. Style and glamour has taken over the fashion world but I want to fly the flag for 'in your face', bold, playful fashion statements.

I hope to evolve, change and stay relevant whilst staying true to my aesthetic. World domination isn't on the agenda but I definitely want to work with new stockists, factories, stylists and performers.

PRODUCTION

Chapter 10
Fabric Sourcing

To begin production, you must find sources for your fabrics and **notions**, develop patterns for your collection and create samples.

Sourcing can be a scary subject especially if you don't have access to a garment district and are limited to high priced chain fabric stores. Let's be honest, if you live in LA or NYC, you shouldn't have a problem, but if you live anywhere in between, where do you find your sources? Don't fret; there are several options for you yet.

When on your search for the perfect fabric, look for more than one source for your supplies. Businesses close down every day and you don't want to be stuck if your supplier ceases to exist. Target to have at least two back up sources, even if those sources are more costly. This will prevent you from getting stuck in an unfavorable situation.

Trade shows

Textile trade shows are the ideal way to source your fabrics. At a show, such as the Los Angeles International Textile Show, you get a chance to see everything in one place. It can be a bit

Notion: *A supply that goes into the creation of a garment. Thread, buttons, zippers, snaps, etc.*

Sourcing: *trade jargon for finding resources for your fabric, notions, and everything in between.*

Notes:

overwhelming, so having an idea of what you are looking for in the first place is a must. Here are some questions to consider:

- What colors are you leaning towards?

- Are you seeking woven fabrics or knit fabrics?

- What quality of fabric are you looking for? Is it fine silks, organic fabrics, or run-of-the-mill broadcloths?

A visit to your local stores should help you narrow your decisions. Don't stop at just one—hit them all. At many places, you can ask for a swatch of the fabric. Make a note of the width of fabric, the fiber content, where you bought it, the price, and any notes on availability. You may need to buy yardage at a moment's notice for a last minute order and it's a good idea to know whether, and where, you can get the fabric quickly.

At the end of this chapter I've added a textile and trim sourcing form to help you organize this information.

After you've done a local run and narrowed down your choices, plan a trip to the nearest textile show. These shows carry everything from notions and cheap polyester to high quality laces, "green" fabrics, and everything in between. If you aren't prepared, you could get lost in the chaos.

Jobbers

What is a "jobber"? A jobber is a wholesale distributor who buys fabric lots from leftover productions or last season fabric. This can be a great choice for you if you are doing smaller quantities. One question you may ask is, "Can I reorder this fabric?" The most common answer is, no. These fabrics are seconds, what you see is what you get. If you like something, buy as much as you can.

It is possible for a jobber to track down fabric for you, but it will often be at retail prices. So if you see something you like, buy it, and buy all of it. On occasion, if you develop a relationship with a jobber, he or she may offer to buy fabric back from you or trade it out, but usually at pennies on what you paid.

Some fabric stores may also act as jobbers. Your local mom and pop shop may offer merchandise for purchase at wholesale prices or at a discount for small businesses.

Fabric reps

A fabric rep will usually represent several different textile companies and travel around the country to secure new clients. If you attend a textile show, the show guide should list the fabric reps who exhibited. Strangely enough, fabric reps are generally listed in the yellow pages, so you can locate one near you. You can also search online for companies that carry the textiles you want. Contact them to see if they have a fabric rep that covers your area. If they do, you are in luck. If they don't, ask for a swatch card for the specific type of fabric you are looking for.

Be specific when requesting for swatches, asking for a sample of silk is like asking a baker for a slice of bread. There are several types of fabric that can be silk (for example, dupioni, charmeuse, chiffon, organza, etc.). Educate yourself on fabric types before leaving a bad impression with your possible source.

Notes:

Notes:

Online

If you are at your wits' end and cannot make it to a fabric show, and can't find a jobber or a fabric rep to help you, try the internet. Ebay.com and Etsy.com can sometimes have just the fabric you need, but there are many other resources available, so do some googling with specific criteria and search beyond the first pages of results.

The Big Q's

Once you have found the sources for your fabric, you need to know what questions to ask. This also pertains to fabric show reps and jobbers.

What are their minimums? Many companies you find at fabric shows require a ridiculous minimum yardage, some in the quantities of 1000 yards or more. You can sometimes get around this by ordering sample yardage. Sample yardages can be as low as one yard or as much as 100. Sample cuts are usually more expensive, or they may charge you a fee to cut the smaller yardage.

A second way to get around ordering minimum fabric in each color is to order the fabric as PFD (prepared for dying). PFD refers to the fabric's dye-ability. If you plan on offering several designs in the same fabric but in different colors, you can have your garments dyed after being sewn. Buying PFD will often help you reach the supplier's minimum. This can also cut down the cost of sewing because your seamstress doesn't have to change thread. But there's a catch: your thread must also be dye-able; if not, you must choose a thread color that will work with every color that your garments will be dyed.

If you have to order a large quantity and you know you will have fabric left after your production run, talk to your local fabric shops, they may in interested in purchasing your left over fabric. You could also try reselling on the internet.

Is this fabric readily available and how quickly can you reorder it? If there is a long waiting period or if the fabric is an **end lot**, you might want to rethink your choice or find another company as a backup for sourcing.

End Lot: The end of the fabric batch by a supplier, and it will not be produced again.

What is the minimum amount of fabric you should buy? Buy enough for at least three prototypes, plus one yard for testing. The prototypes can be used for marketing purposes—one for photographing, one for your sales rep, and one extra for any last minute needs (or in case of emergency).

Do they have the recommended care instructions for this fabric? If they do, that saves you a little work later on when writing your care instructions and gives you a heads up before testing your fabric.

Testing

You will need to test the fabric for shrinkage as well as for dye-ability, dry-ability and dry cleaning-ability. If you plan to dye your garments, send samples of the fabric to the dye house for color matching. To determine shrinkage, cut one yard, measure it exactly, wash it, measure it, and dry it. And re-measure it. The difference, if any, will help you account for shrinkage in the pattern. You will also need to put care instructions on your finished garment, and this is a good starting point to determine the appropriate care.

Notes:

Fabric/Trim Detail Sheet

Item Name: .... Item Number: ....

Cost Per unit: .... Minimum Purchase: .... Supplier: ....

Size: .... Width: .... Weight: ....

Colors Available: ....

Content: ....

Care Instructions: ....

....

....

Testing Results:

....

Swatch/Sample

Fabric/Trim Detail Sheet

Item Name: .... Item Number: ....

Cost Per unit: .... Minimum Purchase: .... Supplier: ....

Size: .... Width: .... Weight: ....

Colors Available: ....

Content: ....

Care Instructions: ....

....

....

Testing Results:

....

Swatch/Sample

Case Study: Fabric/Trim Detail Sheet

Item Name: *Bamboo Linen*   Item Number:

Cost Per unit: *$5.35*   Minimum Purchase: *100 yds* Supplier: *Bamboo Suppliers*

Size: Width: *54"*   Weight: *7 oz*

Colors Available: *PFD or any color for a $75 color setup*

Content: *95% Bamboo, 5% Organic Cotton*

Care Instructions: *wash cold*   Swatch/Sample
dry low heat

Testing Results:
Shrink 1%

Case Study: Fabric/Trim Detail Sheet

Item Name: *Invisible Zipper*   Item Number:

Cost Per unit: *$1.25*   Minimum Purchase: *20*   Supplier: *ZZ Zippers*

Size: *7" – 36"*   Width: Weight:

Colors Available: *many, see color chart they provided*

Content: *100% Nylon*

Care Instructions: Swatch/Sample

Testing Results:

Chapter 11
Patterns and Samples

The next step is to create samples and sewing patterns for your collection. Let's face it; some of us aren't as skilled in drafting patterns as we'd like to be. If your background isn't in fashion, you won't even have the choice to develop your own patterns (and don't even consider using a home sewing pattern such as Butterick or Easy Sew – the use of those in your production is copyright infringement). Whether you attended school for design or business, there may come a time when you need to hire a technical designer to create your patterns.

I have focused this discussion on pattern making, further in this chapter, I will discuss sample making. How do you find or select a pattern maker? Some options include searching posts on 24seventalent.com, haute.net, guru.com, launchmyline.com, local design school employment offices or even Craigslist.org.

In selecting your contractor/pattern maker, consider their qualifications and experience. In a tough market, some pattern drafters may take on projects that are beyond their experience. The result may be you paying for their learning experience. At the same time, don't be afraid to work with a newcomer. You could discover an excellent pattern maker who doesn't yet

Notes:

Notes:

charge like the pros. Here are a few questions to ask.

How long have they been making patterns? Experience counts, but having a newcomer isn't necessarily bad. All pattern makers have to start somewhere. Decide if experience is what you need for this particular project. If the person is new to the industry, their prices should reflect it.

What is their pattern specialty? Do they work with knits, wovens, or both? Plus size, juniors, mens, childrens, or womens? Pattern drafting for each fabric type is very different, as well as the drafting for different markets, so you need to know what their experience is with each. Ask to see examples of their past work.

Have they worked with one of your competitors? If they have worked with a design line similar to yours, that may be a plus.

Can they give you client references? This is a great way to find out how they work before your initial consultation. This may not always be available due to confidentiality agreements, but they should be able to provide some sort of reference.

Do they charge by the project or by the hour? If it is a project price, find out how many samples are included in the price and what additional samples will cost over and above the project price. Likewise, if they charge hourly, ask for an estimate of how long each pattern may take.

Do they charge for consultations? Many pattern makers may offer 30 minutes free for consultations, but if you go over this time, expect to pay their fees.

Do they have a minimum charge? Oftentimes, pattern makers can be very efficient and may complete a project faster than anticipated. To make a project worth while to this individual, they may have a 2-3 hour minimum per project or per garment.

What is their turnaround time and do they charge extra for rush projects? This will most likely depend on their other projects at hand, so this time line may vary for each project you have them work on.

If you find a pattern maker who does not sew samples, get a referral from her for a sample maker who is familiar with their work. Finding an individual who is both a pattern maker and a sample maker is oftentimes better because she can translate the pattern into the most practical construction methods and can modify the patterns according to the production method needed.

Preparing for your pattern maker
Before you meet with your pattern maker, determine for yourself how you would like your sizing and your fit. For example, is there a particular brand in which their fit and sizing impresses you? This is a great starting point. Have your sketches, or pictures of similar designs, and bring them to your first meeting.

Notes:

Pattern maker Questionnaire

Name:

Address: ....   Website: ....

....

Phone: ....   Email: ....

Rates: ....   Hourly or Project

Minimum Charge: ....   Rush Charges: ....

Turn Around Time: ....

Design Specialty:

Grading Experience:

References:

Additional Notes:

Case Study: Pattern maker Questionnaire

Name: *Jennifer Lynne*

Address: _____   Website: *lafashionresource.com*

_____

Phone: _____   Email: *jennifer@lafashionresource.com*

Rates: *$45/hour (friend discount)*   (Hourly) or Project

Minimum Charge: *2 hours*   Rush Charges: *1 week – $150 extra*

Turn Around Time: *2–3 weeks*

Design Specialty:
missy, maternity, woven, knit, lingerie, sportswear

Grading Experience:
moderate – hand grading only

References:
FIDM Instructor, her own lingerie and clothing line, development for other designers

Additional Notes:
Allow 2 weeks for each garment development sample, she will do patterns and samples

Notes:

Sample Making

Your pattern maker may not do both patterns and samples, so if you are working with a sample maker too, consider that the process of creating these samples may take longer. When meeting with your pattern maker or sample maker for the first time, you should have a small quantity of the fabric chosen for your collection available for your samples. It is important to create your samples in the fabric you are going to use for pattern accuracy (or use an inexpensive substitute until the final design has been completed). Every fabric type works and fits differently, so using something close to your final fabric is required.

At the end of the consultation with your pattern and sample makers, you should be given a ballpark figure for the creation of two to three samples. If there are numerous unplanned changes in the design and fit between each sample phase, this would not be accounted for in the original quote and you should expect to pay for it.

Disorganization on your part can cause frustration for the pattern maker and will cost you money. She will basically be starting over each time, doubling her time and your cost. Most seasoned pattern makers will overshoot the quote for that reason. Treat your pattern maker as a professional and respect her time and labor.

You should not expect to receive a perfect sample on the first try. (If you do, this person is a keeper and please pass her information to me. I would like to hire her.) More commonly, expect the first sample to need revisions and don't expect it to be sewn at 100% quality. You are aiming for fit and are testing the initial design with the first sample. Your second and third sample should fit well, but you may still need revisions. If you can't get a good working sample by the fourth go, you might want to find another pattern maker. It is normal to shop around. If you have a few items, test out a couple individuals with different projects. It is always better to have more than one option.

Sample Sizes

If you have not previously worked with a pattern maker and are just starting your business, you should develop a set of blocks or slopers of your sample size. Once you create these, your pattern maker should be able to create your designs relatively easily.

Blocks or Slopers: The basic pattern shapes for you market. All patterns are drafted from these basic shapes. This usually includes a skirt, pant, bodice, torso and sleeve. This may also include a bias torso and a knit torso and sleeve.

I know it is your instinct to use yourself as your sample size, but it may not be appropriate for your collection. Your sample size should be a medium or a size 8 and fit your target customer. Juniors have a different shape than missy, plus sizes or petites.

Creating samples in the middle size is complimentary for when you begin *grading*. Mediums have hips and curves, so making the pattern larger incorporates those shapes. XS and Small sizes don't usually have the same curves, so growing your size from a XS to a XL will not translate well into the larger sizes.

Notes:

Grading: The size range of the garments. This is expressed by a numerical standard. For example, small/medium/large numerical standards will vary from the 2/4/6/8/10/12 size range.

You will also need to work with a fit model. A fit model isn't a fashion model nor doesn't she need to be drop dead gorgeous. A fit model has the proportions, both height and width, of your target customer. This fit model will be used to determine how each of the samples fit on the body. It will be important that the fit model wear the same shoes and foundations (i.e. bra and type of underwear) for each fitting so the clothes hang the same way each time. Fit models usually get paid as much as fashion models, but you can sometimes entice a friend who is the ideal size to be your model in exchange for free clothes (or baby sitting if she is a mother).

Make sure to keep copies of your blocks on hand even if your pattern maker has a copy. Block are a valuable commodity and it could be disastrous if you develop a great fitting sample block and your pattern maker accidentally gives them to another customer or their dog has their way with them.

Grading

Pattern. Check. Samples. Check. What's next in line? Grading. Grading refers to graduated sizes. In other words, you need to create a size range out of your pattern. Your pattern maker may be experienced in grading patterns, but the costs will add up quickly. A cheaper alternative is digital pattern grading. The price is usually per pattern piece and will cost pennies to what your pattern maker will charge.

Computerized grading, however, is not always the most accurate. If you get your garments graded digitally, I highly recommend creating a sample in each size. It doesn't have to be a pretty sample. You just need to make sure it fits your targeted sizes. If you are working in foundation clothing such as bras and underwear, you will need to find a specialist in grading these items to create **grading rules** for all your future designs.

Grading rules are a set measurement between sizes. Your grading rules will vary depending on whether you use knits or wovens and will also vary depending on your market and size range. For example, plus sizes use very different grading rules than missy sizes. The larger the sizes go in plus sizes, the greater the difference becomes. Missy sizing on the other hand, is usually consistent between sizes. All these are things that you can ask your pattern maker to help you with. There are also books entirely on grading, so consider reading them, or seek a professional to do the work for you.

Grading Rules: *The percentage and standard of change between each clothing size. Mathematical calculations are used to create proper grading rules.*

Block Development

Select the blocks needed for your collection:

☐Bodice ☐Torso ☐Bias Torso ☐Jacket ☐Fitted Sleeve ☐Straight Sleeve

☐Jacket Sleeve ☐Skirt ☐Pant ☐Jean ☐Knit Pant ☐Knit Torso ☐Knit Sleeve

Market Classification - Be specific (e.g. juniors, plus size, etc.)

☐Women ☐Men ☐Children

Measurement Description		Sample Size ____	
Upper Torso		Front	Back
Across Shoulder (shoulder tip to shoulder tip)			
Across Chest (1" higher than mid armhole)			NA
Across Back (1" higher than mid armhole)		NA	
Bust Arc (side seam to side seam over bust)			NA
Back Arc (side seam to side seam continuing from bust arc position		NA	
Bust Span (bust point to bust point)			NA
Waist Arc (narrowest point side seam to side seam)			
Abdomen Arc (3" below waist, side seam to side seam)			
Bust Radius (from bust point to below bust on rib cage)			NA
Below Bust (side seam to side seam directly below the bust)			NA
Hip Arc (widest point of the hip from side seam to side seam			
Hip Depth (from waist to hip point			
Center Length (neck to waist over bust bridge)			
Full Length (waist to side neck)			
Shoulder Slope (center waist to shoulder tip			
Bust Depth (shoulder tip to bust point)			NA
Side Length (underarm to waist)			
Shoulder Length (shoulder tip to side neck)			
Side Hip Depth (waist to widest point at hip			
Lower Torso		Foot (over heel and instep)	
Upper Thigh		Knee Depth (waist to mid knee)	
Mid Thigh		Ankle Depth (waist to ankle)	
Knee		Floor Length (waist to floor)	
Calf (widest point below knee)		Crotch Length (front waist to back waist	
Ankle		Crotch Depth (sitting - seat to waist)	

Case Study: Block Development

Select the blocks needed for your collection:

☐Bodice (☐Torso) (☐Bias Torso) ☐Jacket ☐Fitted Sleeve (☐Straight Sleeve)

☐Jacket Sleeve (☐Skirt)(☐Pant) ☐Jean (☐Knit Pant)(☐Knit Torso) ☐Knit Sleeve

Market Classification - Be specific (e.g. juniors, plus size, etc.)

(☐Women) ☐Men ☐Children

_____*Missy*_____

Measurement Description			Sample Size ____	
Upper Torso			Front	Back
Across Shoulder (shoulder tip to shoulder tip)			15	15
Across Chest (1" higher than mid armhole)			12.5	NA
Across Back (1" higher than mid armhole)			NA	13.75
Bust Arc (side seam to side seam over bust)			19	NA
Back Arc (side seam to side seam continuing from bust arc position			NA	17.5
Bust Span (bust point to bust point)			3.75	NA
Waist Arc (narrowest point side seam to side seam)			13	12
Abdomen Arc (3" below waist, side seam to side seam)			17	15.5
Bust Radius (from bust point to below bust on rib cage)			3	NA
Below Bust (side seam to side seam directly below the bust)			13	NA
Hip Arc (widest point of the hip from side seam to side seam			18	20
Hip Depth (from waist to hip point)			8	8.5
Center Length (neck to waist over bust bridge)			14.75	17
Full Length (waist to side neck)			17.5	17.75
Shoulder Slope (center waist to shoulder tip			17	16.75
Bust Depth (shoulder tip to bust point)			9.5	NA
Side Length (underarm to waist)			8.5	
Shoulder Length (shoulder tip to side neck)			5.25	
Side Hip Depth (waist to widest point at hip			8.5	
Lower Torso		Foot (over heel and instep)	9.75	
Upper Thigh	20.5	Knee Depth (waist to mid knee)	22.5	
Mid Thigh	17.5	Ankle Depth (waist to ankle)	37.5	
Knee	13.5	Floor Length (waist to floor)	39.5	
Calf (widest point below knee)	11.5	Crotch Length (front waist to back waist	25.5	
Ankle	9	Crotch Depth (sitting - seat to waist)	9.75	

Sample Development

Style Name: .... Style #: ....

Estimated Labor Cost: .... Actual Labor Cost: ....

Prices per hour: Drafting: .... Sewing: .... Fitting: ....

Sample #1

Drafting Time: .... Sewing Time: .... Fitting Time: ....

Materials	Quantity Used	Materials	Quantity Used

Comments:

Sample #2

Drafting Time: .... Sewing Time: .... Fitting Time: ....

Materials	Quantity Used	Materials	Quantity Used

Comments:

Sample #3

Drafting Time: .... Sewing Time: .... Fitting Time: ....

Materials	Quantity Used	Materials	Quantity Used

Comments:

Case Study: Sample Development

Style Name: __Swing Dress__   Style #: _____

Estimated Labor Cost: __$400__   Actual Labor Cost: __$300.75__

Prices per hour: Drafting: __$45__   Sewing: __$45__   Fitting: __NA__

Sample #1

Drafting Time: __2.5__   Sewing Time: __.75__   Fitting Time: __.5 (self)__

Materials	Quantity Used	Materials	Quantity Used

Comments:
__lower neckline, lengthen 2"__

Sample #2

Drafting Time: __1__   Sewing Time: __.75__   Fitting Time: __.5 (self)__

Materials	Quantity Used	Materials	Quantity Used

Comments:
__good fit, make next in real fabric with overlocked edges and blind stitched hem__

Sample #3

Drafting Time: __.25__   Sewing Time: __1.5__   Fitting Time: __.5 (self)__

Materials	Quantity Used	Materials	Quantity Used

Comments:
__maybe have some top stitching in contrasting colors.__

Notes:

_____

_____

_____

_____

_____

_____

_____

_____

Technical Sketch or Flat Sketch: *An illustration of a garment with finished dimensions including all sewing details, seam lines and garment finishings.*

Spec Sheets

After the process of developing your patterns and grading, you need to create garment specification sheets (or spec sheet for short). A spec sheet details everything about your garment in terms of finished measurements and sizes. Your pattern maker should be able to assist you in creating one. It details the finished measurements of each part of the garment for each size available.

The spec sheet also contains a detailed ***technical sketch*** as a reference for sewing. The technical sketch is usually created by the designer on a computer program such as Adobe Illustrator. If you prefer not to go the digital route, a technical sketch may also be done by hand. A technical designer can assist you in developing a technical flat sketch.

A spec sheet helps each person in the process of production to understand the expectations of your finished garment through measurements and stitch lines.

Spec Sheet

This spec sheet should accompany the Pattern Production Card and should be given to the sewing contractors.

Date: _____   Season: _____

Style Name: _____   Style #: _____

Size Range: _____   Yardage: _____

Notions: _____

Technical Flat

Measurements	Sizes						
	XS/2	S/4	M/6	L/8	XL/10	12	14

Case Study: Spec Sheet

This spec sheet should accompany the Pattern Production Card and should be given to the sewing contractors.

Date: *October 30, 2010*　　　　Season: *Spring 2011*

Style Name: *Urban Knickers*　　　Style #:

Size Range: *2–12*　　　　　　　Yardage: *2.73*

Notions: *5'' zipper*

Technical Flat
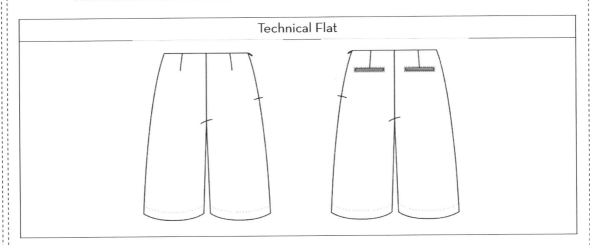

Measurements	Sizes						
	XS/2	S/4	M/6	L/8	XL/10	12	14
Front Waist	12	13	14	15	16	17	
Back Waist	13	14	15	16	17	18	
Across Hip Front	15.5	16.5	17.5	18.5	19.5	20.5	
Across Hip Back	17.5	18.5	19.5	20.5	21.5	22.5	
Side Seam	19	19.5	20	20.5	21	21.5	
Inseam	13	13.25	13.5	13.75	14	14.25	
CF Seam	7.25	7.5	7.75	8	8.25	8.5	
CB Seam	9.5	9.25	9.75	10	10.25	10.5	
Leg Hem Front	9	9.5	10	10.5	11	1.5	
Leg Hem Back	10.5	11	11.5	12	12.5	13	

Chapter 9
Cutting and Production

You are one step closer to production when you reach the stage of cutting. Cutting is not as straightforward as pulling out a pair of dressmaker shears and chopping away at some fabric. The patterns must arrive at the cutters organized and prepped on a digital marker.

Markers

A marker is a paper representation of all pattern pieces to determine how many garments can be cut from the fabric with the least amount of waste. If you had your patterns digitally graded, you are ahead of the game and your marker will be easy to create from those digital files.

If you had a pattern maker size your patterns by hand, you will most likely now need to get them digitized. The reason? Many of the cutting services have grown with technology and now create digital markers for cutting various widths and lengths of fabrics.

One advantage of digitized patterns is that they can be emailed, saving you the hassle of hand delivery or snail mail.

Notes:

Notes:

Digital markers are a great advancement in the garment industry and your savior in figuring out how many garments you can create from your yardage. Why would a company prefer to do markers digitally rather than manually? To do it manually, you will have to lay out the pattern pieces by eye and trace them off by hand. With digital markers, the computer creates the layout automatically, depending on the width of fabric – saving you both time and material. This layout is then printed and spread out over the fabric for cutting multiple layers at a time.

Fabric Width: *Different fabrics come in different widths. The norm is between 45" and 60" wide.*

For costing purposes discussed later in Chapter 35, you can use a marker and the **fabric width** to determine the exact amount of fabric needed for one garment. You can get help from your pattern maker to get an accurate amount.

Costing of fabric: *Determining the exact amount of fabric used for the creation of your garments*

In order to make sure you are allowing for enough fabric in your **costing**, have your pattern maker take into consideration all sizes in which you plan to make the garment and calculate the average amount of fabric used per garment. Use this amount in Chapter 35, Variable Costs.

Notes:

Cutting

Your cutters may sometimes also be your production contractors, so you may not need to worry as much about cutting being a separate step. Some cutters may also offer grading, marking, and digitizing. A company that offers cutting, sewing and all of these pattern services under one roof is referred to as being vertically integrated, or as CMT (cut, make, trim).

If you are shopping around for cutting services, get two or more quotes for different quantities. Find out what the minimum cut charge is. Use the higher quote for costing purposes in Chapter 35. You will need to know how many pattern pieces are in each garment for your quote to be accurate.

Be clear when working with a cutting service by providing a detailed cut sheet for each garment. The cut sheet details the fabrics and pattern pieces that need to be cut for each garment, as well as the technical flat for reference.

Notes:

Cut Sheet

Date: _____ Season: _____

Style Name: _____ Style #: _____

Size Range: _____ Yardage: _____

Delivery: _____ Contractor: _____

Technical Flat	Swatches	
	Self	Contrast
	Lining/Facing	Interfacing

Pattern Pieces			
Self	Contrast	Lining/Facing	Interfacing

Quantity

Colorways	Sizes						
	XS/2	S/4	M/6	L/8	XL/10	12	14
Total							

Case Study: Cut Sheet

Date: _November 5, 2010_   Season: _Spring 2011_

Style Name: _Swing Dress_   Style #:

Size Range: _2–12_   Yardage: _2.95_

Delivery: _7 days_   Contractor: _Domino Cutting_

Technical Flat	Swatches	
	Self	Contrast
		NA
	Lining/Facing	Interfacing
	NA	NA

Pattern Pieces			
Self	Contrast	Lining/Facing	Interfacing
Front Top			
Front Skirt			
Back Top			
Back Skirt			
Center Strap			
Side Strap			

Quantity

Colorways	Sizes						
	XS/2	S/4	M/6	L/8	XL/10	12	14
Mushroom	4	6	8	10	8	8	
White	4	4	4	6	4	4	
Orchid	4	4	6	6	4	4	
Total							

Notes:

Production

We are down to the last step in getting your product made—the actual production of your garment. You have screened your pattern maker and sample maker. Now you need to screen your sewing contractors.

Not every sewing contractor will work out for you, and the referrals you get may not always pan out. There are several things you need to determine about the contractor you are considering including the machinery they have, if they have cutting abilities and what their capabilities are for production.

You should know, from your final samples, what types of machines are needed to produce your garment. Not every sewing contractor has every specialty machine. Buttonhole, zigzag, blind hem, flat lock, or rolled hem machines are special equipment that may not be in every contractor's inventory. Know what you need before settling on a contractor.

Don't limit yourself to one contractor either. Try a few until you get one that will work well with you. Follow your instincts. I tried three before I settled on the one I currently use.

Production Card: A chart that includes a technical flat of the finished garment, trims to be used, pattern pieces, finished measurements, and construction details.

My present contractors and I have mutual respect for each other and our relationship has grown with my business. They were willing to work with me and my deadlines. When I began working with them, I don't think I had a properly sewn sample, let alone a *production card* to go with the garments. They were very helpful and walked me through the whole process. I still forget to drop things off at times, but they respect me enough not to put me on the back burner, and we continue to meet my deadlines. I now give them everything bundled properly with swatches and specs.

This trust and recognition came with time. The first production they did for me was not that great, but as I stuck with them and communicated my expectations, my production became more efficient and of a higher quality.

When choosing your contractors, see how much work they have lying around. If it looks like they are busy, ask if you will get the priority you need. Get price quotes. Have realistic ideas of how much you want to spend on each piece. The per-piece price is usually negotiable, but don't insult them. They have to make a living and recognizing this will help develop mutual respect. You will oftentimes get better prices if your production is larger.

There are listings of sewing contractors in the printed and online version of the Business-to-Business yellow pages. Call around, ask questions. Not every factory has English speaking laborers, so make sure there is someone with whom you can communicate. Language barriers are sometimes a problem. Finding the right factory for your production takes patience.

International Trade

Manufacturing or sourcing internationally has many restrictions. These restrictions pertain to the materials and merchandise and which country it is originating from. Sourcing and manufacturing overseas may appear to be less expensive, but in many cases, after you calculate all the fees included for transport, storage, handling, customs, brokers and manufacturing, pricing may equal what you would pay for domestic sourcing. Weigh all your options before choosing to work internationally.

If you do plan to work with a company internationally, contact a customs broker to handle the transport and delivery to your business.

Notes:

Listings of customs brokers can be found on the U.S. Customs and Border Protection Website www.cbp.gov

Production Facility Information

Contractor: _____   Contact: _____

Address: _____   Phone Number: _____

_____   Fax Number: _____

_____   Referred By: _____

Cutting Services Yes / No   Referrals: _____

Turn around time: _____   Minimums: _____

Prices: _____

Comments: _____

Digitizing Services: Yes / No   Referrals: _____

Turn around time: _____   Minimums: _____

Prices: _____

Comments: _____

Sewing Services: Yes / No   Referrals: _____

Minimum per style: _____   Minimum per order: _____

Turn around time: _____

Machinery needed: _____

Machinery available: _____

Comments: _____

Case Study: Production Facility Information

Contractor: _ABC Sewing_   Contact: _Sandy_

Address: _____   Phone Number: _____

_____   Fax Number: _____

_____   Referred By: _Porcelynne_

Cutting Services Yes (No)   Referrals: _Domino Cutting_

Turn around time: _____   Minimums: _____

Prices: _____

Comments: _____

Digitizing Services: Yes (No)   Referrals: _____

Turn around time: _____   Minimums: _____

Prices: _____

Comments: _____

Sewing Services: (Yes) No   Referrals: _____

Minimum per style: _50 pieces_   Minimum per order: _200 pieces_

Turn around time: _21 days_

Machinery needed: _blind hem, overlock, coverstitch_

Machinery available: _all available_

Comments: _clean space, friendly, English-speakng contact_

Production Pattern Card

This form accompanies the Spec Sheet and goes to the sewing contractor

Date:_____   Season:_____

Style Name:_____   Style #:_____   Size Range:_____

Delivery: _____   Contractor:_____

Technical Flat	Swatches	
	Self	Contrast
	Lining/Facing	Interfacing

Pattern Pieces			
Self	Contrast	Lining/Facing	Interfacing

Quantity

Colorways	Sizes						
	XS/2	S/4	M/6	L/8	XL/10	12	14
Total							

Packing Method: _____   Hangtag:_____

Construction Details:_____

Case Study: Production Pattern Card
This form accompanies the Spec Sheet and goes to the sewing contractor

Date: _November 5, 2011_   Season: _Spring 2011_

Style Name: _Wrap Dress_   Style #: _____   Size Range: _2–12_

Delivery: _21 days_   Contractor: _ABC Sewing_

Technical Flat	Swatches	
	Self	Contrast
		NA
	Lining/Facing	Interfacing
	NA	NA

Pattern Pieces			
Self	Contrast	Lining/Facing	Interfacing
Front Top Left	Tie Right		
Front Top Right	Tie Left		
Front Skirt Left			
Front Skirt Right			
Back Top			
Back Skirt			

Quantity

Colorways	XS/2	S/4	M/6	L/8	XL/10	12	14
Mushroom	4	6	8	10	8	8	
White	4	4	4	6	4	4	
Orchid	4	4	6	6	4	4	
Total							

Packing Method: _Hanger_   Hangtag: _____

Construction Details: _stitch at 1/2'' SA, overlock finished seams_

Designer Profile: Simplicio Michael Luis

Simplicio Michael Luis, a.k.a. "M", has been designing for over 15 years, internationally. He has a design studio called Haus of "M" where he works with corporate clients, and M The Movement, an eco-friendly designer street wear line.

What is your Design Philosophy?

To create environmentally sound pieces that are contemporary and thoughtful. I love the mix of organic and earthly with a sleek and modern presentation. I like to incorporate wooden hangtags for my clothing with paper finish leather scrolls inside them with my philosophy imprinted on it.

What general process do you go through when developing a collection?

Each season it really depends. First is the inspiration, which comes from anything from music, a city I visit or a new film. Then from there, I do some sketches via computer and organize some images from the web that give the vibe of the newly found inspiration. Then I render some CADs and play around with colors and prints. After the pieces are done, I step back and look at it all. I add and edit as needed. Final steps are the Tech Packs. I then send them off to be made. The prototypes will normally come back about 80% correct, and I go through two more steps to make them perfect. From there I duplicate them into salesman samples and let work on taking orders while I market the line via fashion shows, advertisements, etc.

When designing your collection, do you limit yourself knowing how much something might cost in production?

We do that in the final steps of the design, right before the Tech Packs. It is very necessary to make items that are feasible structurally both physically and financially. But this cannot be part of the initial design phase. You need to be completely free from all restrictions in the beginning because in the first step it's all about the inspiration. Starting the process is already hard enough!

What was your first experience of manufacturing overseas like?

It was fun and exciting. I learned and experimented a lot. I traveled to the factories to see how they operated and treated their employees. It is quite interesting how disciplined the process of garment making is.

Did you have to figure it out for yourself or did you have assistance?

I had assistance. The factories are always there to help. They want your product and company to be successful. The more successful you are, the more they would be. Even though I did get help, I still had to learn a lot on my own. It was a great process. I am very much the entrepreneur and love the challenge to solve problems creatively.

What is your most accomplished piece of press and how did you get it?

I was featured on WGSN, which is an ultimate source for who's who. It's a predictive for fashion, online connecting the international fashion both in education and retail. They did a profile on my career that was seen by their many subscribers. I also received some great press from the Mercedes Fashion Weeks.

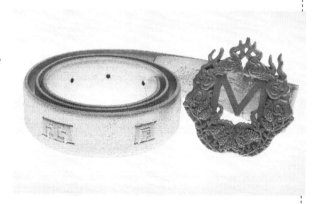

Do you find social media helps in promoting your business?

Yes, in this day in age, it is much more effective than printed materials. It receives more distribution and the number of "eyes" that receive it.

Chapter 10
Fast Fashion vs. Slow Fashion

What does fast fashion and slow fashion mean to you and your business model?

Fast fashion is what many of us shoppers are familiar with; it is when buying seasons don't follow the traditional pattern of four seasons a year. Typically new merchandise is available every few weeks. Fast fashion hits every trend and makes clothing available at a moment's notice. Fast fashion is possible when companies work closely with their factories and closely track customer trends and demands. The lead time for fast fashion can be as little as two weeks.

Where might you see fast fashion? Examples include big retailers such as H&M and Zara. What makes these companies capable of this "fast" turn around, is that they have buyers in each of their retail locations and then place orders based on local demand. Buyers can make purchases directly from their own company factory and have immediate local results regardless of what other locations are doing. This process makes a two week lead time possible.

Notes:

Notes:

Another example of fast fashion can also be seen with smaller design companies. Many small companies have a close relationship with their manufacturers, enabling them to react to local fashion trends quickly, often through road reps or local buyers.

Fast fashion is difficult and typically not possible for companies that produce internationally because of lead times, quality control and import travel times. (H&M and Zara are the exception because they manage the factories that produce inventory.)

At the other end of the spectrum is slow fashion, although this concept may not be as extreme as you might think. Your company might be best suited in both levels.

Slow fashion is about creating quality garments over quantities of garments. Slow fashion typically uses local resources over outsourcing, focusing on making contributions to the local economy. This is a newer movement that has become more popular in recent years and could be a result of the current economic climate. Let me explain.

One such reasoning for this new perspective can be traced to 2008, when the US economy began to suffer, gas prices rose from $2 a gallon to $5, and this made freight charges untouchable by those that once produced internationally. As the gas prices rose, it produced a chain reaction began. People stopped buying goods, forcing many companies to react fast and smart. The idea of focusing on necessity and promoting local industry was reborn.

Similar to the slow food movement which formed in 1989; restaurants bought from local farmers and restored local traditions to their communities. The restaurant patron knew that their dollar was helping local farmers, and in turn, returning their money back into the local economy. The focus of slow food is quality and sustainable living.

Slow fashion is similar. The focus is redirected on design, quality of the garment, quality of fabric and the benefit to local producers. Slow fashion is done locally, so quality is controlled first hand.

When I was a designer living in the San Francisco Bay Area, I was part of the slow fashion movement. I produced all my products locally. I knew my contractors; I joked with them, learned about their lives and oversaw their work in every aspect. I knew my dollar was going back into my community. In the same respect, I sold to local retailers and had many local customers - they got to know me and my business practices. They preferred to pay the higher price for my garments than spending their money at Target, on a lower quality mass produced item. They knew that their money was going back into the community.

The idea of knowing all aspects of a garment's origin, from design, to production and sales is the rise of slow fashion. Slow fashion could mean that the designer is making everything by hand and spends three weeks on one garment, but it could also mean that the designer's relationship is so strong with their local manufacturer that they could produce new designs within two weeks.

Notes:

Notes:

Does this mean that a slow fashion designer could also be a fast fashion producer? One design firm that comes to mind that falls into both categories is American Apparel. They have their own retail establishments. They are also their own wholesaler and manufacturer, which mean they have the means to produce orders on demand as a fast fashion company. They also promote local enterprise and produce everything in Los Angeles. Taking care of their employees and educating the public on sweatshops, places them into the category of slow fashion. In the most basic terms, American Apparel is both.

Chapter 11
Sustainable Fashion

Can fashion be sustainable? Fashion is something that is trendy and disposable. Sustainable describes something that lasts.

So what is sustainable fashion? It is the part of the fashion industry that recognizes social and environmental responsibility. Another name is eco-fashion, a term which was once affiliated with hippy clothing, but now has a larger meaning in everyday clothing.

Sustainable fashion can be described as the fabric used in production, the process of creating a garment or the life of the garment itself.

Sustainable Fabrics

The first part of explaining sustainable fashion is through the origin of the textiles and notions that are used to put a garment together. To produce fabric through current industry processes, a portion of the environment is affected. Designers who practice sustainable fashion are very conscience of their carbon footprint and consequently choose products that will have the least amount of impact on the environment. There are advantages and disadvantages to all types of fabrics, so

Notes:

familiarizing yourself with each one of the products you use is important if you choose to go this route.

Cotton is the largest contributor to the carbon footprint of the garment industry. This single plant is responsible for over 25% of the world's consumption of insecticides and 10% of pesticides, which all contribute to global warming. Organic cotton is more sustainable, it's better for your body and the environment because no chemicals were used. However, organic cotton also uses more than twice the amount of water of regular cotton which could be detrimental in periods of drought. Organic generally means no pesticides, insecticides or genetic alterations are used in the resource.

Bamboo is an example of an easily renewable resource because it grows fast and it absorbs greenhouse gasses during its life cycle. However, negative effects can be seen when rainforests are cut down to house bamboo fields. In addition, the chemical process to make the plant into textile fibers is even more detrimental to the environment than cutting down those forests. The process is toxic and without the proper equipment and machinery to regulate the chemicals, the environment can be harmful to the health of humans, plants and animals.

Polyester has a bad reputation being associated with those 1970's itchy un-breathable garments. It won't break down over time like cotton or bamboo can, but it can be made from recycled plastic and can be mixed with other fabrics to have a lasting, wearable quality resulting in less of an environmental impact.

Fabrics that contain Spandex or Lycra are comfortable and provide a flexible fabric. These fibers allow for clothing to fit more than one size, but they wear out faster than no-stretch fibers. This is do to the stretching of the fabric and care of the fabrics (washing in hot water and the use of high heat driers cause the threads to disintegrate rapidly). Because of these factors, garments with Spandex or Lycra have a shorter lifespan.

Sustainable Fashion

Fabric isn't the only part of fashion that can be sustainable. The longevity of your finished garment is also important. We have all heard the words disposable fashion used. Fast fashion guru's H&M produce fashion that is poor in quality and is what I call "wear, wash and throw away." On the other hand, quality garments can be repaired and fixed and live longer in our closets.

Sustainable fashion products are destined for reuse through a thrift store or second hand store, rather than the rag bin. The sustainable movement in clothing use needs to start with the designer educating the public on what happens to your clothes when they land in the trash. Donating used clothing for reuse or recycling need to become a norm. Many businesses offer discount incentives for the return of old worn out merchandise. And what might they do with them and who offers this service?

Apple does it. They analyze whether the product returned can be refurbished and resold; or whether the product needs to be dismantled in order to recycle the metals, glass or plastic into new products.

Notes:

Bonded Logic:
www.bondedlogic.com

Hickory Springs:
www.innotherm.com

Recovery Insulation:
www.recovery-insulation.
co.uk

Notes:

Some clothing can be recycled, but the facilities aren't very common. Your old 501 blue jeans can now be turned into building insulation. Three companies that currently do this are Bonded Logic, Hickory Springs and Recover Insulation, Ltd. Another philosophy that some designers follow is creating designs from second hand clothing, upcycling them into new innovate creations. Repurposing used clothing into new innovative merchandise is following a sustainable philosophy.

Other designers have adapted the idea of no waste designs, meaning that there is no fabric left after cutting the design. Julian Roberts, a fashion designer and educator uses this method and creates unique and original designs that can actually be recreated. To see his amazing work, go to julianand. com. His website is only open for business on Wednesdays from 10am to 8pm. The method he designs by is called Subtraction Cutting. See his website for more information.

When did it become acceptable to get rid of a garment instead of sewing on a button? Repairing isn't a new trend, but a very old idea that has been forgotten. On a personal note, I get my black strappy sandals re-soled every year or so. I love these shoes. I can't remember, but I don't think I paid much for them, they are classic and comfortable. I have had them repaired over 5 times at almost $10 each time, but I have to say it was worth it. I mentioned to one of my students about getting new heels put on them and they thought it was the coolest idea that you could get something repaired. Why does this generation think everything is disposable?

Ethical Fashion
Ethical fashion is related to the treatment of employees and

work conditions while garments are being manufactured. Despite the efforts of government agencies and celebrities, sweatshops are more abundant than Starbucks in NYC. (There is one every three city blocks.)

I'm sure you've heard talk about sweatshops, but how much do you really know? I have stood against them in the past, but (on a personal level) I never actually had first hand experience with them. A common misconception is that all factories are sweatshops.

Back in 2008, I began following the Centre for Sustainable Fashion at the London College. Their program is about educating the public about conditions at sweatshops. They have some fabulous fact sheets worth reading. I don't think I even had a clue as to how bad sweatshops could be until I came across this resource. The following information was obtained from these fact sheets. If you are interested in learning more, check their website **www.sustainable-fashion.com**.

Sweatshops are all over the world, including China, India and even the United States. Although governments have set forth restrictions on pay, hours and employee rights, many still elude officials and their customers. Factories have been known to do double books, one for them and one for the government enforcers.

The women who work in these factories get treated the worst. They work long hours (12-16 hour days, 7 days a week), receive low pay (sometimes as little as 50 cents an hour) and are often treated poorly. There are some establishments known to not

Notes:

Notes:

allow women to drink water, use the bathroom and even subject them to pregnancy tests to prevent having to pay maternity leave.

In the last couple years, a few large fashion houses were caught using sweatshops; one in particular was The Gap*. In 2007, a sweatshop comprised of 14 children in New Delhi, India was raided in an inspection and was found to be in violation of labor laws. The questions are: Did the Gap know? Did they check the factory before doing business with them? Or did the factory lie to them to get their business? According to Gap officials, they hired one factory to do that work but another was subcontracted for the work without their knowledge.

These questions bring up another issue regarding international production - subcontracting. This means that the factory you hire to do the work may hire another factory to do the work (which is cheaper) and the customer has little knowledge of this manufacturing transition.

How can you monitor your outsourcing and know what the work conditions are in a factory you have hired? The best way is to go and check the factory out for yourself. There are organizations and unions that regulate factories on a regular basis which can assist you in finding a reputable company.

Next time, when you see a tee for $2 or find a dress for $5, question how they can afford to sell a garment for that price and make a profit. Consider the conditions in which that garment was produced.

I have heard arguments between tee shirt designers and fashion

Articles: http://www.cnn.com/2007/WORLD/asiapcf/10/29/gap.labor/index.html
http://www.telegraph.co.uk/news/worldnews/1567849/Gap-sweatshop-children-saved-in-India-raid.html

Chapter 12
The Tee Shirt Business

designers and it isn't pretty. Yes, a tee shirt is a wearable item that designers add graphics to, but it is not considered fashion design.

I felt it was important to include a chapter on the tee shirt business because much of what we do as fashion designers, (selling, marketing and running a business) is similar to running a graphic tee business. There are however a handful of differences, namely that most of these businesses use blanks as a way of displaying their art.

Sourcing

Graphic tees are made from clothing blanks. These **blanks** are adorned by works of art placed on them that were created by graphic designers. Much in the way that fashion designer source fabrics, graphic designers source their blanks, whether it be tee shirts, onesies or coffee cups. There are companies that specialize in these items such as American Apparel or Alternative Apparel.

Once the sources have been found for the blanks, the designer needs to search for a printer. Traditionally, the only options

Notes:

Blank: A stock garment used for adding graphics to. A blank can be a tee shirt, hoodie, bag or any other item that is ready made for printing.

for creating graphic tees was to either screen print if yourself or hire a printing company to do it for you. If you are hiring a company to print, they will often give you the option to source the blanks for you. Something to note when screen printing – each color you have in a graphic requires a separate screen, more screens mean more money. This amount can be a variable amount depending on the complexity of the graphics and the company you choose.

Technology is leading to new innovations. You can now purchase a heat press machine, inkjet printer and specialized paper and do it all at home. These machines start around $200, but can go up to a couple grand. Pro World offers many options for the tee shirt entrepreneur. There are also machines that will print directly to fabric that can then be sewn onto the garment. There is also printable transfer paper where all you need is a $20 iron.

Fulfillment Options

While some designers may opt to create their own tangible goods, there are options to allow others to create them for you and on demand. This is a good option when selling online. Fulfillment options are available through companies like Café Press and Zazzle. You can even create your own online store with these companies, and then they market your designs on their website. One upside to this option is not having to carry any inventory. This could also be an option for the fashion designer who wants to print promotional tees for an event without the hassle of sourcing the tees and the printers.

Other than those differences, a graphic designer can develop a collection in the same manner as a fashion designer, create a customer profile and brand, market it and run a business.

MARKETING

Chapter 13
Introduction to Marketing

How does the world find out about you? Through the mighty wonders of marketing. Marketing may sound like a mysterious universe that everybody but you knows about, but you might be surprised by how much you actually know. Independent designers typically overlook this segment of the business, but it is marketing that makes a small business thrive and survive.

Marketing is the process of getting your name, brand and product out in the marketplace. It is an extension of branding and a bridge to sales. How might one achieve successful marketing? For independent designers, the common ways are through press releases, social media, email marketing campaigns, and personal networking.

Advertising

I am not sure whether or not you noticed, but I have not included a chapter on advertising. Setting aside budgets for large advertising campaigns may not be feasible in your start up phases and may not even be realistic in the long term. If you

Notes:

Notes:

are seeking to launch an advertising campaign, be aware of the audience that is targeting. Print advertising can cost upwards of $20,000 for one month of advertising. Television advertising can surprisingly be more affordable, but is still a large ticket item when you factor in the film crew, talent and editing.

Co-op advertising could be an affordable and realistic option. Co-op advertising is sharing in the expense on a larger ad. Many boutiques have advertising campaigns in print and in other means. If you are selling in one of these boutiques, you can work together with the boutique in getting exposure for your line and their store.

Banner advertising on blogs and online news sites can also be another affordable form of advertising. Just make sure that the customer you target is reading those blogs or websites. There is no sense in advertising where you won't be seen by your target audience.

There is also - free advertising. Free advertising comes from media coverage: magazines, newspapers and blogs. In order to pitch to these outlets, you will need to develop marketing materials. In the next few chapters I discuss attaining this form of advertising. Review these chapters then complete the following form.

Marketing and Promotion

List all possible marketing opportunities. List the frequency, the estimated cost and the expected revenue from each avenue.

Marketing or Promotion	Description	Frequency	Projected Cost	Revenue Projected

Case Study: Marketing and Promotion

List all possible marketing opportunities. List the frequency, the estimated cost and the expected revenue from each avenue.

Marketing or Promotion	Description	Frequency	Projected Cost	Revenue Projected
Facebook Advertising	Maintain business page and advertise to target audience	Ongoing	$50 a month	$100 a month
Sponsored Listings	Marketing based on search key words on adwords, yahoo, bing, ask and youtube	Ongoing	$100 a month	$300 a month
Twitter	Maintain business updates to target customers	Ongoing	Time only – 2 hours a week	$100 a month
Blogging	Pitch to bloggers on current products and promotions. upkeep a personal designer blog	Quarterly Pitches – ongoing personal	Time only – 2 hours a week	$500 a month
Email Marketing	Email announcements to customers who sign up for mailing list about business happenings, new merchandise and sales	Monthly or on collection releases	$20 a month	$1000 per email sent
Website	Update the website with new merchandise events, press and awards	Quarterly	Time only – 3 hours a week	NA
Sample Sales	Promote brand awareness, build a customer following, sell samples and seconds	Quarterly	$200 a quarter – time only	$2000 each sale
Direct mail postcard promotions	Sent to retail buyers, follow up with calls	Before trade shows	$100 twice a year	pickup 1–3 stores each mailing
Press Kits	Samples, press releases and marketing materials to targeted media to encourage editorial and feature use	Beginning of release of collection	$200 twice a year	$2000 each press coverage
Trade Shows	Exhibit at trade shows in Los Angeles and Las Vegas	2 a year	$3500 twice a year	$40,000

Chapter 14
Marketing Materials

When launching a product line, one needs to consider all forms of marketing materials. This includes business cards, press releases, line sheets, look books, promotional postcards and banners. Does your business require these things? Which ones and why?

Business Cards

This should be a no-brainer. Business card should be at the top of your to do list after you develop your business name. Whether you are networking, meeting with a potential customer or being introduced to a colleague's friend, it is important to have current business cards available. You should always be promoting our businesses. Include your full name, your title, company name, website, email address and business address (if you have one other than your home). Many business cards also offer Twitter, Skype and Facebook contact info. Your card should also include your company logo.

One can get very innovative with their business card design. There are business cards that contain seeds, so they can be planted and others that have portfolio images on the backsides. Look to your mission statement and choose a business card

Notes:

Notes:

style that fits the personality of your business.

Press Releases

Press Releases are the most popular way of getting the word out to the press about your business happenings. Press releases are written as news articles and are used to announce a newsworthy business event. Before you spend your time and money on a release, make sure your news is important. Not everything is news. Newsworthy stories include business launches, new products, and special business events. Announcing an ordinary event, such as a 20% off sale, is not really worthy of a press release.

A good release will answer the questions who, what, where, when, why, and how. Your headline and first paragraph should summarize your story. It is sometimes easier to write this part last. The rest of your article should provide all the details.

Think of whom you want to be interested in the story—this is your audience—then focus on the news that is relevant to them. Use an active voice and strong verbs. Most releases are usually under 500 words, so make every word count. Include opinions as direct quotes, otherwise, use facts. Your release should conclude with a short paragraph about your company history, products, and services.

Many channels distribute your releases by headline and summary only, so be sure to prepare a one-paragraph summary.

Make sure your article is brief and to the point. Reporters are bombarded with news these days – the faster you can give the details, the more grateful your readers will be!

Distribution of your Press Release

There are a several ways you can distribute your press release. The most expensive way is to use a Public Relations (PR) firm to send out your release. One step down is to use the actual services that the PR firm submits your press release.

Two of the largest online distribution channels are BusinessWire.com and PRNewsWire.com. Their news distribution is over 10 times larger than the less expensive companies or those that offer free distribution. This is one area where going with the cheaper option may cost you. If you are going to invest time and effort in writing a press release, you might want to consider making the investment on the distribution service.

Prices for services can range up to $500 per release, so this makes it even more important to submit a thorough, specific, and timely release. There are many companies that offer writing services—if you are not sure about your writing abilities, this might be a time to hire one.

Another way to submit a press release is to send it directly to the press outlets that you want to cover your business, perhaps your local paper or Lucky Magazine. If you contact them directly, make sure to follow up afterwards, but if you haven't heard back from them after 3 attempts at contact, let it lie. If using email, send the release in the body of the email, not as an attachment. Most publications have contact info for editors on their websites or printed circulars.

A recent company of interest to you might be Vocus. It is an online database of all the media contacts you could ever want

Notes:

Notes:

to use. They have services that can send your press release to all of the contacts directly either through email or snail mail. It is costly, but might be the perfect option if you have the budget for it.

One thing to remember is that your press release may need to be altered for each media outlet you reach out to. Be sure to know about the publication and make sure it is appropriate for that publication. When pitching to a blog, pay special attention. Many bloggers have details on how they like to be contacted and how to pitch to them. You would not pitch to them the same way as you would a magazine. Bloggers are all about the readers and the content and if your release isn't timely or related, you will not be covered.

Press Release Information

Who is the target audience of this press release?

What news is relevant for this press release?

Where is this newsworthy event taking place?

When is this taking place?

Why is this news important?

How do you plan to get your message out?

What company information do you wish to include in this release?

What contact information is to be included in this release?

Contact Name: _____   **Phone Number:** _____

Address: _____   **Website:** _____

_____   **Email Address:** _____

_____

Case Study: Press Release Information

Who is the target audience of this press release?

Newspapers, trade magazines and magazines

What news is relevant for this press release?

Launch party for collection of a rural northern California designer

Where is this newsworthy event taking place?

Eureka, California at Origin Design Lab

When is this taking place?

Weekend after Valentines Day 2011

Why is this news important?

It it the featured business in the book Fashion Unraveled, bootstrapping designer from small town

How do you plan to get your message out?

Book Release, Launch party and trunk show, origin design lab, FB business page

What company information do you wish to include in this release?

Business has been around since 2002, handbag designer launching clothing line after 8 years

What contact information is to be included in this release?

Contact Name: Andrea Baker

Phone Number: 707-834-6911

Address: 426 3rd Street

Eureka, CA 95501

Website: acbapparel.com

Email Address: andrea@acbapparel.com

Press Release Template

The Headline Announces Your News

The summary paragraph summarizes the news being presented in the full release. Many readers will decide from the summary paragraph whether they will continue to the remainder of the release. Keep this under four sentences.

City, State, Date – The lead sentence contains the most important information in your release. Grab your reader's attention here by stating the news you have to announce. Do not assume that your reader has read your headline or summary paragraph.

A news release is like a news story. Keep your sentences and paragraphs short, about three or four lines per paragraph. The first couple of paragraphs should answer who, what, when, where, why and how.

The standard press release is between 300 and 600 words. Topics for a press release can include announcements of new products, the publishing of a book or a launch of a new business.

"Adding a quote to provide editorial content is acceptable," said lama Coolcat. "You can convey biased information in a quote that you can't include in the rest of the release."

Conclude your press release with a little background on you, your company and your products.

Contact Information: Joe Smith
1234 5th Street
Somewhere, USA 00000

Contact Phone: (123) 456-7890

Website: www.lafashionresource.com

Case Study: Press Release

Origin Design Lab Launches A.C. Baker Apparel Spring Collection with Celebration

A.C. Baker Apparel celebrates the launch of her spring collection at Origin Design Lab this February with a launch party comprising of entertainment, food and drinks.

Eureka, California, January 12, 2011 – A.C. Baker Apparel, a northern California based fashion design business, launches their debut collection at Origin Design Lab this month. Origin Design Lab, the retail showroom for A.C. Baker, celebrates with a launch party on Friday, February 15, 2011. This celebration will feature a trunk show, live music, food and drinks.

A.C. Baker Apparel has become known for their handbag collections over the past 5 years. Designer Andrea Baker launches her eco-friendly spring collection with a variety of linen and organic cotton dresses, pants and tops.

Ms. Baker's featured spring collection was designed to be a staple in every woman's closet. Throughout the business and design development, Ms. Baker consulted with Jennifer Matthews, of the best selling book Fashion Unraveled and designer of Porcelynne Lingerie.

"Andrea's collection is romantic in nature mixed with a comfort lifestyle. I feel comfortable going out in her designs as well as lounging around the house. I wish I had a pair for every day of the week." Teresa Johns explains, "The first pair of A.C. Baker pants I ever purchased, sold me forever."

Contact Information: Andrea Baker
426 3rd Street
Eureka, CA 95501

Email Address: andrea@acbapparel.com

Contact Phone: 707-834-6911

Website: acbapparel.com

Line Sheets

Lines sheets are a way of organizing your collection for a prospective buyer. Line sheets contain flat images and sometimes photos of the pieces in your collection. Line sheets give information about the company, buying options, minimums, prices, fabric details, colors, size charts, and care instructions.

It is wise to keep a copy of your line sheet in a PDF format so it can be emailed to prospective buyers. If you wish to add a link on your website to your line sheet, you may want to password protect it, so only retail buyers can have access to it.

A.C. Baker Apparel Spring 2011 Line Sheet
426 3rd Street * Eureka, California 95501* 707-834-6911

Start Delivery: January 15, 2011
Stop Delivery: February 28, 2011

Order Close Date: November 1, 2010
(For guaranteed delivery during our seasonal delivery dates.)

All opening orders require a $500 minimum. Reorders require a $250 minimum. Each style has its own specified minimum quantity for wholesale purchase. All new accounts will be set up with COD payment terms. To qualify for Net 30 payment terms, a credit application must be completed.

Style Name: Baby Doll Dress	Style Name: Cigarette Pants
Style Number: 10000	Style Number: 7000
Fabric: 100% Organic Cotton Sateen	Fabric: 100% Linen
Colors: Mushroom, White, Orchid	Colors: Mushroom, White, Orchid
Sizes: 2-12	Sizes: 2-12
Wholesale Price: $53	Wholesale Price: $53
Retail Price: $106	Retail Price: $106
Minimum Order: 5	Minimum Order: 5

Style Name: Obi Dress	Style Name: Silk Cover Up
Style Number: 9000	Style Number: 4000
Fabric: 100% Linen	Fabric: 100% Silk Organza
Colors: Mushroom White Orchid	Colors: Mushroom White Orchid
Sizes: 2-12	Sizes: 2-12
Wholesale Price: $53	Wholesale Price: $53
Retail Price: $106	Retail Price: $106
Minimum Order: 5	Minimum Order: 5

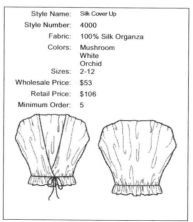

The following example is typical of a traditional line sheet with flats and product details. This example defines the season, the date range for delivery and pricing (both wholesale and retail).

Look books

Look books are mini catalogues of your collection. Some look books carry detailed information that can be found on a line sheet; these are photographic representations of your work and are produced at a high quality. These are ideal for use on your website and displays your collection in a tasteful manner.

The price for putting together a look book can be expensive. The composure of the book is not likely to be free. Booking the models, photography, hair and makeup and the layout of the book are expenses you need to budget for. That is, unless you have an endless resource of friends who do all these and are willing to work for free or trade.

Printing look books may not be financially feasible, but displaying the look book online is. If you print books, they can become wasteful if they are not distributed in a timely manner. Look

Photography by James Reid/Studio 424, Model Jillian Yerby

books are usually distributed at trade shows or by direct mail.

Promotional Postcards

An alternative to creating a mailing of your entire look book is to get postcards printed of select images for mailing and distribution. Promotional postcards can be handed out at sales events, offer sales discounts for online sales, announce your presence at a trade show or just to use as a blind mailing to prospective stores. These cards can be informative as well as displaying your collection.

SPRING 2011

ORGANIC COLLECTION

STYLES SHOWN:
BABYDOLL DRESS
SILK COVER UP

A.C. BAKER APPAREL
CLOTHING & ACCESSORIES

Banners

If you plan on selling at events, whether it be a trade show or street fair, you may opt to have signage to display with your name, logo and catch phrase. These banners can cost from $50 to $300 depending on what you choose to have on the banner.

Notes:

Notes:

Chapter 15
Email Marketing Campaigns

Email marketing is a great tool to help grow your business. Companies such as Constant Contact and Vertical Response offer services that can help you organize and design your email marketing campaign. These services also offer tools for tracking how many people open your email and how soon after you send it that it is opened. You can use this information to fine tune and sharpen your email campaigns.

These companies do not sell email lists. In fact, selling or buying an email list is illegal and the **Can-Spam Act** prohibits it. You are responsible for growing your email list yourself. One way to do this is to add an email sign up option to your website. These services allow you to use the list you've generated to send out professional looking company announcements.

Be sure to keep the email addresses you collect private. This information is proprietary and it is illegal to share it without permission.

Notes:

Can-Spam Act of 2003:
Requires an unsubscribe option, the subject to relate to the context of an email, and a physical address for the email sender. This act prohibits the harvesting or selling of email lists.

Notes:

When I ran a store, I developed a strategy for email marketing that worked for my needs. I would schedule my emails to be sent between 9:30 and 10:30 in the morning on weekdays. Before 9:30, I felt that they would get lost in somebody's inbox amidst all the other emails that come in overnight; after 10:30, I felt that the person would be working and wouldn't get the opportunity to read them. Sending my emails at those times kept them fresh in my customers' inboxes as they were responding to the previous day's emails.

I also kept in mind the day that I sent these emails out. I had many Friday art openings at the boutique, so I would send an email one week in advance to let them know it was coming up and then again on Wednesday when people are planning out their weekends. I also offered sales on the website and special sales in the store. I sent emails for these events out on payday (or the day after). Each of these strategies worked and I received an influx of sales because of them.

You will discover that my strategies may not work for you. Your customer is specific and you will learn what people respond to as you experiment with your email marketing. Many programs will allow you to create different emails for the same campaign and send them to different people on your list. This is a good way to see how many people open each email and how many click through to your links. Another advantage of using one of the email marketing programs is that you can design your emails days in advance and schedule the time for release accordingly.

Email Campaign Etiquette

Take this bit of advice from an email campaign savvy entrepreneur.

There's a good change your name is part of an email list, and probably more than one. Some we signed up for voluntarily and others we just ended up on one way or another.

How do you end up on an unwanted email list? Easy. We all get them, the emails from a friend or colleague who sends an email to a large group of people and places all recipients in the "To" box or the "CC" box.

Yep, you know what I mean and you have probably done it too. I've been guilty of sending a simple email to a group of friends asking about the best restaurant or inviting them to an event with everybody openly cc'd. With friends, it not a big deal.

Where things can get problematic is if you send an email promotion of your business or an event with an open line of contact information for a large number of people you know vaguely or not at all, such as customers who signed your email list. All it takes is for one person on that list to say "hey, this is free information and I'm taking it," and start spamming your list with their promotions. It happens.

This is not only unethical but illegal. It's stealing someone's proprietary information without their consent and it is punishable by law. What's the law? This is the classic definition of spamming.

Chapter 16
Creating a Web Presence

Everybody's on the web these days, whether they have something to say or something to sell. Truth be told, your business will not be taken seriously without a website.

There are a few ways you can create your website. One is the traditional way using HTML code with or without the help of a web designer. The second way to get a website quickly is through templates provided by sites such as Yahoo.com.

Another form, and more popular because of the ease in use, is setting up a blog as your website. You can use sites such as Blogger.com or Wordpress.com. I will get into blogging in the next chapter, but just so you are aware, it is an option for web design as well. If you plan on selling your products on your website, you can create a website through a site such as BigCartel.com. If you plan on selling online, but not on your website, there are options for this too. I will discuss those further on my chapter on direct sales.

Notes:

Notes:

Any way you decide to go, you need to figure out what kind of website you need. Look to other sites that sell products similar to yours. What navigation do they have? Do you need the same or better navigation? Do you need an online store where your customers can buy directly from you or will you be marketing via your website to a wholesale market and use your site as a portfolio for your work?

Prepare all the information you'll want on your website before meeting with your web designer or even before you begin your own layout. Compile your bio, your company information, your services, products, wholesale information, links you want to include, and anything else you can think of prior to your meeting. Get all your images ready (give your images recognizable names: "pillow.jpg", not "image22.jpg"). Have ideas about a color scheme. It should be consistent with your branding.

One more thing to consider, a company's "About Us" page is the most traveled page on a website, so make it extraordinary.

Search Engine Optimization

The most beautifully designed website would be worth zilch if your customers can't find it. How do you ensure that your website shows up in search engines? Here are a few simple tricks to help you out.

Search Engine Optimization (SEO) is what web designers call the little tweaks you do to make your website easy for search engines such as Google and Yahoo to find.

- Make sure your page titles are descriptive and contain your business name. Limit your title to 60 characters.

- Make sure your website has page descriptions. Your descriptions will appear in the search engines along with your page titles and will be your first selling point with those browsing for info. Limit your description to 150 characters.

- Use key word phrases (e.g., empire waist dress) rather than just key words (e.g. dress). Limit your key word phrases to 10.

Just one more tip for a better website: Hire a professional to do all this if you feel it's too much for you to deal with.

If you are unsure what keywords to include, search the engines for the products that you want your website to come up on. Look at the top sites and take a peek at their source code. All browsers have a menu command for viewing the source code. Scroll down on the source code page to see what the page's keywords are. Use this as a guide for developing your own key words and phrases. Do not copy another site's keywords, word for word; this would be plagiarism. More importantly, do not use your competitor's name in your keywords; if the name is trademarked, you could be in for a lawsuit.

Analyzing Your Website's Traffic

Once your site is up and running, you may wish to implement a statistical tracking tool such as Google Analytics. Other programs are available, although Google provides one at no charge. This form of tracking allows you evaluate your customers and traffic in many different ways.

Notes:

Notes:

This type of web tool shows you what countries people are visiting your website from. The program shows entry pages, exit pages, length of time on the site and which pages are visited most. Besides this data, the browser customers reach you through and referrals are captured by this statistical data.

You can use this data to help you target your marketing campaigns. You can test to see whether certain online advertising campaigns are effective. This data can be used in conjunction with your online advertising campaigns to track traffic to your site.

Web Site Competition

Look to your 3 competitors and evaluate their web presence.

Competitor 1:

What navigation do they have on their site? Where is the navigation located (top, side and/or bottom)?

How is their home page titled?

Looking at their source code, what page description do they use in their meta tags?

What key words do they use?

Search their company name in your favorite search engine. What sites does your search pull up?

Competitor 2:

What navigation do they have on their site? Where is the navigation located (top, side and/or bottom)?

How is their home page titled?

Web Site Competition - continued

Competitor 2 (continued

Looking at their source code, what page description do they use in their meta tags?

What key words do they use?

Search their company name in your favorite search engine. What sites does your search pull up?

Competitor 3:

What navigation do they have on their site? Where is the navigation located (top, side and/or bottom)?

How is their home page titled?

Looking at their source code, what page description do they use in their meta tags?

What key words do they use?

Search their company name in your favorite search engine. What sites does your search pull up?

(Due to copyrights, we cannot print our case study on web site competition)

Web Site Organization

After reviewing your competitors' websites, what would you like for your own site?

Will you be setting up your website as a blog or through traditional web site hosting?

Where will your navigation be located and what will it include?

What general description would you like for your site?

What key word phases are appropriate for your site?

Home Page

What information would you like to include on this page?

What images would you like on this page?

Web Site Organization - continued

About Page

What information would you like to include about your business?

What information would you like to provide about yourself?

What images would you like on this page?

Contact Page

What information would you like to include on this page?

What images would you like on this page?

Web Site Organization - continued

Link Page

What links would you like to include?

What images would you like to include on this page?

Page-

What information would you like to include on this page?

What images would you like on this page?

Web Site Organization - continued

Page-

What information would you like to include on this page?

What images would you like on this page?

Page-

What information would you like to include on this page?

What images would you like on this page?

Case Study: Web Site Organization

After reviewing your competitors' websites, what would you like for your own site?

Will you be setting up your website as a blog or through traditional web site hosting?
Traditional Hosting - I own acbapparel.com

Where will your navigation be located and what will it include?
Home, About Us, Gallery, Stockists, Press, Contact
It will be located on the left side of the site.

What general description would you like for your site?
Andrea Baker's women's wear collection provides an alternative to everyday clothing with her
innovative designs and eco-friendly fabric.

What key word phases are appropriate for your site?
Eco friendly, green fashion, sustainable fashion, organic clothes, women's wear, linen dresses, sustain-
able, independent designer, fashion designer, eureka designer

Home Page

What information would you like to include on this page?
it will contain major new, links to sign up for the email list, and a link to my online store.

What images would you like on this page?
I'd like to include images from my collection - maybe the images from the promotional fliers or the
look book

Case Study: Web Site Organization - continued

About Page

What information would you like to include about your business?

I would like to include my mission statement, about the involvement in the book Fashion
Unraveled

What information would you like to provide about yourself?

I need to work on creating a web based bio

What images would you like on this page?

My bio picture

Contact Page

What information would you like to include on this page?

This will include my design studio/showroom address and phone number, email signup list
sales contact info

What images would you like on this page?

A picture of Origin Design Lab

Case Study: Web Site Organization - continued

Link Page

What links would you like to include?

I do not plan on a link page

What images would you like to include on this page?

Page- _Gallery – A.C. Baker Apparel: Spring 2010 Women's Wear Collection_

What information would you like to include on this page?

This page will feature the current collection and offer links to past collections

What images would you like on this page?

This will include all images from my collection in Look Book form

Case Study: Web Site Organization - continued

Page- Stockists – A.C. Baker Apparel: Where to purchase our eco-friendly collections

What information would you like to include on this page?

This page will contain the retailers, both online and brick & mortar shops

What images would you like on this page?

This will include pictures of my past work or a picture of Origin Design Lab

Page- Press – A. C. Baker Apparel: Press and Accolades

What information would you like to include on this page?

This page will contain all the press I've received, both for the clothing line and for my other endeavors

What images would you like on this page?

This will include a picture from our grand opening at the store.

Chapter 17
Blogging

Blogging so easy to do, even my father is doing it. With no or very little web knowledge, anyone can create a blog and post online. Some companies have abandoned traditional websites to use a blog as their main web presence.

Why would someone prefer to write a blog as opposed to a website? Blogs often show up higher in search engines since they are updated regularly. Many companies use blogs as a way to provide regular updates about their products. Here is a little article about blogging covered by San Francisco journalist and (new mother) Lorraine Sanders, explaining the basics of this popular medium.

Notes:

A Little Blog Know-How

By Lorraine Sanders

Don't think of your company's blog and accompanying social media as just an online journal or series of status updates. Instead, look at them as a dynamic catalog, public relations maven, branding pro, marketing diva, and never-ending networking event that's working 24-7 to get your voice, your products, and your message out into the world. Better yet, they're free—and you are in complete control of them.

Whether you chronicle the trials and tribulations of a hectic production cycle, post images of fabric swatches and sketches to preview upcoming collections, or highlight your company's latest news and events, maintaining a blog and using social media platforms such as Facebook and Twitter allow you to show fellow bloggers, fashion journalists, shop owners, and customers a side of your company that would otherwise remain hidden.

The beauty of blogging, tweeting and Facebooking is that they work both ways. Not only do they allow you to broadcast your message outward, but they also pull people in, and that, in turn, increases your chances of being discovered by even more people.

When you blog and use social media, you create an ever-growing series of pathways for people to find you through search engine results, RSS subscriptions, other blogs and their blogrolls, favorite links lists and via their friends and followers. Of course, building relationships online doesn't happen overnight – or without an ongoing effort to reach out. But over time, you're likely to find that your company's blogging and social media efforts have paved the way for new relationships with fellow designers, journalists, retail buyers, and everyday customers.

Ready to get started? You can easily set up a free blog using platforms such as Tumblr.com, Blogger.com or WordPress.com. If you want a look that's integrated with your company's existing web site, and you don't know how to do that on your own, save yourself the headache and hire a professional to do it for you. Don't forget to look at other blogs for inspiration, and add your favorites to your blogroll (don't forget to ask them to reciprocate). You're ready to start posting. See you in the blogosphere.

Five Habits of Successful Bloggers
The most successful bloggers:

- Blog often.
- Use social media such as Facebook and Twitter to grow readership
- Have a consistent point of view.

- Know the power of a good photograph or image.
- Network like mad, online and off.

Five Social Media Tools Every Blogger Can Use to Grow Readership
- Twitter
- Facebook
- StumbleUpon
- BlogLovin'
- Blogged

What Does That Mean?! Weird Blogging Words Defined.

Blogroll: A blogroll is really just a list of links to other blogs and web sites. Think of it as a list of favorites or friends. You can fill your blogroll with any site you choose, but most bloggers populate their blogrolls with blogs they read or want to endorse.

Blogrolls will help you grow readership if you make a habit of asking other bloggers to reciprocate whenever you add a new blog to your blogroll.

Pinging: When your blog pings another site or service, it is simply saying, in tech-speak, "Hey, I've updated my content." Most blogging platforms have pinging capabilities built in and notify blog search engines and blog directories every time you create new content.

RSS: Formally known as Really Simple Syndication, RSS technology allows anyone with a web site to syndicate content. In a nutshell, it allows you to make your blog posts available to anyone who subscribes to your feed using a program like Google Reader. In turn, you can use these programs to subscribe to other blogs. It's an easy, convenient way to receive content from all your favorite blogs in one place—instead of having to check multiple sites daily or wade through a slew of emails.

Tags: Tags are simply relevant keywords you choose and attach to your posts in order to help more readers find your blog and locate specific content once they're there.

Tags can appear in "tag clouds", which are basically groups of keywords. Use a tag often, and the keyword in your tag cloud will grow larger in size relative to other tags you've used less often. Sites that monitor and search blogs – like Technorati –group blog posts from many blogs according to their tags in huge tag clouds. Tag a post with the word "fashion," for example, and your post will appear alongside other posts tagged with that word.

Lorraine Sanders is a San Francisco based writer, blogger and media consultant. She is the founder of SF Indie Fashion, a web site and resource covering the San Francisco Bay Area's wealth of independently run fashion labels, local designers and independent retailers. She writes for 7x7 Glamwatch, the San Francisco Chronicle, Daily Candy, NBC Bay Area, KQED and many others. Ms. Saunders is a part-time fashion journalism instructor at the Academy of Art University. She freelances as a copy writer and media consultant and works in developing online content and social media strategies.

www.LorraineSanders.com

Using Blogs Even Further

Not only is blogging great for you to do, but it is also great to be mentioned by one—especially if the blog has industry clout. Bloggers are the new journalists of our time. If a respected blogger mentions or recommends a product, that product can become highly sought after overnight. How might you get mentioned on someone's blog? Send your pitch and make sure it is applicable to their blog. If they show interest, they may request a product to evaluate first hand.

Chapter 18
Social Media

Social media is vast, varied, and ever evolving. By the time this edition is available there will likely be several dozen more social networks on the rise. One of the first social networks I remember is Friendster.com. It was a way to connect with friends and high school buddies.

These days social networking has taken on a life of its own. The sites themselves have become active verbs in our vocabulary. For example, "I'll facebook you." No longer are we using these networks to stay in touch with friends; but we're also using them to share news stories and promote businesses and products. Social media can enable you to connect to potential customers, and network with other professionals in your area of expertise.

Not all social media is suitable or relevant to every industry. You could spend countless hours searching through all the different networks. I have chosen not to include all of the relevant sites at this time due to the nature of social media. One minute you are hot, the next you are not. The following are a few in which you should be familiar.

Notes:

Notes:

Facebook

So many people are on it, including my father. Although most people are familiar with individual pages, it can be more useful for its business page. You can set up a business page and build a fan base. When you update your business profile status with news or products, those updates appear on your fan's news feed. It is a great way to stay in touch with your customers without hassling them.

You can also advertise with Facebook to promote your business page or website. To advertise, you set up a list of statistics based on geography, sex, age and interests. Your ad then appears to individuals who fit into those categories. Use your customer profile to narrow your options. (This is similar to the tools used to create an advertising campaign with Google Adwords and Microsoft adCenter.)

If you have ever wondered why certain relevant advertising appears on your pages, it is because of the listed interests and businesses you are a fan of.

Twitter

You can use twitter in many of the same ways you use Facebook. It enables you to follow other businesses and even monitor your competition. It's a great way for you to see what other people are saying and how they say it. It is expected that users post updates regularly. There are also applications that can take your twitter updates and post them to Facebook. Be wary of doing this, users of Facebook and Twitter are different. Twitter users check updates multiple times a day, where Facebook users may only check once. Facebook users may get annoyed by 20 status updates from your business on a given day.

Twitter is also a tool that will allow you to monitor mentions of your own brand or company through their alerts. This is one of the major differences between Twitter and Facebook.

YouTube

Videos are viral. They spread through our virtual worlds like a virus. Have you seen the dancing wedding and the frat boys singing Lady GaGa? How did you come across them? Possibly through email or through your social media outlets.

Creating a video to promote your products or your business can be just as viral. They are your own personal commercials, whether you hire a film crew or you use your iPhone to film it, video can be a big opportunity for your business.

Plan what you would like to advertise and write a basic script for it. Who is your target audience? What message do you want to convey? Where will you film it? What is involved in the production of the video? It can be as basic as a slideshow with text, or more complex such as a stop motion film or skit. Peruse YouTube and see what other companies may be doing and determine if a video could work for you.

Notes:

Designer Profile: Colleen Quen

From the start of her earliest collections, Colleen Quen created a strong visual language of beauty and art, defining her own interpretation of fashion. Quen graduated from the Fashion Institute of Design and Merchandising in 1986. She went on to study at Simmone Sethna School of French Couture, adding to her repertoire of refined fashion discipline. She graduated with a certificate in French Couture in 1996. Quen decide to open her own Couture design company in 2000.

Colleen's designs have drawn much attention, both in the art world and in fashion; her gowns have been featured in WWD, The New York Times, Forbes and the International Herald Tribune, and have been seen on America's Next Top Model, The Tyra Banks Show and has dressed Melissa Rivers at Grammy events and Tyra Banks at the NY Emmy Awards. Many of Colleen's collections have been exhibited internationally in museums and countless magazine editorial layouts and PBS Documentaries.

www.colleenquencouture.com

What is your Design Philosophy?

To create designs that have a message of emotion through me and my experiences I wish for the world. To be continuously inspiring our world with creation, beauty and harmony.

What general process do you go through when developing a collection?

I am inspired by my theme or intention for the collection. For example, my "Compassion" collection: Each piece in the collection reflects the message in the fabric or shape of the garment that describes the emotion of Compassion. I feel my work is like words of Poetry. It expresses emotion through the cut of my design and the color and drape of my fabric.

My words are in my Designs.

What do you think has been your most successful form of marketing for your business?
Being genuinely honest to your work, with that, your work speaks and communicates out to the public. My marketing is by word and by recommendation. I feel this is the best way for my work to be commissioned

Do you find that social media networks help your business?
Definitely it does. It helps the credibility and the exposure of your work to be seen all over the world. It touches people all over the world.

How do you approach the media outlets?
I've been fortunate to reach media through my fashion show events and the exhibitions I participate in. Also, through "by word" of my clients and supportive followers.

What is your most accomplished piece of press and how did you get it?
The Butterfly Dream art piece. It was recently exhibited at the Shanghai MOCA 2009 during the Shanghai Biennale. The curator Victoria Lu, so graciously invited me to participate.

What would your recommendation be for a newbie in creating a successful marketing campaign?
Is to wear your work everywhere you go. Be truly living in your designs.

Chapter 19
Networking

Before blogging and social media became the norm, there was
the traditional form of networking where people meet face
to face. Networking is one of the most powerful tools you can
use to grow your business. Networking can happen anywhere,
but the easiest way may be to join a group. There are industry-
specific networking groups, entrepreneurial groups, gender-
specific groups, and cultural groups. Try more than one group.
I belong to two different networking groups: a fashion industry
group and a women's entrepreneurial group.

To find a networking group of your interest, try Craigslist. org or
Meetup.com. Both contain links to all kinds of groups.

Many groups invite speakers and seasoned professionals to talk
on topics that may be relevant to your business. Chances are,
at a talk or a meeting, you'll meet other professionals you can
brainstorm with, share resources and gain valuable feedback.

I joined a women entrepreneurial group which I found to be
incredibly resourceful; not only in the topics they cover at
meetings, but because it helped introduce me to women in my
community. These are people whom I would have never had
the opportunity to meet otherwise. The women I met have

Notes:

Notes:

become wonderful friends and mentors. They have proven to be a reliable and useful support group. Some have gone on to participate in television shows, appeared on Oprah and others have opened up new enterprises.

I also participate in a fashion industry networking group. This group has led to several media opportunities and partnerships that I might not have otherwise created. The group is attended not only by designers, but business owners, photographers, models, media, and everyone in between. Networking groups create an opportunity to be on the same playing field as others, whether you are a student or a professional.

The Elevator Pitch
A useful skill to have down before attending a networking event is delivering your "elevator pitch". The elevator pitch is a 30-second pitch about what you do, why you do it, and why someone else would want to know more about you and your business.

Why the goofy name? It comes from the situation of being in the elevator and being asked "What do you do?" Most elevator rides are in the 30 second realm, so if the publisher of "The Greatest Magazine in the World" got on your elevator and you had 10 floors to say your spheal, are you going to let this opportunity cross your path and not take advantage of it? Of course not, you want to introduce yourself, give the hot shot a card and make an unforgettable impression. You think this may never happen to you? Opportunity comes to those who are ready for it, so why not be ready?

What's in a successful elevator pitch? Answers these questions in as few words as possible:

- What does your business do?
- Who is the target market?
- Why is it important to your market?
- How are you different from the rest?

Be sure to cater your pitch to your listener. If you are speaking top a friend's aunt who once saw project runway, don't speak to her in a technical voice. That may only be appropriate if you are speaking to another designer or crafts person.

> "I design and sell clothing for mothers who want to feel good while doing good for the environment. My dresses provide an eco-friendly alternative to the masses and I offer a garment reimbursement incentive for all my creations once they are past their prime."

This is a fictional example, but aren't you curious about that garment reimbursement program? Make your pitch grab their attention and leave them wanting more information.

Always be prepared to give your elevator pitch, whether you are going to the grocery store or a networking event. Just as you would leave your house with your wallet and keys, always carry business cards with you. You could also carry around any promotional fliers you may be using, or even your product. If you can wear your creations, that could prompt conversations leading to your elevator pitch and a possible sale.

Last bit of advice, if you exchange business cards, follow up with an email or a call to say it was a pleasure to have met them and refresh them about your conversation. Hand written cards can also a nice touch. Many people don't receive snail mail as often anymore, so a card could leave a lasting impression.

Notes:

Elevator Pitch

What does your business do?

Who is your target market?

Why is it important to your market?

How are you different from the rest?

Summarize all of those answers into 40 words or less?

Restate your summary for a colleague who is familiar with your industry?

Restate your summary for an individual who is unfamiliar with your industry?

Restate your summary for a child?

Case Study: Elevator Pitch

What does your business do?

We design women's wear, romantic and timeless designs, stellar fit, fabrics are eco-friendly, designs are contemporary without being too trendy, everything is made in the USA

Who is your target market?

Customer is a woman in mid 20s-40s, women who care about what they wear and where their garments came from

Why is it important to your market?

The garments fit well for the design aesthetic and doesn't cost a fortune.

How are you different from the rest?

Same as above

Summarize all of those answers into 40 words or less?

Designer of eco-friendly women's wear that is romantic and timeless in nature, fits well and is made from Belgium linen, the original eco-friendly textile.

Restate your summary for a colleague who is familiar with your industry?

I design romantic eco-friendly women's wear that is made from an eco-friendly textile from Belgium The fit is stellar, feels and looks are flattering to the missy figure and is made in California.

Restate your summary for an individual who is unfamiliar with your industry?

I design women's clothing that has a romantic feel and fits well. I manufacture everything here in the United States and use environmentally friendly fabrics.

Restate your summary for a child?

I design comfy clothes for women so they feel and look pretty.

SALES

Chapter 20
Introduction to Sales

How do I actually make money with my product? It wouldn't make sense to have a business if you didn't, would it? If you are getting to this point and your reaction is "I don't care about the money," my recommendation is to consider making this a hobby rather than a business. For those who say, "Yes, I want to make money and live off of it," the following chapters are about selling your creations.

Sales can be split into two categories: direct and indirect. Simply, some sales you have direct control over and some you don't. Starting with the obvious, selling directly to your customer is going to give you the highest profit margin. You act as the retailer. Whether you are selling online, at street fairs, or taking custom orders - you control your profit. In the following chapters I discuss different avenues for selling your product, both direct and indirect. Before we get to that, we need to discuss a more important issue – how to sell yourself. This subject was touched upon in the previous chapter on networking and your elevator pitch.

Notes:

Notes:

Selling yourself

When dealing with either a potential customer, whether it is with a wholesale account or a consumer, you need to be able to sell yourself. Showing passion in your product and believing what you are preaching are both equally important. You need to love it and it needs to show.

When you sell your product, you are selling a piece of yourself. Whether you are conducting a traditional elevator pitch or meeting with a client, you must sell all that is you. Your enthusiasm will be carried on to the buyer and will be more likely to purchase your product if your personality shows through in your sell. Know your product inside and out, including all features and the benefits.

What reasons would someone want to buy your product as opposed to going to Target? The personal connection a person makes to you helps sell your product and allows that buyer to take that connection and pass it on their customers.

Treat every possible customer as your best customer. Offering excellent customer service can be one of the best ways to market your business.

Chapter 21
Direct Sales

Online Sales

Online Sales are not only a possibility, but for many, it is a necessity. In addition to having a website to maximize your exposure, you can easily set up an online store. There are several companies who help promote independent artists and designers through their online communities. Etsy.com, SmashingDarling. com, ArtFire.com, and IndieDesignerLabels. com are just a few examples. Another option to sell online is using Ebay.com. Ebay's focus has changed over the years and unless you are selling at dirt cheap prices, you may end up wasting time taking this route.

Amazon also offers sellers opportunities, but they have restrictions on clothing (you must apply and be accepted through a juried process). You may need to purchase a barcode for your items to sell through this outlet.

If you choose to sell on one of the sites I mentioned, you have automatic exposure through their marketing efforts. This could be ideal if you want to test the market with sample merchandise or if you want to keep your website as your portfolio for your collections and press.

Notes:

Notes:

You may also consider hosting a webstore directly on your website. There are several ways to do this. Some hosting companies offer shopping carts, for example, Prostores.com and BigCartel.com. The monthly charge is much higher than for regular hosting, but may be worth it if you know how to generate your own web traffic.

Another way to host a store on your site is to purchase a ready made shopping cart component and integrate it with your normal website hosting. You maintain a low monthly charge, but you purchase the shopping cart software outright.

Shopping cart software can cost anywhere from $100-$5,000, which is in addition to your web hosting and payment processing charges. Depending on the time you have and the amount of money you wish to spend on setting everything up, you have many options. Be realistic in assessing your ability to set up and manage your online store. If you are not computer savvy, I recommend you hire someone to tackle this for you.

In addition, you will need to set up payment processing for your sales. Paypal.com is one option that is accepted worldwide. It is not the least expensive of all that is available, but it is the easiest to set up.

The obvious advantage of having an online store is that you have direct contact with your customers and receive immediate payments. The drawback is that you must keep merchandise inventory updated and ship out the orders soon after they are received. This requires a fair amount of organization. Again, if you are not that kind of person, or can't hire somebody to handle it, online sales may not be the best option for you.

Street fairs

Street fairs can be a great way to sell your product. You receive 100% customer interaction and instant feedback on your merchandise. Street fairs are the fastest way to develop your sales skills. These sales skills will help you with pitching your product to stores, reps, and the media.

Most cities have craft and art fairs where vendor space is available, as well as many of the farmer's markets. Contact your city or neighborhood associations for information on participating. Fees can range from $75-$1,500 depending on the event and the amount of promotion by the organizers.

Vendor space is also available at most jazz festivals, wine fairs, and music events. Keep in mind that while your audience at these events is everyone, most people will expect to pay a fairly small amount. Use street fairs to sell seconds, and your lower priced items.

You will need to own your set up including a 10x10 tent, tables, mannequins, clothing racks and signage. Spaces are usually a 10x10 space.

Sample Sales

A sample sale is an organized event where designers sell off samples, seconds, and last season's merchandise. They are like street fairs, in the sense that you have full customer interaction. The audience often consists of a specific targeted market and customer. The businesses that organize these sales will advertise to a specific customer. This is why it is so important to know who your customer is. You could have the best million dollar product idea, but if you hit the wrong market

Notes:

for the sample sale you'll end up wasting your time and money. Attendees usually pay an entrance fee, so they are there specifically to shop. Sample sale participation can range from $50-$2,000. Some well known sample events on the higher end of the spectrum are Shecky's, Million Dollar Babes, and Thread. Sometimes these events are called trunk shows, but that is not the true definition of a sale like this.

You may be required to provide your own tables or racks. Space is more limited at a sample sale and sometimes there is only space for a rack. These are usually hosted indoors and some form of entertainment is provided by the organizers.

Trunk Shows
The name "trunk show" comes from way back, when designers used to take a trunk of designs to a clothing store and sell directly to the customers. A trunk show these days can describe either a direct or indirect sale. Direct sales are when a boutique offers a designer to come and sell merchandise at their business as a promotion, with the store taking a small percentage. If you are at the store doing the actual selling, the store should not take more than 30% of your sale, because you are the sales person.

Indirectly, a store may run all sales through the store and give you 50% of the purchase price after the sale is complete. Trunk shows can be a nice opportunity to expand your client base. You get a captive audience in the store's clientele, and the store may also end up carrying your designs if they appeal to their customers.

You may be asked to provide your own table or rack, although most stores have additional display materials than what is on the floor.

Home Parties

Oddly enough, this seems to have become the newest rage in selling. The idea is the same as with a Tupperware party or a Pleasure party.

Tupperware parties started as one of the first direct marketing programs in 1946, where housewives got together to buy and sell the latest Tupperware products. Pleasure parties (also referred to as candle parties) are newer and started in the late 1970s as a way to sell intimate toys and accessories to women, sparing them the embarrassment of going into a store.

More recently, home parties have emerged as a way to sell products that are not available in stores or online. This is a great concept and has gotten more recognition by the media recently. One of the more recognizable names that have taken this route is Carol Anderson by Invitation (CABI for short).

With home sales, designers usually seek out reps that sell lines out of their own homes to friends and family, and take a percentage. Usually, the designer requires the rep to purchase a sample kit at wholesale price; the rep then takes orders, collects the money, and the designer ships directly to the customer or to the rep for distribution.

Retail Store

At first glance, opening your own retail store sounds like a great idea. You can control the way your designs are displayed, you receive direct customer feedback, and you get 100% of the

Notes:

Notes:

profit. Sounds good, but do you know what it takes to run a store? A store is a full time job, and because you are reading this book, I assume you are planning for a full time job as a fashion designer. A store is possible, but without the help of a full time staff to manage and run the store, you could easily lose your focus and cause your design work to suffer.

"If you build it, they will come,"* is not as much of a reality as you might think. That only happens in the movies or with the right PR firm. To make your sales, you need to bring traffic to your store. If you score a prime location in an area with lots of retail shoppers (and can afford the 3-5 year lease), then you have nailed the traffic situation, but what about your time? If you will be in the front of the store selling your merchandise, then what has become of your design business? These are all questions you need to ask yourself before you get much further with the retail idea.

Operating a retail store could be another book entirely, but for now, know that it is not as glamorous as it looks, and the profit isn't as much as you think either. There is a reason why the markup from wholesale to retail is so much. It costs that much to run a shop. From the labor to the fixtures to the million unexpected expenses, it adds up quickly.

Once your business is going steady, then you may want to consider opening a store, but running your clothing line is usually a full time job in its own.

Something you may often hear about are "pop-up" shops. It's where a designer rents a commercial space on a limited basis for a store. This has become rather popular in shopping areas

* "Field of Dreams" with Kevin Costner

where there are many vacant store fronts. One can usually negotiate a short-term lease from anywhere from 1-6 months if a space has been vacant for some time.

If you are lucky, the previous renters may have left a cashwrap, built in racks and dressing rooms. Moving in could be made simple and inexpensive.

Cooperative Boutiques

This type of boutique is very popular where there are large concentrations of independent designers. It allows several different designers the opportunity to run a store together. A true co-op divides the store responsibilities, including sales, merchandising, marketing and finances between all members. This can be a great seg-way into the operation of your own boutique.

This type of boutique gives you the experience of what it's like to have a boutique without all the risk. Once your line is in production and you've survived your first collection, this could be something to look at.

Mail Order

The mail order business is dying down with the rise of internet business. You may have noticed that you are receiving only one Victoria Secret catalog a month instead of the usual four. Even the Ikea catalogs aren't being sent out automatically anymore. It's costly to print catalogs, not to mention targeting your mailing list to those likely to order. By contrast, email marketing campaigns are easy and inexpensive, and they receive the same response, if not more.

Notes:

Designer Profile: Candice Gwinn

Candice Gwinn owns and operates Trashy Diva (a women's clothing boutique with 4 locations) and Truck Stop (a men's clothing store) in New Orleans. Trashy Diva carries the Candice Gwinn label and also features jewelry, lingerie, and shoes. www.trashydiva.com

What is your design philosophy?

I just make what I like. I REALLY love the fashion, art and history of 1890's-1950's, ethnic textiles, and a little bit of kitsch. I like natural fabrics, bold prints, spangles and a glamorously body hugging fit. I design fanciful and fun retro inspired clothing. I am on a never ending quest to make the perfect dress that can flatter any shape!

How many pieces do you create for a collection? How many collections do you do a year?

Usually I create 5-6 pieces per fabric group and maybe 2-3 fabric groups making a collection. I'd ideally like to make 4 or so collections a year, but usually fall/winter/holiday gets lumped into one small collection and resort/spring/summer is ongoing through 9 months of the year due to the New Orleans climate! The collections are presented at trade shows twice a year, so to most buyers it looks like 2 collections anyway. I am continually working on my timing!!

Being a store owner, as well as a designer, how are you able to balance them? Do you spend an equal amount of time on each?

I run 5 boutiques and a retail web site as well as a clothing line, so the stores are a HUGE pull on my time. I have lots of wonderful people to help me, but I do all the buying from other vendors which is really time-consuming. I've just recently taken on an accountant to help on the finance end, and am in the process of hiring someone to take over the web site updates.

I also have a 3yr old son, so I'm always being pulled in a million different directions. I pretty much have gotten to the point of locking myself in my design studio for days at a time to get my designs finished in time!

Do you find it challenging to own both the store and the line?

It is challenging to manage my time with both, but I think it is much easier to own a line and the shop to sell it in. If you own both, then you can design for the real needs of your end customers. I don't have to rely on other companies to buy my pieces so that they get manufactured. I make what MY customers want.

How long did you have your store before you decided to launch a line?

I opened Trashy Diva as a vintage clothing store in 1996, and started my first 2 piece collection in 1999. It wasn't until 2002 when Trashy Diva had evolved to sell only my clothing and I no longer carried the vintage.

Why did you decide to launch the line?

After dealing in vintage clothing for a few years, it was basically a financial decision. I couldn't find any vintage dresses from the eras that I loved that weren't falling apart, stained, trashed, or too expensive. All of my customers were saying the same things. Why buy a vintage 40's rayon dress for $200 just to have it tailored, wear it once and have it fall apart at the seams while still smelling like mothballs? It just didn't make sense to have a store filled with dresses that only came in one size (and never the size you need!). It was a pretty easy choice.

Chapter 22
Indirect Sales

Indirect sales are sales that others control. When you sell your product wholesale, you no longer have control over how your merchandise is presented or sold. Although direct sales might seem to be the better option at first, wholesale or indirect sales should be your goal. Wholesale is beneficial to you in that you take orders, produce what is ordered, deliver to your retailers and receive your payment when you deliver. You don't have to wait for the customer to make the purchase before you get paid.

Things may not always go as planned. Retailers may cancel or go out of business before your delivery date, but that is something that may happen. Turn those canceled orders into direct sales. How does one acquire a wholesale account? In the following pages I briefly discuss several possibilities.

Trade Shows
There are two major trade show seasons. The first one is in January/February and features Fall collections; the second is in August/September and features Spring collections. There are

Notes:

other trade shows throughout the year, but these are the two main times buyers travel for shows.

MAGIC Marketplace
www.magiconline.com

The best known trade shows are the ones held in Las Vegas known as **MAGIC Marketplace**. To find the listings of all trade shows, look to the calendars on WeConnectFashion.com (formerly Infomat.com). Their list is comprehensive and includes all shows stateside and international.

MAGIC is ginormous and houses over 20,000 product lines. 80% of the exhibitors are large name designers and typically do not exhibit at other venues. Some of the larger exhibitors have show budget upwards of $50,000 for their exhibits. Independent designers do not have that budget and can easily get lost in the shuffle at a show of this magnitude.

Project
www.projectshow.com

Pool
www.pooltradeshow.com

It's a good idea to walk any show prior to signing up for it to find out if your product fits into the targeted market for the show. The last thing you want to do is invest $10,000 in a show that turns out to be the wrong show for you. During MAGIC, several smaller boutique shows take place, such as **Pool** and **Project**, so check those out as well.

Notes:

Ten thousand dollars for participation is not an exaggerated figure. The cost can be upwards of $5,000 for a small booth, and large companies may pay up to 20 grand for the large display spaces. Some of the smaller shows may cost slightly less, but can also run as high as $3,000.

Those are just your space fees; you also need to consider your display, transportation to the show, food, and lodging. Most trade shows will also not let you load up your booth through the front door. You will probably have to arrange for delivery to the show and there is a charge per piece for load in. Fixtures (racks and shelving) may not be included in the space rental. The show organizers may offer these at an additional charge, or you may wish to provide your own.

Preparing for the shows can also be costly. Printed material, website updates, and samples all have to be made ready. You'll also need someone to help run the business while you are out of town for the show, and possibly help with all the follow up calls after you come back.

While this sounds overwhelming, it's not unrealistic for you to consider being in a show. Take two seasons to walk the shows. Fall shows are different than Spring shows. Shows usually last about three days, so my advice is to take the first two days to see what is there, and the last day to talk to the vendors. The last day is usually quiet and the vendors are naturally exhausted. Ask them how they did. Some may share, some won't, but it doesn't hurt to try and get as much info as you can. (Hint- you may find more competitors to keep your eyes on.)

Talk to some first time vendors and some seasoned ones. You can probably tell right away who is a first-timer and who is seasoned – just look at their footwear (stilettos = first-timer, slippers/comfort shoes = seasoned). You will hear a difference in their sales figures. Most first timers don't sell as much as the ones who have braved it a few times. This is due to their lack of selling experience in a trade show environment, as well as to buyers being cautious.

Buyers are hesitant to buy from a new vendor without a history. Once buyers get used to seeing a vendor more then once, they'll feel more confident and may purchase a new line. A

Notes:

continuing presence shows that the designer will be around for more than one season. Buyers of retail establishments cater to their customers and usually have a loyal following. The last thing a buyer wants to do is find an outstanding line or product, have the customer love it, want more, and find out the next season that the designer has gone out of business.

You've walked your shows, decided which ones work, now its time to commit. When deciding on a show, check the map and location of the booth. People tend to be too tired to walk that last row, so be careful when signing up for a space.

If you have an opportunity to be in the first booth in a row towards the front, chances are, you will get enough sales to cover the cost of a full size booth. Get your best sales person (whether a friend, family member, employee or customer) to help you out. You need to give a great first impression, and the enthusiasm of someone who loves your product will help you sell more. If you have compiled a list of potential stores, send them a postcard inviting them to visit your booth. People are more likely to visit an unknown vendor if they have a little enticement to direct them to your booth.

Last bit of advice. FOLLOW UP. No kidding here. Many vendors do not follow up with people who visit their booths – you can chalk these in the column of lost sales. Take business cards, email signups and snail mail signups from everyone so you remember who to follow up with. And remember that it's not only buyers who visit your booth; sales reps, media and the press walk these shows too.

Showrooms

A showroom is a "store" that houses your designs for retail buyers. It is not open to the public and may be by appointment only. Being carried in a showroom allows buyers access to your collection all year as opposed to the 3 days for a trade show.

The ultimate hope of any designer at a trade show is to get into a showroom. Sales reps from these showrooms often attend the trade shows to find the next biggest brand. Many showrooms won't take you until you've reached a certain number of stores that already carry your collection. Showroom space is high staked real estate. Some showrooms charge a monthly rack (or space) fee and then a percentage of sales. Showroom cuts can be 10-25%, plus the monthly fee. The fees and commissions will vary, and there are many items that can be negotiated in your contract with the showroom.

Virtual showrooms have become a popular medium for showcasing young design businesses. Trunkt.com offers such services and caters to smaller design entrepreneurs. In the past few years, Trunkt has changed their focus from a retail marketplace to an online showroom. With this service, you can even produce and print personalized line sheets.

Road Reps

Road Reps are basically traveling salesmen. Road reps work a specific region and have a regular route of boutiques with which they have set up accounts. These reps will take samples to the stores for orders. Road reps can sometimes charge a higher commission (25-35%) to account for their travel expenses, but I know there are still road reps out there who still charge 15% commission.

Reps and showrooms will both have contracts for you to sign.

Notes:

Notes:

Look over the contract and negotiate the terms of payment, exclusivity, percentages, and length of the contract with each account you acquire. Don't just sign on the dotted line. Geographic limitations are always good to look for.

If you are working with a new rep on the scene, you need to make sure you are covered for possible loss of your samples, so I suggest you take a credit card deposit for your samples until they are returned. You can include this in a contract of your own. Use your best judgment in requesting this information. If you ask this of a showroom that has been around for 10 or more years, you may be laughed at; research and be sure to check up on any references. This will help you establish a relationship of trust without appearing too difficult.

Finding a rep can be a difficult task. Sometimes they find you; sometimes you need to do the hunting. There is a new company that works to connect reps with clothing lines and vice versa. FindFashionRep.com is one option and for a monthly subscription fee, designers and reps can find each other.

Boutiques

Another way to nail a wholesale account is to be your own rep and contact the boutiques directly. In order to do this successfully, you need to approach or solicit the stores before they head off to market and use their entire buying budget. Approaching stores requires some tact. Store owners and buyers are very busy. It may not appropriate to just walk in and start pitching your line. One way is to call in advance, ask for the name and email address of the buyer, and email her information on you line; then follow up with a phone call a week later. This also works with snail mail.

However, the approach I recommend is to visit the local boutiques personally, see if your product will work there, then ask for the card and name of the buyer so you can contact her at a later date. Because buyers are busy bees, disrupting their schedule can be frustrating to them and can possibly leave a bad first impression. (This is a recommendation based on my personal experience as a store owner.)

One advantage of selling directly to a boutique is that it creates a personal connection, one which the store owner can carry into selling your product.

Consignment Boutiques

Another well known option is consignment. While many seasoned designers shudder at the word, for a newcomer, this could be a great first step. Consignment is an arrangement where a store agrees to carry a product without purchasing it up front, and pays the designer only after sales are made, usually on a monthly basis. Many small boutiques will offer a new line the consignment option. It presents little risk to the store owner and gives a new designer an insight into what customers are looking for and whether the designer has targeted the correct market.

If you choose to do consignment, make sure you have a signed agreement with the store and a payment schedule. Consignment rates can vary from 40%-80% depending on the boutique. Make sure you find out what the percentage is before setting your price. It is also very important to rotate your merchandise regularly.

Many shoppers return monthly to boutiques to see what is new, so keeping merchandise in a boutique on consignment for more

Notes:

than 60 days can cause your clothes to go "stale." Boutiques will usually keep merchandise for longer than 60 days, but at that time, they are generally marked down to make room for new arrivals. If you keep your merchandise fresh and new all the time, your products have a better chance of selling.

When entering into a consignment arrangement, find out who else has worked on consignment with the store and talk to them. Unfortunately, some boutiques don't pay up, and others may close unexpectedly and keep your merchandise. There will always be a risk in consignment, for you and none for the store. You are going into business on the honor system.

Department Stores

You may score a department store order, but be wary. There are hidden costs and requirements that department stores follow which can really be unsavory for an independent designer. All large stores require bar-coding of your product. Barcodes can be purchased individually or you can purchase the system that generates them. Individual barcodes run $15-30 each (versus the $800+ for the barcoding system). Even after you get your barcode, the stores require merchandise to be packaged a certain way, in plastic wrap and on hangers. They are also very picky about delivery dates. If they do not receive a product on a specific date, they may refuse your shipment and you can be left with a whole lot of inventory on your hands.

Once you jump all the hoops and get into a department store, there is yet another trap to watch for. Payment dates. Some may pay up to 120 days after receipt. That's four months of no income. And of course there is the chargeback.

Chargebacks (otherwise knows as Markdown Money) are a nasty surprise to newbies in the business, so you should know a little on how they work. Let's say you sell 1,000 items at the wholesale price of $10 each to Macy's and they marked the garment up to $40 retail. 30 days later they mark down the garment to $30. Macy's is still making a profit of $20, but that $10 they marked down they now consider a loss and they make you responsible for half of that markdown, which is $5 (half your wholesale price). 60 days go by and they mark the merchandise down to $10 to move it. The markdown is $30, and you are still responsible for half of it or $15. You could now owe money to the department store for the merchandise you sold to them!

There is no way around chargebacks, but there are ways you can protect your profits from being eaten by a department store. If a department store expresses an interest in your line, limit their orders and don't put all your eggs in their basket. Diversify your sales channels. Make sure you target smaller boutiques where there is no chance of a chargeback. Consider your merchandise in a department store as part of your advertising budget. It's great exposure to sell in a department store, but decide how much you would spend on advertising and limit their orders to that expected expense.

Payment terms

Whoever you end up working with—a rep, a showroom, or a store—you need to be clear on your payment terms. If you are up front with your accounts, there should not be an issue with this. You should require COD or credit card payment until you have a steady cash flow or you establish a relationship with a store. You can explain to the stores and reps that you are a small business and can't wait 30 days for payment. Once you have the

Chargebacks: charges to the design company when discounts are given by the retailer. A practice used by department stores.

Notes:

product and you are ready to ship, call the stores to let them know it is being shipped and their credit card is being charged.

Once you have established a relationship with a store, changing your payment terms to Net-30 is recommended. Your stores will be grateful that they don't have to use those nasty credit cards anymore with you.

Collecting Debt

What do you do if a store – for example one where you have merchandise on consignment—doesn't pay up? I personally had a consignment arrangement with a boutique that went AWOL without paying. When I went to switch inventory I discovered that the store had closed, and my inventory had gone with it. I later found out they liquidated their entire inventory on eBay, kept the cash, and ran. Did I ever collect? No. The amount I lost was miniscule compared to the other designers in the store. Some of them took the owners to small claims court and settled. I felt my time was more valuable than the price of the merchandise I lost in comparison.

How do you avoid getting into this situation? You can't avoid the risk entirely, but you can take steps to reduce it. If you are doing consignment, check up on your inventory every two to four weeks. Stop by the store and rotate your inventory regularly. Do your homework – get to know the stores and compare notes with other designers who might have consignment agreements with those boutiques. Your last option is to take the store into Collections or to Small Claims Court. There are agencies that will facilitate collections for you in exchange for a percentage of the amount they collect for you. This can be done for consignment boutiques as well as for stores where you have an arrangement of Net 30 or more.

Designer Profile: Mallory Whitfield

Mallory Whitfield is the founder of Miss Malaprop, an online store/blog for handmade and eco-friendly goods. Mallory designs recycled clothing and accessories, including reconstructed denim skirts, and designs made from recycled FEMA tarps. www.shopmissmalaprop.com

What is your design philosophy?

Clothing that is fun and comfortable to wear everyday. It is unique and made in the most sustainable way possible. I love basic styles, but with vintage-style details. I am self-taught in my craft. I consider myself more of a crafter who designs clothing and accessories than a true fashion designer.

Do you create collections or one of a kind designs?

One of a kind. I work primarily with recycled materials, so while I do some designs that have a similar theme or style, each one is always slightly unique. My favorite material to work with is denim. I make upcycled denim skirts out of past-their-prime blue jeans. I add details, lace overlays or appliqués, and repair holes or stains on the denim. I love to breathe new life into old clothes and keep something out of the landfill just a little longer.

How do you spread the word about your work?

I participate in many local events and markets, including design competitions and fashion shows, all with the focus on recycled fashion. They are all great for generating publicity. I have a blog that I have upkept since 2006. It focuses on handmade & eco-friendly design. I use it to promote like-minded designers, but I also show off my own projects. I've built up a pretty large following through it. I also network with other bloggers and designers as much as possible.

You have recently changed your focus from concentrating on your own designs to promoting other designers and crafters. How did this change come about?

I first started selling my own work in 2004. For the first few years I concentrated mainly on promoting my own work. As I got more involved in the indie craft community, I saw these great little boutiques for handmade goods that were popping up all over the country.

When I was young, I dreamed of owning a boutique one day. I started my blog in 2006 with the store being the long-term goal. From day 1, with Miss Malaprop, I intended to focus on building a community and a brand. In the summer of 2009 I started feeling a little frustrated... I felt like I had built a good brand and I had a fairly large following, but I didn't feel any closer to my goal of opening my boutique. I usually find that getting really frustrated spurs me into action and I decided to just go for it.

I contacted a few designers and started selling their work alongside mine at local events. I continued to add more lines. In the fall of 2009, I contacted the local Small Business Development Center. I was lucky to meet some great people who helped me turn my ideas into a reality through a grant and created my online store. I'm just continuing, full steam ahead, to build my business by promoting work of some amazing artists.

As a blogger and a designer, what advice do you have for designers who want to be noticed by bloggers?

Contact bloggers who may like your aesthetic. Look for blogs and websites that feature work similar in style to what you do. Send them a friendly email introducing yourself and your work. Most bloggers like to be addressed by first name (please make sure you have the CORRECT name!). Most bloggers like to feel that the content they are covering is exclusive, so instead of sending out a mass email to every blogger you have ever encountered, I recommend spreading out your emails. If you can create a real friendship and connection with a blogger, they'll be more likely to help promote your new collections and the developments that occur with your line.

STARTING YOUR BUSINESS

Chapter 23
Business Entity*

Way back, when we wore corsets and top hats, all you had to do was hang a shingle over your front door touting your services in order to start welcoming customers into your business. You could spend the business' revenue as you saw fit, and business receipts were kept in a hat box under the bed. Today, only a fool would follow that path. There are many eyes watching where your revenue comes from – think IRS, state sales tax departments, potential investors or partners, lenders, etc. There are formalities required to operate a successful business and much is tied to the formal structure of your business. Thus, you need to think about your business structure before you begin operating your business.

Sole Proprietorship

If you do nothing in the way of setting up your business, by default, you are a sole proprietorship. Under this form of business, the government, and your business creditors see you and the business as a single entity. Your personal assets are treated as the assets of the business and the liabilities of the

Notes:

*This Chapter 23 will focus on the critical issues relating to the legal structure of your business and the type of income taxation you wish to apply under that structure. By formal structure I mean whether you will do business (and hold your business' assets) as a sole proprietorship, partnership, corporation (C and S corporations), limited liability companies (LLCs) or one of the other legal structures approved in your state. A fashion business could be structured under any legal form, however each legal form – also called business entity – will be treated a bit differently from the other under both state contract law and state and federal income tax laws. The purpose of this chapter will be to illustrate the differences between each business entity to help you select the entity that is best suited to meet your long-term personal and business goals.

business are treated as yours, alone. If you ever baby-sat or cut lawns for some spending money, you technically operated as a sole proprietorship, although one that probably operated outside of the income tax laws. When your sole proprietorship buys inventory, signs an agreement, or signs a lease, those obligations are personal obligations. When you obtain a business license or buy a piece of equipment to be used in the sole proprietorship, the license and title of the property are in the name of the owner -- not the business.

Sole proprietorships are "flow-through entities." Meaning all taxable income created by the business flows through to the owner(s). That means that the owner reports their share of business profits (or losses) on his or her Form 1040. This will not always be the case with other business structures where the business has to pay its own income taxes.

Owners of a sole proprietorship do not receive wages because they are not employees. They are the business. Basically, any cash from the business is theirs. Cash can be withdrawn and used to pay the owner's personal expenses (e.g., Starbucks on the way to work) without the need to process a payroll check. There is no withholding, but the owner will generally need to report and pay self-employment taxes.

Sole proprietors who are employed while they grow their business will include their business profits on their personal income tax filing Form 1040, Schedule C. For a typical new business with expenses that exceed revenue, the owner will generally be allowed to apply some or all of the business' net-loss as a deduction. You should understand that the amount of the losses that may be deductible can be limited. For example, individuals who show consistent loses for seven years can have all of their past deductions disallowed by the IRS and the business treated as a hobby. There are no deductions allowed for a hobby loss.

A sole proprietorship can be the easiest way to run a small business, but complexities in operating this way get worse as the business grows. When there is a need to establish a business line of credit with a bank, there is a general feeling among bankers that a business structured as either an LLC or a corporation is a lower credit risk than a sole proprietorship. For that reason, many small business owners, who could otherwise operate as a sole proprietorship, elect instead to operate under one of the other forms, such as an LLC or a corporation.

Notes:

Sample Organizational Chart - Sole Proprietor

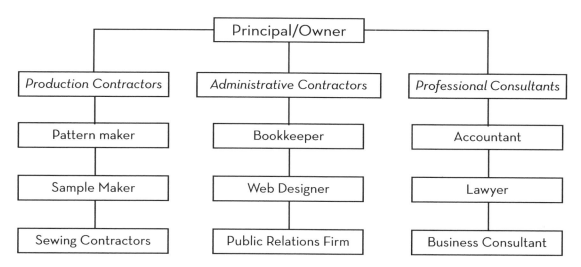

General Partnerships

When any two individuals work together on a single commercial enterprise, they have created a partnership. So a partnership is very much like a sole proprietorship, except that there are two owners. Generally, both owners have equal rights over the operation of the partnership and share equal responsibility for payment of debt. Most set their agreement as to who does what in a formal partnership agreement.

The laws relating to what a partnership can and cannot do are controlled under state law – with most states following the provisions of the Uniform Partnership Act (UPA). It should be noted that many states do not require a partnership to register with the state, though most states do allow for this type of registration. The registration in part tells the public (e.g., potential vendors) who owns the business and who can commit the entity under a contract.

Without a formal partnership drafted by an attorney, disagreements over management issues and partnership assets generally ends up being settled in court. Most partners who are serious about the business sign a partnership agreement defining the general terms of their business relationship.

With general partnerships, management of the partnership's business and how the profits and liabilities are split between the partners is based upon the agreement. Without an agreement, personal liabilities can be tied to the business as well as each partner. You do not want to write your own partnership agreement or download one from the Internet without having it reviewed by an attorney. Your attorney will likely recommend that it be revised to comply with your state's laws.

Now on to the most critical question on the partnership agreement; "When does it end?" If you have a well-drafted partnership agreement, the answers will be addressed there. That means that before you get the partnership agreement written you have to agree with your partner as to what is to be included. What will happen to the partnership if there is a death, disability or loss of interest by one of the partners? You have to discuss what happens to the business, the assets and the liabilities when you end the partnership.

Sample Organizational Chart - General Partnership

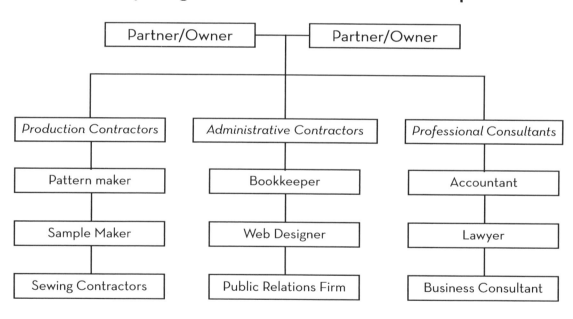

Limited Partnerships

Let's distinguish the difference between a general partnership and a limited partnership. A general partnership exists when partners share in management responsibilities and liabilities. There is sometimes a desire to have all the responsibilities and liabilities assumed by only one partner. This is where the

Notes:

limited partnership becomes an option.

The general partner of a limited partnership – and there must be at least one – is the party who runs the business and assumes all responsibilities. If the business goes bust, the limited partner only loses what he or she invested. The exact relationship between the general partner and the limited partner will be spelled out in the limited partnership agreement. Unlike general partnerships, most states require limited partnerships to be registered. You will see some limited partnerships in the fashion industry, but the trend seems to be moving to the use of LLCs, LLPs and similar entities with different classes of owners.

Sample Organizational Chart - Limited Partnership

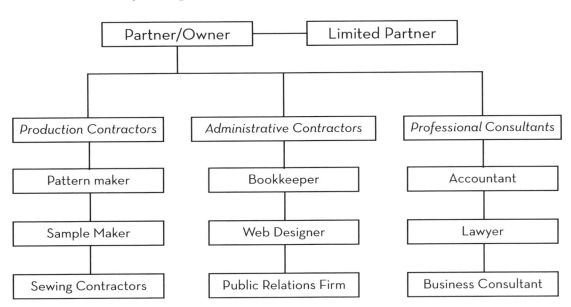

Taxation of Partnerships*

CPAs whom I have talked with on the pluses and minuses of various business structures tend to agree on the following statement, "The taxation of partnerships is one of the most complicated areas of the US Tax Code." It would take a book much thicker than this one to give you a thorough overview of the laws and regulations relating to partnership taxation, I'm sure you would prefer to use it as kindling over bedside reading. In this limited space I will provide broad generalizations on partnership taxation.

- **Flow-Through Entity:** A partnership is treated as a "flow-through" entity, meaning that the profits made at the partnership level flow through and are taxed to the individual partners. That is, a partnership does not pay income taxes, though it must report on its profit, revenue and expenses annually to the IRS. That reporting will also report on how the partners are to be taxed on those profits. The partnership agreement may specify that profits are shared evenly or it may give different percentages to be allocated to each partner. The partners will include their share of profit or losses on their own individual tax filings, much as a sole proprietor does.

- **Draws:** Partners do not receive paychecks; they take "draws." Here is the difference. When the partnership writes a paycheck to an employee, that amount is immediately taxable to the employee. The cash draws that partners receive from the partnership require no withholding or FICA tax payments, which paychecks do require. Partners are taxed on profits at the end of the year. Like a sole proprietor, the partner pays self employment taxes. The total taxes can be deposited in quarterly payments with the IRS.

*A partnership can elect to be taxed as a corporation or a partnership. I will assume for the remainder of my discussion on partnership taxation that an election was made to follow the partnership taxation rules.

Goodwill: A business term that refers to the real value of a business beyond its cash, inventory, property

Notes:

- **Capital Accounts:** Each partner has a capital account which is determined by the amount of capital that he or she contributed – cash, inventory, raw materials or equipment – to the partnership, plus his or her share of annual profits, less the total amount of their draws. Theoretically, when a partner departs, he or she is entitled to the value of his capital account – which does not include any business **goodwill**.

Perhaps I should take a moment to help you understand the difference between capital and goodwill. Knowing the difference should to be important to any business owner. Goodwill can be much more than capital, it is the "value" of an organization like Starbucks, whose reputation is worldwide. Starbucks, as a brand, has a value greater than just the cash and property that it owns. That goodwill is recognized by investors and is reflected in the value of Starbucks' stock. It is more than the total capital that Starbucks holds as business assets. In a similar way, a fashion partnership that develops a label with nationwide recognition has a value that is more than the partnership's cash inventory and business assets. This increased value is not a tangible item, but it can be sold as its goodwill.

It is important to know the differences for this reason. If you are a partner forced out at a time the partnership is beginning to make a bushel of money, you will likely want the partnership agreement to spell out how you share in that goodwill value. You shouldn't settle for just your capital account.

Needless to say, know the person whom you will be going into a partnership with. Personal differences and misunderstandings can easily arise when working to meet a difficult deadline. Aggravation can arise and that could eventually bring a business down. Remember, if one partner makes improper decisions for the business, the other may end up on the hook for those decisions.

Joint Ventures

Individuals working together may describe their business as a joint venture, but it is probably a general partnership. "Joint ventures" are temporary associations to accomplish a specific project (say, a one-time fashion show). When the project is over, the joint venture ends. So it is a specialized form of partnership. A joint venture can be a general or limited partnership. Joint ventures do require a written agreement to spell out the way the business will operate and what happens when it ends. I won't go into much more except for saying that a joint venture is generally not suitable for a fashion business because most fashion businesses are intended to grow and last for an unspecified amount of time.

Limited Liability Company (LLC)

This is a rather new business form that was created about 15 years ago as a way for professionals to take advantage of the benefits of both corporate liability protection but not be subject to rigid tax rules that apply to corporations. My general comments on LLCs also apply to LLPs (limited liability partnerships), and similar named entities. The use of these entities is growing, and is rapidly becoming the entity-of-choice for most new businesses. The reason for this growth is their flexibility in structure. A diverse range of needs for the owners and the business' investors. The last business that I set up I did so as an LLC, with one member, being myself.

The owners of an LLC are called "members." Each LLC has

Notes:

Notes:

managing members who are responsible for the company's operations. Business owners choose an LLC to obtain personal liability protection for the members that may arise (whether it is from the business operation or a screw-up of another member). With an LLC, none of the members are theoretically liable for the business' debt. However, understand that most banks and many vendors giving credit to the LLC may ask for one or more of the members to be personally responsible for such debt. LLCs generally provide liability protection to their members from business related activities – such as slip and fall lawsuits. Another reason for the popularity of an LLC is that the managing agreement of the LLC can allow the LLC a great flexibility in the way it allocates and distributes profits and the business ownership. Many states permit an LLC to be owned by a single managing member; however, there can be restrictions in some states.

Sample Organizational Chart - Limited Liability Company

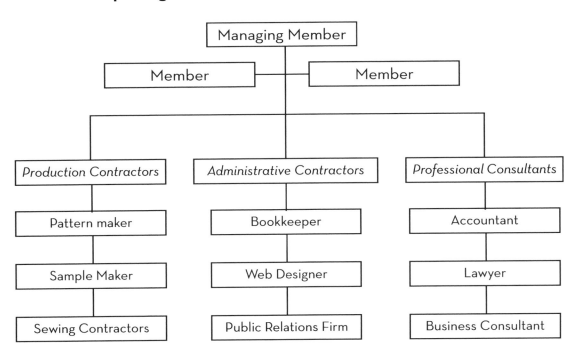

Taxation of an LLC

An LLC – other, than a one member LLC – is generally taxed as a partnership unless it elects to be taxed as a corporation. This election is made at the time the LLC is formed, by filing Form 8832. LLCs are usually required to file annual reports and pay annual fees to maintain status.

Corporations

Corporations are unlike any other business structures. They have been in operation for many years and are used by most businesses that are in operation today, although the numbers of LLCs are growing. The main reason for selecting a corporation is to create a separate entity under the law. Interests can be bought and sold without impacting the operation of the business. These business owners are called "stockholders." The officers of a corporation operate the business and can enter into contracts.

With a corporation, the entity owns property and is responsible for its business liabilities. Setting up a corporation is more complicated than setting up an LLC. A corporation is also more costly to maintain. There are stringent record-keeping and governmental reporting requirements. Because the corporation is not required to be run by its owners, the stockholders elect a board who, in turn, hires officers to run the business. Officers are generally hired with an employment agreement that spells out their duties and responsibilities.

Corporations pay their own taxes, unless an election is made to be treated as an S corporation. With an S election, the corporation does not pay taxes but is a type of flow—through entity. The business profits flow though to the shareholders.

Notes:

Notes:

With an S corporation, profits are taxed to the stockholders regardless of whether they are paid in cash. The shareholders of a non-S electing corporation (otherwise referred to as a "C corporation") who work in the business are paid wages. At the end of the year a C corporation pays taxes on its profits. For that reason most small businesses make the S election. Generally, a C corporation's tax rates are more than an individual's tax rates during the formative years of a business. An S election can result in less income tax paid. The Tax Code imposes very strict rules on S corporations. Violate one of those rules, and penalties can be the result. One requirement is that the profits be distributed in the ratio of stock ownership. If the 1% owner does 99% of the work, he or she can only get 1% of the profits. He or she would receive wages to make up the difference.

Most small businesses who incorporate make the subchapter S election, though more and more are looking at the benefits of operating as an LLC, which allow for similar treatment of profits.

If you are pulling your hair out or have already pulled it out, I'm right there with you. Writing about this stuff is just as stressful as reading about it.

Sample Organizational Chart - Corporation

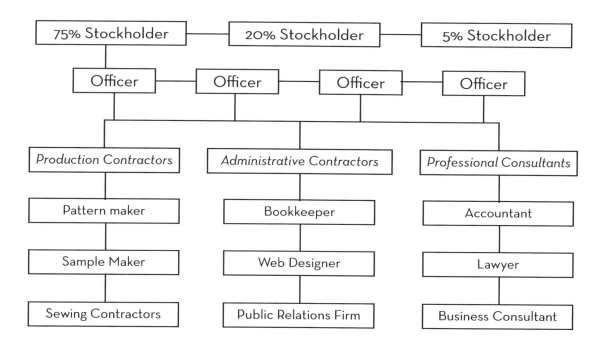

Business Entity

Who will be the owner or owners?

If there is more than one owner, will it be an equal partnership?

What will the partners be contributing to the business? Time? Money? Expertise?

Will you be asking others - family or investors - to provide the cash, inventory or equipment to get up and going?

Should these individuals be treated as investors with an ownership in the business or as lenders with you being personally responsible for repaying that obligation?

If you are starting this business on your own, do you plan on bringing a partner into your business down the line?

Will that decision cause you to change your business entity when the partner joins? [Note: a change in form could require redoing contracts, leases and agreements]

Case Study: Business Entity

Who will be the owner or owners?

Just Me: Andrea C. Baker

If there is more than one owner, will it be an equal partnership?

_NA_

What will the partners be contributing to the business? Time? Money? Expertise?

_NA_

Will you be asking others - family or investors - to provide the cash, inventory or equipment to get up and going?

No, but I will be using the equipment purchased for the studio/store that I co-own.

Should these individuals be treated as investors with an ownership in the business or as lenders with you being personally responsible for repaying that obligation?

_NA_

If you are starting this business on your own, do you plan on bringing a partner into your business down the line?

No, I will eventually hire my kids as employees and I expect them to take it over, but I don't plan them to be partners with me

Will that decision cause you to change your business entity when the partner joins? [Note: a change in form could require redoing contracts, leases and agreements]

_NA_

Notes:

Choosing your Legal Council

The formation of a business in a format other than a sole proprietorship is not something that you should do on your own, at least not the first time around, and maybe not the second, either. Sooner or later something may happen that forces you to seek some "reliable" legal advice. When that happens, you will want to be working with an attorney who knows something about you and your business.

You need to determine if the attorney you are considering will be the right person for the job. This individual will be guiding you through the process of getting your business set up. Seek out a tax attorney who will be there for you as your business grows. You shouldn't assume that all lawyers are equally knowledgeable in all facets of the law. You will want to look for an attorney who specializes in working with small, start-up businesses, and likely has an LLM in taxation (LLM is a Masters of Law, or MLT for Masters of Law in Taxation). Bottom line, you'll want to make sure you are not talking about business and tax structures with a divorce attorney, even if she is the wife of your Monday morning yoga instructor.

Give the attorney you are considering working with a phone interview. Find out about his or her practice, and ask how billing is calculated. If you prefer to meet face to face, ask for your first meeting to be an interview, so that you can get to know the nature of the practice and how you will be billed. Most business attorneys will agree to meet and talk without a charge for half an hour or so, to find out if there is a mutual relationship. Attorneys working with business owners tend to have a lasting relationship, so getting your business set up is only the first step in your relationship. The point here, get an understanding of how you will be treated by the attorney before any hiring is done. Think of this as a first date, but with a lawyer, not Prince Charming.

Once you have made a decision on your business entity, your lawyer will then guide you through the formalization of the business under your state's laws. Your attorney will draft basic business forms to form the business, file the required documents with federal, state and local agencies, and most likely direct you to speak to an accountant. Yes, you will also want to speak to an accountant when you start your business. The accountant's role will be to guide you through the practical process of how you keep track of all of your business transactions. We will talk more about accounting records in Chapter 33.

Before you visit a law office to have any discussion, write down your goals for the meeting, including all questions you may have. When you get to the attorney's office, forget about where he went for vacation last year or how healthy his pet ferrets are. Get down to business and ask your questions. Most attorneys charge in quarter hour chunks, so if you take 40 minutes to discuss an issue, you will be charged for · of an hour. Spending 40 minutes on the breeding habits of his pet ferrets costs the same! You will likely be paying $200 an hour, and getting updated on those ferrets could cost you $150.

Write down what you discuss. If you don't understand what was said, ask for a better explanation. It is not your responsibility to understand a bunch of legal jargon; instead, it is the attorney's responsibility to explain things in way that can be understood by the client no matter what. Don't ever let the attorney try

Notes:

Notes:

to intimidate you. If you feel intimidated, get up and leave. Remember, you are buying advice from this individual and if he or she cannot clearly provide an understandable answer in a non-threatening manner, go elsewhere.

I have worked with many attorneys and thanks to an introduction by my father; I have one of the country's best tax and business attorneys. I continue to learn along the way and to be truthful, there are some legal tasks I now do without an attorney, but I know the limits of my knowledge. I have learned that you cannot scrimp on good legal advice.

Comparison of Business Entities

Owner Objectives	Sole Proprietorship - Partnership	LLC (taxed as a partnership)	C Corporation	S Corporation
Sole Worker	A possible choice; Owner does not take a paycheck; Pay quarterly estimated taxes	A possible choice; Owner can issue self paychecks; Owner can take a draw; Draws are subject to self-employment taxes	Not recommended; Profits must be paid as a salary	A possible choice; Pay small salary when profits are available; Profits can be taken as distributions at the end of the year
Contributing equipment, inventory and cash to get the business going	Owner and business are one and the same	Single Owner LLCs permitted in most states and property can be contributed to start up business with no taxation.	Contributing cash or property to a corporation requires reporting for tax purposes; Property becomes ownership of the corporation	Same as a C corporation.
You plan to bring in a partner later on; Partner may or may not have capital to contribute	No partners with a sole proprietorship; 2 or more would form a partnership and this would create a new entity	Easiest format to bringing in another owner; You can have different classes of ownership with different rights.	Not recommended; Equal rights to all shareholders; May have different rights; Costly to deal with.	Same as a C corporation; Restrictions on number of shareholders and all shareholders need to have rights.
May lose your initial investment in the first year and will hold a job on the side until you start making money	Not a problem with a sole proprietorship; Any loss will be offset against other income	Not a problem with LLC; Loss flows through to the owner like a sole proprietorship and is offset against other income.	The loss is generally not deductible because it is at the corporate level.	Not a problem with S corporation; Profits and losses flow through to the stockholders in the ratio of their stock ownership
Sell your business within 10 years and turn the business over to that buyer to run	Not the best choice; Determining exactly what is being sold can be difficult.	An appropriate solution	The tax issues here can be disastrous for an organization formed as a C Corporation; so it is not a good solution.	Generally S corporations work without too much of a problem; Taxation is similar to that of a LLC
Creditor protection for manufacturing and a business lease	No protection signing as owner	No personal liability; Owners may be required to personally guarantee any liability	No personal liability; Stockholders may be required to personally guarantee any liability	Same as C corporation.
Protection from liabilities arising out of business operation	Owners are personally liable	The members are not personally liable for the debts or other obligations of the LLC	The stockholders are not personally liable for the debts or other obligations of the Corporation	Same as a C corporation
Change to another type of business entity	Yes, and normally without a tax penalty	Maybe, see attorney for advice	Difficult and fraught with lots of penalties for not doing things correctly, see an attorney.	Even more difficult and more penalties, see an attorney.

Notes:

Setting Up Your Business

By now I am sure you have googled some of the terms discussed to see if there were any low cost services to help you set up your legal entity. You wouldn't be an entrepreneur if you hadn't. There are lots of online services that advertise legal or paralegal services to set you up at affordable prices. They exist, some do a fair to good job, but most offer highly generic forms and agreements and may not protect you as you have intended. Go see a competent lawyer and get started correctly. If you are well prepared, the legal work won't cost a whole lot more than one of the web site options, and you'll know the entity has been set up right. That means you'll be legal to do business in your state and won't have to worry about penalties at a later date when you find out your web-based advisor forgot to tell you to do something for the city where you do business. If you do decide to take a do-it-yourself legal approach, check out any services you use with the Better Business Bureau in your home locale.

Chapter 24
Licenses and Permits

There are many licenses and permits that one must receive when beginning a business. The following are generalized. Your city and state may require additional permits for you to conduct your business. Check with your state's government website for more details on setting up a small business.

Fictitious Business Name

You will need to file a Fictitious Business Name Statement if you plan on operating your business with a name other than your own legal name. This statement allows you to operate with a business name when you don't setup your business as an LLC or Corporation. This name statement is filed with your city or county government. Make sure to conduct a search for the name you are planning on using before actually filing it. These searches are usually available online and can be found on your city or county government website.

There is a minimal registration fee for this, and you are required to post the fictitious name in a local paper. Many papers specialize in this type of posting. When you register for the fictitious name, you also register your address as your place of business. Because of this, your mailbox will be flooded with

Notes:

Notes:

offers on where you can have it posted, so don't worry about planning out which paper to post it in advance.

Business License and Taxes

You will generally need to file for a business license with the city you are operating your business in. You will need your Fictitious Business Name Statement, incorporation papers or your LLC documentation in order to do this. You may also need to file for zoning permits. The zoning permits regulate the type of business allowable in your area. If you are operating out of your home, your business may have to be designated a home occupation or hobby. Your city government can point you in the right direction.

The business license is usually not a large investment. You may have to pay for any zoning permits that go with the license. Your business license is reviewed annually, and to do that, you must file your business taxes with your city each year. Forms will be mailed automatically to you, so make sure to let your city business office know if you are moving.

Sellers Permit

You are required you to have a Sellers Permit/Resale Number through the State Board of Equalization if you sell merchandise. This is sometimes called a "Use Tax." There is a nominal fee, and the permit allows you to purchase your fabrics, notions, and other goods at wholesale prices without being charged sales tax. It also requires you to collect sales tax on goods sold directly to the public. If you sell directly to a retailer with the intent of your goods being resold, you do not need to collect sales tax; it becomes the retailer's responsibility to collect it. It is your responsibility to obtain your retailers' numbers for audit purposes. You will be required to file your Use Tax Return with the state either annually, quarterly, or monthly, depending on what you chose when you filed for your number.

Employer's Identification Number

If you are operating your business as a sole proprietorship, you may use your Social Security number for your business, or you may file for an Employer's Identification Number (EIN) from the IRS, using Form SS-4. Forms are available online at IRS.gov, and filing is free.

Any filing made for your business with the federal government must have a tax payer identification number. Sole proprietors are the only types of businesses that may use the owner's SSN rather than an EIN, however when the sole proprietor hires an employee, the owner will need an EIN for the business.

Notes:

Chapter 25
Financial Basics

Business Bank Accounts

You'll need to get a separate business checking account as soon as you have filed for your business license. You will need these documents in order to set up your accounts and demonstrate to Uncle Sam you are following the tax laws. Once you set up a business checking account, apply for a business credit card. To keep things orderly, use your business credit card only for business purchases and personal credit cards for personal purchases. You might want to apply for a business credit card at the same time you set up your checking account. You can sometimes link the two together for overdraft protection and you can only do that if they are with the same bank.

If you ever charge personal things like groceries on that card, you will need to reimburse the business the same as if you use your personal card to pay for business needs. Understanding that mixing business and personal does more than make keeping track of your business accounting difficult, it can become an IRS issue.

Without getting into a discussion of IRS regulations, you

Notes:

Notes:

should know that when a business reimburses an employee for business expenses, that reimbursement must be through an "accountable" plan. This is a term for reimbursements that can be clearly documented (keep your receipts). Entertainment expenses must include the parties involved, what was discussed and the date it occurred. A reimbursement not meeting these requirements may be treated as a payment from the employer that is taxable to the employee. In order to avoid this issue, remember to use your business account for business purchases and your personal account for Starbucks.

Taxes

There are all sorts of tax payments and tax reports that fall upon a business name. There can be city, county, state and federal filings, each with a separate due date, that if missed can result in penalties. Set reminders on your calendar. Put post-its on your door. Write yourself notes on your mirror with lipstick. Do whatever it takes, but remember to file your taxes. If you don't, those wonderful people at the IRS can come knocking on your door asking to audit you. You will be fined if you do not file your taxes and reports in a timely manner. You will need to check with your county and state government to see what additional filings you are required to make.

Depending on the business entity in which you will be operating, there are several types of reporting that needs to take place on a regular basis. The IRS compiled everything you need to know as a small business into several different publications. It is recommended that you read them and start with Publication 583. It contains the most relevant information. I have summarized the key points in the following paragraphs.

Almost all businesses are responsible for filing both business income tax reports and payroll tax reports. These are in addition to the business owner's individual income tax return. You may estimate your taxes to help anticipate taxes for the upcoming year.

Any business with paid employees must withhold income tax and certain payroll taxes from their employee's wages. These include federal unemployment taxes (FUTA) and Social Security and Medicare taxes (FICA). If you are using a payroll service, you can have them file the taxes for you, relieving the burden of figuring the math out on your own.

For sole proprietors, filing self employment taxes can be paid quarterly or sometimes annually. You can estimate a portion of your self employment taxes based on your profits. Social security is 12.4% and Medicare is 2.9%. Income tax estimates for flow through entities are a little more complicated. It is calculated in tiers. For example, the first $8400 of profit is taxed at 10%, the next $2500 of profit is calculated at 15% and so on. These numbers change annually, so check with the Form 1040ES for the most current monetary breakdown.

Sales tax depends on your state's laws. This can usually be paid monthly, quarterly or annually depending on the estimated sales of your business.

Notes:

Comparison of Taxes on Business Entities

Business Entity	Income Tax Filing	Estimated Tax	Employment Taxes	Owner's Reporting
Sole Proprietor	Business income is reported on the business owner's tax return	Form 1040 ES for estimated taxes if applicable	Form 941, Employer's Quarterly Federal Tax Return Form 940, Employer's Annual Unemployment Tax Return Form 8109-B, Federal Tax Deposit Coupon	Form 1040, Schedule C-Business Reporting Schedule SE - Self Employment Taxes
Partnership & Limited Liability Companies	Form 1065, Annual Partnership Return Schedule K-1 to report a partner's share of income, deductions and credits.	Form 1040 ES for estimated taxes if applicable	Form 941, Employer's Quarterly Federal Tax Return Form 940, Employer's Annual Unemployment Tax Return Form 8109-B, Federal Tax Deposit Coupon	Form 1040 Form 1065 Schedule K-1 on Schedule E that is filed with form 1040 Partnership taxes are 15.3% of profits distributed from the business Form 1040ES for estimated taxes if applicable
C Corporation	Form 1120 Annual Income Tax Return, reports income, deductions and credits	Form 1220 W, Estimated Corporate tax Form 8109-B Estimated Tax Deposit Slip (if no reportable profits, where all profits are paid as wages to shareholders and employees, no deposit is required)	Form 941, Employer's Quarterly Federal Tax Return Form 940, Employer's Annual Unemployment Tax Return Form 8109-B, Federal Tax Deposit Coupon	Form 1040, Schedule B, dividends from a corporation, Form 1040ES for estimated taxes if applicable Form 1040ES for estimated taxes if applicable
S Corporation	Form 1120S, Annual Income Tax Return Schedule K-1 for reporting the shareholder's share of income, deductions and credits	No tax at the corporate level. The shareholders of an S corporation may need to make deposits of estimated income taxes using Form 1040ES	Form 941, Employer's Quarterly Federal Tax Return Form 940, Employer's Annual Unemployment Tax Return Form 8109-B, Federal Tax Deposit Coupon	Form 1040 Form 1065 Schedule K-1 on Schedule E that is filed with form 1040 Form 1040ES for estimated taxes if applicable

Make note of when these are due:

- Your business tax return needs to be filed annually, but you may need to file quarterly estimated returns.
- Use and sales taxes need to be filed annually, quarterly or monthly.
- Business property taxes are annual.
- Unemployment Taxes (if you have employees) are filed monthly.
- Social Security and Medicare Taxes are filed immediately after they are collected from payroll.
- Income tax filing date is April 15th.

If you collect sales tax from customers, set this money aside and keep an accurate record of what you owe to the state. Do not commingle it with other accounts or make the mistake of spending it on some urgent expense. Not paying all of your sales tax when it comes due can get you some stiff penalties.

You may want to open a business savings account for setting aside your collected sales tax and a portion of your profits for income taxes. This allows you to collect interest on government money. Maybe the interest earned will treat you to a really nice relaxing foot massage.

Insurance

Not having certain types of insurance is like playing Russian roulette with your business. Seek out and invest in business insurance that is appropriate for your business. You may need liability insurance in case somebody gets injured on your property. Liability insurance can also cover you on lawsuits against your business. Ask your insurance agent about coverage of your inventory and business property, and coverage of losses due to theft and loss of business due to a catastrophe (fire,

Notes:

Notes:

storm, flooding). There are many levels of insurance coverage, costing from $50 a month to $300 a month or more. You may also want to consider product liability coverage. This coverage protects you against faulty products and product injury.

If you have employees, you are required by law to have workers compensation insurance. Workers Comp covers employees if they injure themselves on the job or become disabled. Without coverage, the business's owners become personally liable for all injuries incurred at work!

Health insurance is a whole other animal and isn't related to your business operations, that is, unless your business causes so much stress that you develop ulcers. On a more serious note, if you are seeking health insurance, find yourself an insurance broker to narrow down your options. You generally don't pay extra for this service, although the broker usually receives a commission from the insurance company that you choose.

Chapter 26
Funding Your Business

Bootstrapping

Bootstrapping is not exactly funding, but it's what most of us do when first settling on the idea of working for ourselves. Basically, you hold a job, freelance, or take on a position part-time to fund your company. Bootstrapping a business means being self-sufficient without external financial help. If this is how you plan to do it, it's important that you maintain a strict budget and only set a certain amount of funds aside for your business. Spend only what you budget.

Start-up Capital

You have saved up every cent possible - breaking open your piggy bank and working nights and weekends. This savings is now part of your start-up capital, but you may need to raise more. The start-up capital can come from all kinds of sources. Savings accounts, investment accounts (401(k) & retirement accounts), selling a car or other assets, borrowing against a house, borrowing from friends and family, and credit cards can all be used to fund your start-up or as collateral for a business loan. If you can avoid tapping into the last resource (credit

Notes:

cards), please do so.

Using or maxing out your credit cards can not only be detrimental to your credit but can cause banks to turn down your loan applications. Friends and family may be your best bet, but be careful and make arrangements for returning the payment. You can use social lending companies to set up friends and family lending. This will assure them that you will pay them back. Social lending will be discussed a little further into this chapter.

Banking Relationships

Why is a banking relationship important to a new business owner? Consider the following: Bank lending usually doesn't come until after you have established a long term pattern of good financial behavior. While that means not bouncing a check, it also means that you need to establish a relationship with a bank and show that you are a profitable customer. If they don't make money from the relationship you have a low profile to them. There are things you can do to put yourself in a position to get a loan. To build a good banking relationship:

•   Instead of using the drive through every day with your deposits, go inside and meet the bank officer that has been assigned to your business. Make one of those meetings a time to discuss yours and your business finances.

•   If you have a car that is paid for or other collateral, consider getting a small short term bank loan (these are easier to obtain, but will not fund your business operations). It will be your opportunity to show that you make payments when they are due. Then when you need a larger loan the officer will be able to demonstrate to the lending board that you are a good customer.

- Avoid transferring all your money into a money market account; leave it in your bank account. What you will earn on that money market account is minimal. The bank uses your money to lend to others, so when they make money off of you, you are a good customer. From a business stand point, who would you appreciate more, the one time buyer who spends $25, or someone who spends $10 every week?

- Set up annual meetings to discuss your business with your banking representative and wave to them at the grocery store.

Micro-Loans

The Small Business Association works with several banks in assisting small businesses with loans they may not otherwise qualify for. An SBA-guaranteed bank loan is called a micro-loan. The interest rate on these types of loans is usually higher than traditional bank-term loans, but they are easier to obtain. These loans are ideal for startups though existing companies use them too. You will need to have money in the bank in order to qualify for the loan; this is where the start-up capital comes in. You will need to show the bank how much you have already invested or how much you are willing to invest, show them a business plan with your projections, and offer up any collateral available. These loans range from a couple hundred dollars up to $20,000.

Bank-Term Loans

Bank-term loans are usually for established businesses and are typically used to expand a business. These loans start around $25,000. They are not usually an option for small design businesses, but don't rule it out. Talk to your bank about what conditions you must satisfy to qualify.

Notes:

Notes:

Social Lending Sources

Social or peer-to-peer lending is the newest form of lending and is quite different from traditional loans. Applicants get qualified based on their loan application as well as their individual story. Social lending serves two purposes. It allows anyone who chooses to lend, to do so. It also helps many people obtain a loan, who may not otherwise be qualified to get a loan from a bank. There are only a handful of social lending companies participating in this type of lending.

Three companies that currently assist with social lending are Prosper, Lending Club and Zopa.

- **Prosper** – Peer-to-peer lending where each individual makes the ultimate decision on who gets the loans. Loans are available up to $25,000. Lenders "bid" loans on interest rates in a similar way that you would bid on an item on eBay. Having a large amount of bids lowers the interest rate. You set the highest interest rate you are willing to pay.

- **Lending Club** – Much like Prosper, but is not available in every state. Loans are available up to $25,000

- **Zopa** – Based in the UK, Japan and Italy; your credit score is the ultimate factor determining whether you'll get a loan. Loans are available up to £15,000.

There are advantages and disadvantages to social lending.

Advantages: As a borrower, you may qualify for a loan even if you don't qualify when screened by a traditional institution. As a lender, you can invest in other people and build an investment plan to suit your needs.

Disadvantages: As a borrower, your interest rates may be higher than with bank loans if your credit score is blemished. As a lender, you may be at risk if borrowers default on their loans.

Venture Capital

Venture capital is usually provided by professionally managed firms that loan large amount to high growth companies capable of reaching $25 million in sales by the 5th year. Venture capitalists (VCs) expect equity ownership in exchange for the investment. This is not really a practical option for a small design business.

Angel Investors

An angel investor is very similar to a VC, but is an individual rather than a company. Angel investors expect ownership percentage and sometimes require involvement in the business to help create a return on their investment.

Factoring

Factoring is a loan secured by orders taken. Factors are lenders who lend money based on the total amount of orders placed with your company. Factoring may not be an option for you if you have less than lustrous credit or have not built up your business credit.

Traditionally, the loan does not cover the entire amount of your orders. Payment is due as soon as orders are shipped and money is collected. If you have cancellations, you are still responsible for immediate payment. Not all factors will lend on all orders, especially small design firms that don't have business

Notes:

credit. The businesses placing the orders must also have sound credit in order for a factor to cover your orders.

Another form of factoring is where the lender actually buys the invoices. This puts them on the hook if an order is canceled. This is generally done with well known venders such as Macy's, Nordstrom's and other department stores.

Knowing your Personal Credit

When embarking onto your own business venture, you really need to be aware of your credit and the information that the credit bureaus have. Make sure to obtain your credit report prior to applying for any loan and go over it carefully. You do not want to discover a surprise item on your credit report after you've applied for a loan.

Credit scores range from 300 to 850. Any score under a 680 can cause lenders to be less than forthcoming with their money. Once you check your credit, I suggest you keep an eye on it. Credit monitoring services can help in this matter and alert you when new activity appears on your credit file.

However, they may not always alert you in a timely manner when new activity shows up under your name. It can take months for you to learn that a new account has been opened in your name, and that may have been enough time to cause damage. I suggest you get a copy of your credit report regularly (once a year is free), so you can be sure it reflects your profile accurately for future business.

You can obtain one free copy of your report a year from each of the bureaus. Annualcreditreport.com will guide you through obtaining these free copies. Check on all your past credit as well. Are there accounts that are showing open even though you closed those 10 years ago? This can adversely affect your overall credit score. Call or write to the parties involved, request that they fix the error, and keep on them until they do.

What if you discover that your identity was stolen and the thief has run up credit on your name? Contact the company that issued the credit immediately, explain your problem, and stay with it until it gets resolved. This happens more frequently than you might think. When running a business, you will be particularly vulnerable as you will be using your credit cards, bank cards, and checks a lot more than before. Each use is an opportunity for theft.

Here are a few suggestions on how to keep your information safe.

- Purchases online should be done with a credit card and not a bank/debit card. If your bank account is hit, you will feel it immediately and it may take time to get that money back. On the other hand, with credit cards, you're generally not responsible for fraudulent charges, and will not feel a financial impact while things are being straightened out.

- Use certain cards for certain things. Try not to mix up your business card with your personal card.

- Sign up for online banking and check your bank account balances often. Make sure your computer has virus protection.

- Do not send financial information or passwords over email or by cell phone. Emails can be easily hacked and cell phone calls can be intercepted.

Notes:

Dun & Bradstreet
Business Credit Scores:
smallbusiness.dnb.com

Credit for your Business

So far I've discussed protecting your personal credit, but
what you may be interested in is building your business
credit. Business credit scores range from 0–100. 75 and up
is considered to be excellent. Dun & Bradstreet provides
business credit scores, as well as a handful of other companies.
Business credit profiles usually cost a few hundred dollars
to set up. Good business credit is important if you plan on
working with factors or if you plan on establishing credit terms
with suppliers and contractors.

Chapter 27
Protecting Your Work

Most designers' biggest fear is having their designs stolen, and there is a good reason for it. If you pay attention to fashion, you see similarities among clothing lines all the time—from colors to fabrics and designs. The first thing you need to accept is that in fashion there is nothing ever really 100% original. As designers, we pull inspiration from the past, the present, and yes, other designers.

To tell someone that you have never pulled inspiration from another person's clothing is foolish. Artists are inspired by everything, and unless you are blind, you cannot make that statement without holding your fingers crossed. Having said this, where do we draw the line between inspiration and stealing?

Traditionally, "knocking off" a design happened after the design was released out into the world, so it was known who the designer was that originated the design. Although, the bigger question is "Did that designer really originate it?"

Notes:

Big names aren't exempt from "knocking off" designs. Despite all their fame, brand name designers have been caught stealing. Yves Saint Laurent took Ralph Lauren to court in 1994 for stealing a tuxedo dress design and won in a French court.

Design theft happens on all sides of the trade. For smaller designers, it can be a particular concern. How and where can this happen to a smaller company? Trade shows for one. Many larger companies hire their designers to walk the trade shows, find designs that are fabulous, and knock them off or be "inspired" by them. All the big names do it. Maybe it was coincidence, but did that blouse really mean to have the exact same pattern mistake in the neckline?

The second most common way to steal is in the actual production of the garments. The danger lies usually in overseas production, primarily out of Chinese factories. Because the factory controls how and when your product is finished, if they decide to knock off your design, they can get it on the shelf before yours and at a lesser price. This can seriously hurt a designer. To ease your fears, I suggest having any international manufacturer sign an exclusivity agreement to limit their production of your garments to you. Not everyone will do it, but if they say no, think twice about using their services.

Are you scared yet? Are you tossing and turning at night, wondering how to avoid the threat of imminent piracy? You should always be designing new and original pieces for your collection. If you launch your business betting on one design only, what happens to your company if you get knocked off? You'll be out of business in an instant.

The best things you can do to protect yourself against the loss of business is to build your brand loyalty. If you have a loyal audience that loves you and your designs, who cares if H& M steals from you. Look at it as flattery – a big name thinks your designs are worth stealing. Get the word out in your social media networks. This type of news travels faster than TV anyway. Make sure you can back up your claims.

You also have some legal means of protecting your designs, but not as good as you might wish. If you live in Europe, you are in better luck. There are copyright laws there that protect your designs longer than the life of the actual garment. If you live in the US, sorry guys, no such protection yet, although there are some acts in the works. But even if these laws are passed, how will they be enforced? Will there be a large influx of lawsuits? And against who? The small designer who hasn't budgeted for an attorney or the big guys?

Innovative Design Protection and Piracy Prevention Act
The fourth attempt at passing a fashion copyright law has just hit the courts again. This time the law has a name change. It is no longer referred to as The Design Piracy Prohibition Act, it has been renamed the Innovative Design Protection and Piracy Prevention Act. This new proposed legislation will enhance protection of fashion designs by changing copyright law.

A copyright currently protects works of authorship, such as writings, music, and works of art that have been tangibly expressed. The Library of Congress registers copyrights which last for the life of the author plus 70 years. In more recent years, the law has been changed to accommodate design of ship hulls, but limits it to 10 years. Copyrights currently do not

Notes:

Notes:

protect "useful items," which pertains to clothing.

The proposed act would include protection for fashion designs in copyright law, but for three years only. Europe has laws similar to the U.S.'s proposed legislation, and protects their registered fashion designs for 25 years. The U.S. has had the act presented four times in the past few years, never making its way fully through congress. The most recent was presented in August of 2010 by Senator Schumer in conjunction with the Council of Fashion Designers of America (CFDA) and the American Apparel & Footwear Association (AFFA). The first legislation was presented in 2006 as HR 5055, again in 2007 as HR 2033 and once again in 2009 as HR 2196.

To understand what the Innovative Design Protection and Piracy Prevention Act actually protects, it's probably best to discuss what it doesn't protect. It doesn't protect items that are "useful" that have been in the market place more than three months prior to registering the design. In other words, if you don't claim protection at the time you release your design, you are out of luck.

"A designer who claims that his work has been copied must show that his design provides "a unique, distinguishable, non-trivial and non-utilitarian variation over prior designs." And it must be proven by the designer that the copy is "substantially identical" to the original so as to be mistaken for it." Quoted from the New York Times' article by Cathy Horn, Schumer Bill Seeks to Protect Fashion Design, August 5, 2010

The Case Against the Act

Coco Chanel said it best in this famous quote, "If there is no copying, how are you going to have fashion?"

Once you really understand the way this industry works, you will see that to have a law pass like this will not benefit the industry but harm it. Yes, it may halt the fake Louis Vuitton bags from being sold in the alleys of Chinatown, but what about everyone else?

> *FYI – L.V. bags are covered by Trademark protection and the counterfeiting continues to exist. Trademark law has not ceased the production of such merchandise.*

What would the purpose of trends be anymore? What if Marc Jacobs captured the trend of leg warmers by registering them, what would happen to the hand knitters who make hand made leg warmers on etsy.com? Our cultures are defined by trends. The fact that some forms of design piracy happens, is what makes our industry thrive. Think of all the people who would be out of business if the act passes as law. Home sewers, stay at home parents who make things as a hobby, you, me; we will all be out of work. The only people who would make it out unscathed would be the big designers. We would return to a society that makes their own clothes and hires tailors and seamstresses to make clothes for us.

Maybe in the long run, this could benefit us because we would be back to our roots, but honestly that just isn't going to happen. If you look at the companies who are knocking off designers, it's usually the cheapy disposable clothing manufacturers who are knocking off the bigger designers. Who does this hurt anyway? Are the people who shop at H&M going to even be the same customer of Diane Von

Notes:

Furstenberg? Designer brands are made well and are usually made with quality fabrics, so the normal customers of Diane Von Furstenberg who love the feel of her fabrics are not going to wear the polyester rags from H&M.

If you find yourself being a victim of theft by one of the biggies, here is a tip from an insider at Banana Republic: "If a big name company steals your design, get yourself some legal council. They will fold at the sound of a lawsuit or bad press."

European Union Community Design System

In the European Union, such a law is in effect and has been since December of 2001. The law is now part of World Intellectual Property Organization (WIPO). The differences are vast between the EU's laws and the proposed laws in the US. The first difference is who and what it covers. Their design laws are very broad and do not require the novelty of the item to be that unique. Under the EU's law, you can register as an Unregistered Community Design (UCD) or a Registered Community Design (RCD).

The UCD is generally used for portfolios and has to be renewed by the designer each season. The RCD covers garments for a longer period of time and can be renewed every 5 years up to 25 years.

The protection you receive under this law "may be vulnerable when challenged," according to the Community Design System. To qualify under this law, you must meet these 5 requirements.

1. There are no requirements as to the use of the design being registered

2. The design can be descriptive and/or distinctive

3. One application can be filed for a simple design and could cover all of the designer's goods

4. Any member of any nationality or country of incorporation can qualify

5. A registration can be kept "secret" for up to 30 months after filing

As you can see that by this law, there really isn't anything that indicates the originality or uniqueness of a product to qualify for registration. Because of this, very few designers actually register their designs and even fewer designers file lawsuits against infringement.

Japanese Design Law

On the other end of the spectrum, Japan has a law that couldn't be more different. Japan's law offers protection for 20 years and is stricter than a nun at a catholic school. This law was developed in 1959, although it has had several amendments over the years. To be eligible for this protection, there are 6 requirements.

1. The design must be novelty, meaning no identical item can have ever been in the market place.

2. No design without creativity will be registered and this creativity is juried

3. The design must be unique in all matters, no similar item

Notes:

Notes:

United States Patent and Trademark Office
www.uspto.gov

World Intellectual Property Organization
www.wipo.int/madrid

can be registered

4. The item may not breach public order or morality

5. Only one design can be registered per application

6. Priority will be given to the first application filed for a design.

Due to the exclusivity of this law, few designers register their creations. To read more about this law, see the Japanese External Trade Organization (www.jetro.go.jp).

Trademarks

Trademarks can't protect your design, but they can protect your trade name or your logo. A trademark is a type of intellectual property, typically a name, word, phrase, logo, symbol, design, image, or a combination of these elements. Trademarks protect words, names, symbols, sounds, or colors that distinguish goods and services from those manufactured or sold by others and indicate the source of the goods. Trademarks, unlike patents, can be renewed forever as long as they are being used in commerce. Trademarks cost between $275 and $375 to register in the U.S., depending on the classification. You can also register trademarks internationally through The Madrid System at WIPO (**World Intellectual Property Organization**).

Patents

A patent also will not protect a clothing design, but will protect functionality in the design. If you have developed a new way to use a current product, you may be able to have it patented.

If you wish to proceed with a patent, you must have deep pockets and a lawyer who enjoys filling theirs. For smaller designers, patents aren't really an option unless you really have created something new and plan on investing over $20,000 to protect it. You have to pay search fees, registration fees, maintenance, post-allowance fees, and all sorts of other fees. The fee schedule for the US Patent & Trademark Office has a price break for small entities, meaning individuals, so at least there are some advantages of being a small design business.

Confidentiality Agreement and Non Disclosure Agreements
Your best bet, if you're worried about your designs, is to have any contractors you are dealing with sign a Confidentiality Agreement or a Non-Disclosure Agreement. This is customary and protects you from having your contractor sell your secrets to your competitors or share your patterns with them.

The following agreement is an example of one I use professionally in commerce when working with freelance consultants.

Notes:

CONFIDENTIAL INFORMATION AND NONDISCLOSURE AGREEMENT

As a condition of my becoming retained as a consultant (or my consulting relationship being continued) by Jennifer Lynne Matthews and Porcelynne Lingerie organized under the laws of the state of California, (the "Company"), and in consideration of my consulting relationship with the Company and my receipt of the compensation now and hereafter paid to me by the Company, I agree to the following:

1. **Consulting Relationship.** I understand and acknowledge that this Confidential Information and Nondisclosure Agreement (the "Agreement") does not alter, amend or expand upon any rights I may have to continue in a consulting relationship with, or in the duration of my consulting relationship with, the Company under any existing agreements between the Company and me, or under applicable law. Any consulting relationship between the Company and me, whether commenced prior to or upon the date of this Agreement, shall be referred to herein as the "Relationship."

2. **Confidential Information and Nondisclosure of Company Information.** I agree at all times during the term of my Relationship with Company and thereafter, to hold in strictest confidence, and not to use, except for the benefit of Company to the extent necessary to perform my obligations to the Company under the Relationship, or to disclose to any person, firm, corporation or other entity without written authorization of the Company, any Confidential Information (as defined below) of the Company which I obtain or create. I further agree not to make copies of such Confidential Information except as authorized by the Company. I understand that "Confidential Information" means any Company proprietary information, technical data, trade secrets or know-how, including, but not limited to, research, product plans, products, product names, services, suppliers, contacts, customer lists and customers (including, but not limited to, customers of the Company on whom I called or with whom I became acquainted during the Relationship), prices and costs, markets, software, developments, inventions, notebooks, processes, formulas, technology, patterns, designs, drawings, engineering, hardware configuration information, marketing information, licenses, finances and financial data, budgets, electronic communications, graphic communications, marketing information, proposed trademarks, proposed patents, or other business information disclosed to me by the Company either directly or indirectly in writing, orally or by drawings or observation of parts, products or equipment or created by me during the period of the Relationship, whether or not during working hours. I understand that "Confidential Information" includes, but is not limited to, information pertaining to any aspects of the Company's business which is either information not known by actual or potential competitors of the Company or other third parties not under confidentiality obligations to the Company, or is otherwise proprietary information of the Company or its customers or suppliers, whether of a technical nature or otherwise. I further understand that Confidential Information does not include any of the foregoing items which has become publicly and widely known and made generally available through no wrongful act of mine or of others who were under confidentiality obligations as to the item or items involved.

3. **Inventions Retained and Licensed.** I have attached hereto, as Exhibit A, a list describing with particularity all inventions, original works of authorship, developments, improvements, and trade secrets which were made by me prior to the commencement of the Relationship (collectively referred to as "Prior Inventions"), which belong solely to me or belong to me jointly with another, which relate in any way to any of the Company's proposed businesses or products, and which are not assigned to the Company hereunder; or, if no such list is attached, I represent that there are no such Prior Inventions. If, in the course of my Relationship with the Company, I incorporate into a Company product or process a Prior Invention owned by me or in which I have an interest, the Company is hereby granted and shall have a non-exclusive, royalty-free, irrevocable, perpetual, worldwide license (with the right to sublicense) to make, have made, copy, modify, make derivative works of, use, sell and otherwise distribute such Prior Invention as part of or in connection with such product.

4. **Returning Company Documents.** I agree that, at the time of termination of my Relationship with the Company, I will deliver to the Company (and will not keep in my possession, recreate or deliver to anyone else) any and all Confidential Information and devices, records, data, notes, reports, proposals, lists, correspondence, specifications, drawings, blueprints, sketches, notebooks, materials, flow charts, equipment, other documents or property, or reproductions of any of the aforementioned items, developed by me pursuant to the Relationship or otherwise belonging to the Company, its successors or assigns.

5. **Solicitation of Other Parties.** For a period of twenty-four (24) months following termination of my Relationship with the Company for any reason, with or without cause, I shall not solicit any licensor to or customer of the Company or licensee of the Company's products, in each case, that are known to me, with respect to any business, products or services that are competitive to the products or services offered by the Company or under development as of the date of termination of my Relationship with the Company.

6. **Representations and Covenants.**

(a) **Facilitation of Agreement.** I agree to execute promptly any proper oath or verify any proper document required to carry out the terms of this Agreement upon the Company's written request to do so.

(b) **Conflicts.** I represent that my performance of all the terms of this Agreement does not and will not breach any agreement I have entered into, or will enter into with any third party, including without limitation any agreement to keep in confidence proprietary information acquired by me in confidence or in trust prior to commencement of my Relationship with the Company. I agree that, in advance of accepting or agreeing to perform consulting services or other services for companies who businesses or proposed businesses in any way involve products or services which would be competitive with the Company's products or services, or those products or services proposed or in development by the Company during the term of the Consulting Agreement, I will promptly notify the Company in writing, specifying the organization with which I propose to consult, become employed by, or otherwise provide services to, and provide information sufficient to allow the Company to determine if such work would conflict with the interests of the Company or further services which the Company might request of me.

(c) **Voluntary Execution.** I certify and acknowledge that I have carefully read all of the provisions of this Agreement and that I understand and will fully and faithfully comply with such provisions.

7. **General Provisions.**

(a) **Governing Law.** The validity, interpretation, construction and performance of this Agreement shall be governed by the laws of the State of California, without giving effect to the principles of conflict of laws.

(b) **Entire Agreement.** This Agreement sets forth the entire agreement and understanding between the Company and me relating to the subject matter herein and merges all prior discussions between us. No modification or amendment to this Agreement, nor any waiver of any rights under this Agreement, will be effective unless in writing signed by both parties.

(c) **Severability.** If any term or provision of this Agreement or the application thereof to any circumstance shall, in any jurisdiction and to any extent, be invalid or unenforceable, such term or provision shall be ineffective as to such jurisdiction to the extent of such invalidity or unenforceability without invalidating or rendering unenforceable the remaining terms and provisions of this Agreement or the application of such terms and provisions to circumstances other than those as to which it is held invalid or unenforceable, and a suitable and equitable term or provision shall be substituted therefor to carry out, insofar as may be valid and enforceable, the intent and purpose of the invalid or unenforceable term or provision. In the event that any court or government agency of competent jurisdiction determines that my provision of services to the Company is not as an independent contractor but instead as an employee under the applicable laws, then solely to the extent that such determination is applicable, references in this Agreement to the Relationship between me and the Company shall be interpreted to include an employment relationship, and this Agreement shall not be invalid and unenforceable but shall be read to the fullest extent as may be valid and enforceable under the applicable laws to carry out the intent and purpose of the Agreement.

(d) **Successors and Assigns.** This Agreement will be binding upon my heirs, executors, administrators and other legal representatives, and my successors and assigns, including, in the event that Consultant is an entity, any successor entity, and will be for the benefit of the Company, its successors, and its assigns.

(e) **Survival.** The provisions of this Agreement shall survive the termination of the Relationship and the assignment of this Agreement by the Company to any successor in interest or other assignee.

(f) **ADVICE OF COUNSEL.** I ACKNOWLEDGE THAT, IN EXECUTING THIS AGREEMENT, I HAVE HAD THE OPPORTUNITY TO SEEK THE ADVICE OF INDEPENDENT LEGAL COUNSEL, AND I HAVE READ AND UNDERSTOOD ALL OF THE TERMS AND PROVISIONS OF THIS AGREEMENT. THIS AGREEMENT SHALL NOT BE CONSTRUED AGAINST ANY PARTY BY REASON OF THE DRAFTING OR PREPARATION HEREOF.

The parties have executed this Agreement on the respective dates set forth below:

COMPANY:

Jennifer Lynne, Porcelynne Lingerie

Signature: _____

Date: _____

CONSULTANT:

an Individual, on behalf of _____

Signature: _____

Date: _____

LAWS AND REGULATIONS

Chapter 28
Labeling
Requirements

Take a look in your closet. Do half of your garments have labels on them that read "Dry Clean Only"? How many of them have you washed, and discovered they do just fine in the laundry? Do you ever wonder—how does this all-knowing manufacturer came up with the care instructions anyway?

Let's answer the "Dry Clean Only" question first. Many companies think of this as a get out of jail free card. It's no fault of theirs if you wash your garment and ruin it; they warned you to only dry cleaned it. But, is that really why they do it? According to the FTC, if a garment can be washed or dry cleaned successfully, the manufacturer only has to list one. The dry clean instructions are simpler than the washing instructions and let's face it, the more text there is, the more it costs, so to save .0001 cent per label, the manufacturer opted to use the dry clean only label.

Laws of Labeling

Labeling is regulated by the Federal Trade Commission (FTC), though a series of acts, called the Textile and Wool Acts. The FTC requires every clothing item that is sold in the U.S. to be accompanied by a label stating the fabric content,

Notes:

care instructions, country of origin and your own company's registration number (RN).

Fabric Education:
Fabriclink.com

The fabric content needs to be at the top of the list when it comes to your labeling. If you have different fabrics, you need to list the fabric content for each fabric in the garment, starting with the primary fabric used, then the secondary, etc. The fabric content can be on its own label or share the space with the care instructions.

Textile and Wool Acts:
*www.ftc.gov/bcp/edu/
pubs/business/textile/
bus21.shtm*

The Textile and Wool Acts require the fiber content (in percentages) to be either on a sewn-in label or an attached hang tag. The FTC also regulates what fabrics can and cannot be used for specific markets. For example, many fleece fabrics are considered flammable and are not permitted in children's clothing or accessories. Make sure to read the document titled **"*Threading Your Way Through the Labeling Requirements Under the Textile and Wool Acts*"** to see if any other restrictions apply to you.

Notes:

What's another reason to know the fiber content of a garment? Many people are allergic to fibers originated from animals such as wool or angora.

What if you purchase your fabric as remnants or from a jobber without knowledge of the origin or fiber content? How can you disclose your fiber content? The FTC has an exception for use of these items.

"If a textile product is made — in whole or in part — from scraps, clippings, rags, secondhand fibers or fabrics, or other textile waste materials of unknown and, for practical purposes, undeterminable fiber content, the disclosure may indicate that this is the case. For example:

Made of clippings of unknown fiber content

100% unknown fibers - rags

All undetermined fibers - textile by-products

100% miscellaneous pieces of undetermined fiber content

Secondhand materials - fiber content unknown

45% Rayon, 30% Acetate, 25% Unknown fiber content

75% Recycled Wool, 25% Unknown Reclaimed Fibers

60% Cotton, 40% Unknown fibers - Scraps

Made of remnants of undetermined fiber content and origin

Fabric Care Instructions

The care instructions on your sewn-in (or permanently printed) label must include the following 5 items for washing.

- **Wash instructions** by hand or machine, including water temperature: "Hand wash cold water"; "Machine wash warm water"

Notes:

Laundry Instructions and Fabric Care: www.Textilecare.com

Notes:

- **Bleaching instructions**. If any bleach is ok, there is no need to put anything on it regarding bleach, but if testing proves to only be able to use non-chlorine bleach, you need these instructions: "Only non-chlorine bleach, when needed." For no bleach, "No Bleach" or "Do Not Bleach."

- **Drying method**. If any temperature is ok, no need to label this, but if you have special instructions to avoid shrinking of the fabric such as "Hang Dry" or "Dry Flat" or "Tumble Dry Low Heat," these need to be indicated.

- **Ironing Instructions**. If the use of an iron will not harm the product, no need to label this, but if occasional ironing is needed, indicate the ironing temperature such as "Cool Iron if needed" or "Do Not Iron."

- **Warnings** to help the user successfully care for the garment should also be included. If the color may bleed, label as "Wash Separately" or "Wash with like colors." If the garment has a zipper and it washes best when closed, indicate it here as well as "Close Zipper."

Or...... if your garment can safely be dry cleaned, you can label your garment "Dry Clean Only." Now you should see why it is so popular to use "Dry Clean Only."

You may ask, "How do I determine what the care instructions are for my garments?" You should test your fabrics and finished garments by washing, drying, ironing and dry cleaning. Each fabric works differently, so a garment that contains several components could be quite complicated to write care instructions for. Based on the fabrics used, it is possible that you may have a garment label that reads "Do Not Wash, Do Not Dry Clean."

Registration Number

Included on your care instructions, you need to include the country of manufacture, then your Registration Number (RN).

Filing for a RN is probably the simplest form you will ever have to fill out and get this, it's free to file. You can file for this on the FTC's website. You might be asking, "What is the point of an RN anyway?" Every company that creates clothing registers and is listed in a national database, so you will be searchable. So, why would you want one, beside the law requiring it?

Let's say for example you have a brand label and a care label in your garment. Let's also assume that the brand label becomes itchy and the consumer cuts it out. That said garment is then sold at a garage sale or second hand store. A prestigious boutique owner comes across said garment and loves it. They think the aesthetic of the garment would be perfect for their 15 boutiques. Now, what can that person do to track down the origin of the garment? The brand label is missing, but the care label is intact and so is the RN. Here is where the search feature on the FTC site is beneficial in locating a manufacturer. Voila, a million dollar account all due to the person who put the garment up for second sale.

Notes:

Labeling

Style Name: _____   **Style #** _____

Fabric Content: _____

Dry Cleaning   Yes / No

Washing   Yes / No   **Warm water, cold water, temperature?**

Bleach   Yes / No   **Chlorine bleach, non chlorine bleach?**

Drying   Yes / No   **Dry flat, tumble try, air dry, low heat?**

Iron   Yes / No   **Cool iron, any temperature?**

Warnings:

Will the fabric bleed?   Yes / No

Does it need to be washed separately?   Yes / No

Do any trimmings need to be removed before washing or dry cleaning?   Yes / No
----

Other Instructions:

Case Study: Labeling

Style Name: _Wrap Dress_   **Style #**

Fabric Content: _100% Linen_

Dry Cleaning   (Yes) / No

Washing   (Yes) / No   **Warm water, cold water, temperature?**
Cold Water

Bleach   Yes / (No)   **Chlorine bleach, non chlorine bleach?**

Drying   (Yes) / No   **Dry flat, tumble try, air dry, low heat?**
Tumble dry – any heat

Iron   (Yes) / No   **Cool iron, any temperature?**
Any temperature

Warnings:

Will the fabric bleed? (Yes) / No
Wash with like colors and inside out

Does it need to be washed separately?   Yes / (No)

Do any trimmings need to be removed before washing or dry cleaning?   Yes / (No)

Other Instructions:

Chapter 29
State Garment Laws

To deter the persistence of sweatshops, a few states have established labor restrictions for the sewn products industry. The laws are originated by the state's Labor Commissioners and presently exist in California, New York, and New Jersey. Even if you are a business in another state, you may be required to abide by these laws and register if you do any business with contractors in those states. Contact the state's labor board to find out if you specifically need to register.

Garment Registration of California

California implemented its garment laws in 1978 and last revised them in 1999. The laws require that if your company exists in California, or you do business with a contractor in California, you must register with the labor board. Both contractors and manufacturers must register. As a designer or entrepreneur you are considered a manufacturer by law. This classification exists if you contract work from any individual who cuts, sews, processes, repairs, finishes, or assembles a sewn product. These fees range depending on revenue. Manufacturers' fees start at $750 annually.

To register with the labor board, you must fill out an

Notes:

CA Registration:
www.dir.ca.gov/dlse/
howtoobtaingarment
registration.htm

application, pay the fee determined by your revenue to the California Division of Labor Standards (DLSE), and pass a state administered exam regarding labor laws.

Failing to register may result in being charged with a misdemeanor, paying a hefty fine, and having your inventory confiscated. The contractors you use can also be slapped with a fine.

New Jersey Registration

NJ Registration:
www.lwd.dol.state.nj.us/
labor/wagehour/content/
apparel_industry.html

Registration in the state of New Jersey costs $300 annually for manufacturers. Failure to register can bring on a number of charges and penalties. New Jersey laws appear to be the strictest, and they carry the largest penalties. Violations can result in a three year waiting period before being able to begin manufacturing again. Confiscation of inventory, apparel and equipment is a possible penalty.

New York Registration

NY Registration:
www.labor.state.ny.us/
workerprotection/
laborstandards/
workprot/garment.asp

New York has the most lax laws of the three. Registration fees are $200 for manufacturers with a $150 annual renewal. The main purpose of these laws is to regulate the factories and to ensure all factory workers are paid fair wages. The NY labor board hosts an online directory of registered factories. This might be a good place to start when searching for a factory in the state of New York.

Chapter 30
Product Safety Regulations

The latest law affecting you as a manufacturer has to do with product safety. It was passed in early 2008 and became effective on November 6, 2008. It is called the Consumer Products Safety Improvement Act (CPSIA). The law was passed to protect children against recent problems with children's products.

Unfortunately, the law was not clearly written and contains many calls for confusion. Revisions to this act are being consistently made, so by the time this book is in print, more information will be available. I recommend checking the Consumer Products Safety Commission (CPSC) website for more information.

The law targets manufacturers of products intended for use of children age 12 and under. This affects all children's product and garment manufacturers. The law limits the amount of lead and phthalates found in products and their components. These include dyes, buttons, swarovski crystals, zippers and several

Consumer Products Safety Commission:
www.cpsc.gov

Notes:

other embellishments. These components may contain trace levels of lead, so their levels must be tested for compliance.

And on a side note and an interesting tidbit of information that may make you want to either scream or laugh is that the trace amount of lead permitted in children's products is less than what the FDA allows in a piece of candy, which is usually eaten by those same children.

RUNNING YOUR BUSINESS

Chapter 31
Employees and Contractors

Your business is up and running, demand for your product is up, and you discover that you can no longer do all the work yourself and you need help. Congratulations. Knowing you cannot do everything yourself and needing to hire help is the first key to success. When is the right time to hire employees and how do you do it? First let us see what kind of help you need – is it an employee or an independent contractor? What are your responsibilities for hiring an employee or a contractor?

Employees: You must withhold federal, state and city taxes (where applicable), social security and Medicare taxes, match social security, pay workers compensation insurance (where applicable), and pay unemployment taxes. You must do all this on a set schedule and comply with a number of state and federal employee regulations. You must issue a W-2 form annually.

Independent Contractors: Independent contractors pay their own taxes. You hire them for a specific task and pay them an agreed to dollar amount, typically per hour. You report your payments to them on a Form 1099 (for payments over $600 a year).

Notes:

Internal Revenue Service Business Guidelines:
irs.gov/businesses

Notes:

Naturally, you must be asking, "Why would I want to hire an employee, with all the tax work involved?" The Internal Revenue Service has rules as to who can qualify as an independent contractor and who is an employee.

By IRS definition:

"The general rule is that an individual is an independent contractor if (the person for whom the services are performed) has the right to control or direct only the result of the work, and not what will be done and how it will be done or method of accomplishing the result.

"People such as lawyers, contractors, subcontractors, public stenographers, and auctioneers who follow an independent trade, business, or profession in which they offer their services to the public, are generally not employees. However, whether such people are employees or independent contractors depends on the facts in each case."

As you can see, the criterion IRS uses is "Can you or can you not control the work of the person working for you." If the answer is yes, then the person is an employee, if no, you have an independent contractor. There are stiff penalties for treating employees as independent contractors, so be honest in your assessment.

In the fashion industry, you're more likely to deal with independent contractors rather than employees. A person you hire for his or her trade skill, such as a pattern maker, sample maker, or a web designer, is usually an independent contractor. Hiring an administrative assistant for day-to-day operations would be considered an employee.

If you are unable to figure out whether an individual falls into the employee or independent contractor category, the IRS has a helpful Form SS-8, "Determination of Worker Status for Purposes of Federal Employment Taxes and Income Tax Withholding."

Because independent contractors are self-employed and require little obligation on your part, their pay rates are much higher than employee wages. This is true for two reasons. 1. They must pay self-employment taxes. 2. They are saving you time and money, because you don't have to collect and report federal, social security and other taxes, or pay workers compensation and unemployment taxes as you would for employees.

If an independent contractor you hire earns more than $600 from you, you are required to issue them a Form 1099 at the end of the year reporting the amount you paid them. The contractor will then have to report that amount and pay related taxes on that amount.

Let's say that after reading this, you conclude that you want complete control over how and where the work is performed and you decide to hire an employee. Here is a list of steps you need to take to ensure that you set this up properly.

- Have your employee fill out Form W-4 (Employee's Withholding Allowance Certificate), Form I-9 (Employment Eligibility Verification), and Form W-5 (Earned Income Credit Advanced Payment Certificate) if applicable. In some states, you must mail copies of these forms

Notes:

to your state government offices and in others, these forms stay in your possession. You use this information to properly withhold the necessary taxes.

•   Register with your state's new hire reporting program within 20 days of hire or rehire. Check with your state on specific requirements.

•   Sign up for Worker's Compensation Insurance

•   Register to start paying Unemployment Insurance Tax (file with U.S. Department of Labor)

•   Obtain disability insurance if required by your state

•   Post workplace notices

•   File IRS Form 941 to choose whether to report and pay the withholding monthly, quarterly or annually.

To find out more on your state's specific requirements for employers, check your secretary of state's website and search under small business. The IRS and the Department of Labor also have great resources and more forms than you could ever imagine existing.

You may want to hire a payroll company to make your life easier, but be sure to monitor payments of withholding taxes. You are personally liable for the deposit of these taxes.

Interns

I know you hear this word used quite often and it seems every company is offering internships just to help you get your foot in the door. If you ever talk to a seasoned designer, you will hear them say that internships are essential in learning about this industry. The problem is that most of these fashion industry internships are unpaid. You may hear the seasoned designer say you need to pay your dues and take an unpaid internship, but is it truly legal?

In the state of California, you can offer an internship with your company if you work with a school and the student intern gets college credit. The U.S. Department of Labor (DOL) has other ideas about this. They have laid out 6 criterion that you must meet in order to offer an unpaid internship. This is taken verbatim from the DOL website.

1. "The internship, even though it includes actual operation of the facilities of the employer, is similar to training which would be given in an educational environment;

2. "The internship experience is for the benefit of the intern;

3. "The intern does not displace regular employees, but works under close supervision of existing staff;

4. "The employer that provides the training derives no immediate advantage from the activities of the intern; and on occasion its operations may actually be impeded;

5. "The intern is not necessarily entitled to a job at the conclusion of the internship; and

6. "The employer and the intern understand that the intern is not entitled to wages for the time spent in the internship."

Notes:

- - - - - - - - - - - - - - - - - - - -

- - - - - - - - - - - - - - - - - - - -

- - - - - - - - - - - - - - - - - - - -

As you can see from these guidelines, taking unpaid interns can be tricky, so tread lightly when deciding to offer an internship. You may just need to hire them.

Chapter 32
Budgeting Basics

Budgeting your finances may seem daunting, but taking the proper steps will help you see profits in the future. A few words of encouragement before we delve into the nitty-gritty of it. Look forward to your growth. If you plan out your finances and your time well, you should expect your business to grow exponentially by your second year. You are starting at a $0 profit, so growth must be grand.

In your first year of business, you will be busy creating your collections, building your marketing campaign, and learning from your mistakes. But in your second year, your business should have grown considerably in assets, inventory, and status. This does not mean that you will be in the black in year two (making a profit or when revenue exceeds expenses); you may not even see an actual profit until year three. But if you invest your time well, follow the advice in this book, and don't lose sight of your vision, it will happen.

I cannot stress enough how important it is to keep to your budget. It's easy to rationalize spending just a little extra, but it can quickly become a habit. Set limits to your expenses. Simply put, a budget is planning on how to meet your expenses. Your

Notes:

Notes:

first year of business will incur several expenses that will usually not re-occur on an annual basis, these are your startup costs. In an on going basis, there are two major kinds of expenses, variable and fixed. Your variable cost is determined by what you actually produce. Your fixed costs are the costs you incur to run your business.

Fixed costs can be separated into two categories: direct and indirect. Direct fixed expenses include product development, photography and trade show expenses. Indirect fixed expenses are your monthly expenses, or overhead. In the following chapters, I elaborate on each of these costs.

Chapter 33
Start-up Costs

In order to get started correctly, we need to determine what your start-up expenses will be. Your start-up costs are one-time expenses that happen in your first year of business. These can include setting up your business entity, legal fees, logo development and the list goes on.

I've outlined several expenses that may apply to your business, but don't limit yourself to this list. You will need to create a detailed list of start-up expenses for your own business planning.

Business Entity – Set up your business entity legally.

Branding, Identity and Logo Development – If you plan to hire a professional to get your company image set up, include that in your start-up costs.

Licenses and Permits – This includes the cost to register your business, get your resale number and any other permits you need. Register with your state's labor board, if applicable.

Legal Fees – Budget for a legal business setup if you plan on operating as an entity other than a sole proprietorship. If you are seeking a trademark or patent, an intellectual property law

Notes:

professional may be necessary. These fees will vary vastly based on what you are looking for.

Rent Security Deposit – If you are planning on renting office or studio space, include the security deposit in your start up costs.

Technology – Consider purchasing bookkeeping software (I recommend QuickBooks or the Fashion Unraveled Software), graphic software as well as any other software needed to properly run your business.

Utility Security Deposits – If you are renting, you may be required to submit security deposits for electricity, gas, water and telephone.

Website – A nicely designed website can range anywhere from $500 to $5,000, depending of your requirements.

After calculating your start up costs, set aside a cash reserve of at least one-half of your start up investment to use as emergency funds. There will always be unexpected financial expenses that pop up. It's better to be prepared, than caught at the least opportune moment with your pants down.

Equipment

The equipment you purchase to run your business may not be able to be deducted as an expense when starting your business. Your accountant will give you guidance on this, but the value of the equipment you purchase and the value of equipment you contribute will be broken down over several years. This is all equipment you need to operate your business successfully: sewing machines, computers, printers, phones and fax. Create a detailed inventory of your contributions. This will come in handy when dealing with your accountant as well as when you come to the stage of selling your business or acquiring a business partner.

Start-Up Expenses

	Cost
Business Entity	
Branding, Identity & Logo Development	
Licenses & Permits	
Legal Fees	
Rent Security Deposit	
Technology	
Utility Security Deposit	
Website	
Total Start-Up Cost	$

Equipment Purchases and Inventory

Inventory Item	Date of Purchase	Price
Total Inventory Investment		$

Start-Up Expenses

	Cost
Business Entity	$150
Branding, Identity & Logo Development	0
Licenses & Permits	$50
Legal Fees	$150
Rent Security Deposit	0
Technology	$200
Utility Security Deposit	0
Website	0
Total Start-Up Cost	$550

Equipment Purchases and Inventory

Inventory Item	Date of Purchase	Price
Steamer	2003	$75
Hangers	2003	$50
Rolling Rack	2003	$75
Mannequin	2003	$50
Industrial Straight Stitch Machine	2005	$250
Industrial Overlock Machine	2010	$600
Home Serger	2010	$50
Home Sewing Machine	2003	$25
Computer	2003	$1000
Total Inventory Investment		$2175

Chapter 34
Variable Costs

After determining your start up costs, the next stage in developing your budget is to calculate the basis of your variable costs. Your variable costs are your costs of production. To determine this you first need to determine your cost of goods. In the fashion industry, this process is generally described as costing.

Costing

To figure out the actual cost of your garment in terms of materials, you will need to know the cost of fabric per yard and how many yards it takes to make your product, your pattern maker should be able to help you in determining the exact amount.

You also need to know what it will cost to have the garments cut and sewn. For your first production run, you should shop around for the manufacturer who is right for your product. Some contractors will have large minimums (for example, 1000 pieces) and some may have smaller requirements (as few as 25). Get sewing quotes for both.

If you are going to start with a small production run, you

Notes:

Notes:

may also want to find out how much it would cost to hire an independent seamstress. Remember, every scenario and its cost must be considered! This last quote could be important if you get a large enough order that you can't handle personally, but small enough that a contractor won't touch it.

Use the higher quotes when figuring your costs, and price your garments accordingly. As a design company, it is always easier to lower your prices once you establish yourself, but harder to raise them and still keep your clientele. Start high and go down. This can really save you in the long run. Unexpected expenses and emergencies always pop up at the most inopportune moments and its better to have some financial leeway to meet them.

Other than your cost of fabric and sewing, there are a few other expenses you need to take into account when costing your garments. These can include your sewn-in labels, dying costs, screen printing costs, hanger & packaging costs as well as your notions, such as zippers, elastic, and buttons. Your sewing quotes should include the attachment of these items, although certain exceptions may apply when attaching grommets, eyelets and buttonholes, so get those quotes as well.

Woven labels are more costly and many people cut them out. Printed labels are softer, are less likely to be cut out, but may not look as professional. Choose the label that is the most appropriate for your line.

Cost Sheet

Style # _____   **Style Name:** _____

Season: _____

Technical Flat

Materials Cost

Fabric/Trim	Cost Per Unit	Quantity	Total Cost

Total Materials Cost	$
Sewing Cost	$
Cutting Cost	$
Dying Cost	$
Screen Printing Cost	$
Packaging	$
Hangers	$
Total Cost	$

Case Study: Cost Sheet

Style # Swing Dress   **Style Name:**

Season: Spring 2010

Technical Flat
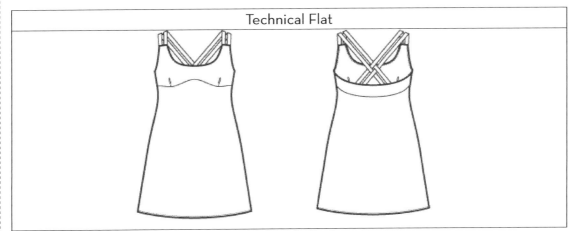

Materials Cost

Fabric/Trim	Cost Per Unit	Quantity	Total Cost
Cotton Sateen	12	1.25	15
Invisible Zipper	.55	1	1.25
Label	.25	1	.25

Total Materials Cost	$16.50
Sewing Cost	$12.00
Cutting Cost	$2.00
Dying Cost	$0
Screen Printing Cost	$0
Packaging	$0
Hangers	$0
Total Cost	$30.50

Production Cost

Calculating your budget for production is directly linked to the amount of sales you expect. If you expect to sell 100 units wholesale to retailers, then you will have to produce 100 units, right? Almost. You should figure that up to 5% of the pieces produced may be flawed and unsellable. Add that percentage to the numbers you produce.

If you plan on selling directly to the consumer through fairs or a website, you will need to produce enough inventory to handle orders and direct sales. One more thing to consider, if your product is a best seller, will you have inventory available for reorders? Let's lump these two scenarios together and estimate that you wish to produce an additional 10% of inventory.

Now for our first production calculation. Let's calculate production costs for one garment of your collection. You will need to create separate production cost sheets for each garment you are producing – a sample is included following this section.

Let's assume you are going to produce 100 pieces of one garment to fill orders that were placed, an additional 5% for damages, plus another 10% for direct sales through your website.

100 pieces x 5% = 5 (Damaged allowance)
100 pieces x 10% = 10 (Allowance for direct sales and reorders)

Your production quantity is 115 pieces. In your cost sheet, fill out the costs for this garment (fabric, trims, sewing, and cutting) and multiply by your quantity (115). This is your production cost for this garment.

Notes:

Garment Production Cost Worksheet

Style #: ---
Style Name: --
Season: ---

Number of items ordered	
__% Allowance for damaged goods	
__%Allowance for direct sales	
Total items to be produced	

Production Cost

Cost of Goods per Piece	
Total quantity produced	X
Total Production Cost	

Garment Production Cost Worksheet

Style #: ---
Style Name: --
Season: ---

Number of items ordered	
__% Allowance for damaged goods	
__%Allowance for direct sales	
Total items to be produced	

Production Cost

Cost of Goods per Piece	
Total quantity produced	X
Total Production Cost	

Case Study: Garment Production Cost Worksheet

Style #:
Style Name: *Swing Dress*
Season: *Spring 2010*

Number of items ordered	75
__% Allowance for damaged goods	4
__%Allowance for direct sales	19
Total items to be produced	98

Production Cost

Cost of Goods per Piece	29.80
Total quantity produced	x 98
Total Production Cost	2920.40

Case Study: Garment Production Cost Worksheet

Style #:
Style Name: *Wrap Dress*
Season: *Spring 2010*

Number of items ordered	65
__% Allowance for damaged goods	3
__%Allowance for direct sales	17
Total items to be produced	85

Production Cost

Cost of Goods per Piece	48.5
Total quantity produced	x 85
Total Production Cost	4122.50

Collection Production Cost Worksheet

Season:

Style #/Style Name	Production Cost
Total Production Cost for Season	

Case Study: Collection Production Cost Worksheet

Season: *Spring 2010*

Style #/Style Name	Production Cost
Baby Doll Dress	1601.60
Cigarette Pants	2277.60
Obi Dress	1320.00
Silk Cover Up	957.00
Strap Top	1548.40
Swing Dress	2920.40
Urban Knickers	1700.16
Wrap Dress	4122.50
Total Production Cost for Season	$16,447.66

Chapter 35
Direct Fixed Costs

At first glance, you may think that items such as development, trade shows and photography are variable costs. In actuality, these items are examples of fixed costs directly related to each collection you produce. Direct fixed costs are linked to your production cycles. Depending on the number of collections you produce, these costs will vary from year to year. Let's break everything down to create a per collection budget.

Development Cost

The most complex direct fixed cost is your development cost. Your initial collection will be the most expensive to develop. You will be creating your blocks and hashing out your fit issues with your pattern maker.

Blocks are your basic patterns for your sample size and type of garment. You will generally create a basic skirt, bodice, torso, sleeve and pant pattern to be used in drafting each pattern in your collection.

With your second, third, and fourth collections you should see a reduction in your development costs. You shouldn't have to redevelop your blocks unless you had major issues in your first collection.

Notes:

Designers often re-release the same design in more than one collection but offer that design in a different fabric or color. In this case, you won't need to recalculate costs for the pattern work and development of the sample, just the sample itself. Below is a general breakdown of costs for the development of each piece.

Fabric cost for creating all samples of that garment. Calculate for the number of samples you expect to generate, including working samples and production samples.

Trim cost for samples. Calculate this in the same manner as your fabric costs.

Sample sewing— Decide how much you plan to spend on each sample and the number of samples. If you do not get a good working sample after you've reached your budget, consider either dropping the design or getting a new sample/pattern maker.

Pattern— You may want to combine the sample sewing with your pattern work in your development cost if you have one contractor do both of them.

Grading services – Include costs for digitizing, grading, and marking services.

Fittings – Using a fit model that meets the criterion of your target customer is a must.

Screen Printing Set-up – If you will be having a screen printed design on your garment, factor in the cost of creating the screens.

Fabric Dying Set-up – Color matching and dying samples of your fabrics will need to be developed for your collection prior to production. The set-up fees for this are generally not free.

Development Cost

Style #: _____

Style Name: _____

	Cost
Fabric	
Trim	
Pattern Development	
Sample Sewing	
Pattern Grading	
Screen Printing	
Fittings	
Total Development Cost	

Development Cost

Style #: _____

Style Name: _____

	Cost
Fabric	
Trim	
Pattern Development	
Sample Sewing	
Pattern Grading	
Screen Printing	
Fittings	
Total Development Cost	

Case Study: Development Cost

Style #: _____

Style Name: _Baby Doll Dress_____

	Cost
Fabric	$18.00
Trim	$0.55
Pattern Development	$0
Sample Sewing	$0
Pattern Grading	$45.00
Screen Printing	$0
Fittings	$0
Total Development Cost	**$63.55**

Development Cost

Style #: _____

Style Name: _Urban Knickers_____

	Cost
Fabric	$23.00
Trim	$0.55
Pattern Development	$75.00
Sample Sewing	$75.00
Pattern Grading	$45.00
Screen Printing	$0
Fittings	$0
Total Development Cost	**$219.65**

Photography Cost

You will need to photograph your collection before you start to sell it. These photos can be used to produce a look book, enhance your website and advertise your business. This needs to be budgeted for every collection you create.

The most obvious expense in photography is hiring a photographer and a model. As a small business, we need to be resourceful and use the services available to us. One way to acquire professional photos is to enter into a TFP (Time for Prints) or TFCD (Time for CDs) arrangement. Many models and photographers are eager to build their portfolios and jump at the opportunity to photograph unique clothing. This arrangement gives everyone in the agreement rights to use the photos with limited expenses. You get your model shots, and everyone gets images for their own use.

To legally use these photos in print or online, you need to have everyone involved sign releases to use the photos. Some releases require all parties' names to be disclosed with the photos. It is to your benefit that you require your company name linked with all photos of your designs.

You may not always receive images that work for you from a TFP/TFCD photo shoot, so it may be worth an investment to hire a photographer and a model for the shoot. You may require a makeup artist as well as a hairstylist to achieve the specific look for your line. Other expenses that may occur as a photography expense are space or equipment rentals and any Photoshop work done by the photographer.

Notes:

Sample Photo Release

I hereby grant [Company Name] permission to use my likeness in a photograph in any and all of its publications, including website entries, without payment or any other consideration. I understand and agree that these materials will become the property of [Company Name] and will not be returned. I hereby irrevocably authorize [Company Name] to edit, alter, copy, exhibit, publish or distribute this photo for purposes of publicizing [Company Name]'s programs or for any other lawful purpose. In addition, I waive the right to inspect or approve the finished product, including written or electronic copy, wherein my likeness appears. Additionally, I waive any right to royalties or other compensation arising or related to the use of the photograph. I hereby hold harmless and release and forever discharge [Company Name] from all claims, demands, and causes of action which I, my heirs, representatives, executors, administrators, or any other persons acting on my behalf or on behalf of my estate have or may have by reason of this authorization.

I am 21 years of age and am competent to contract in my own name. I have read this release before signing below and I fully understand the contents, meaning, and impact of this release.

_____ (Signature)

_____ (Printed Name)

_____ (Date)

If the person signing is under age 21, there must be consent by a parent or guardian, as follows:

I hereby certify that I am the parent or guardian of _____, and do hereby give my consent without reservation to the foregoing on behalf of this person.

_____ (Parent/Guardian Signature)

_____ (Parent/Guardian Printed Name)

_____ (Date)

Trade shows

Trade shows contain many expenses besides the space fees. Load in and load out expenses, hotel, food and transportation all need to be factored in. Don't forget your display expenses.

Show Fee - Many shows have half booths for first time vendors, so ask about them—they are not always published.

Load in/ Load out – Check with the rules of the trade show. Many require setup to be delivered by their preferred delivery service and during a certain window of time.

Display – All big shows will rent you furniture for your space including tables, racks, shelves, chairs and a garbage can. These fees can sometimes cost just as much as purchasing the same items, but when you add in load in/load out fees, it could be costly. Plan your set up and prepare a mock space in your home to test the space and displays. Have friends come in and give you their feedback on what stood out to them. Take pictures of a successful set up and refer to this on the day of set up.

Hotel – Shows usually have deals with hotels in the area for exhibitors. Check around, you may discover that you can get an inexpensive suite down the street which would serve you just as well.

Food – Many shows provide one to two lunches in the show fee. Try to bring snacks of nuts, fruit and water to get you through the day. Water at a show might cost $4, but water bottles down the street at Target will be much lower.

Airfare/Travel – Get your tickets early so you don't end up

Notes:

Notes:

paying last minute prices. Make sure to save your miles! A vacation is well deserved.

Car Rental – Get a car that is appropriate for your travels. If you are staying in the hotel where the show takes place and you can get all your show supplies within walking distance, do you really need a car to get to and from the airport?

Other Costs

Many other costs may occur in conjunction with releasing a collection. Here are a few examples of other direct fixed costs.

Printing – Stocking up on a supply of your look books, line sheets, business cards and postcards are required for a trade show. You could also offer a digital look book and line sheet in a PDF. You could provide this on a CD or maybe even a promotional jump drive with your company name on it.

Print Design and Layout – Look books and line sheets should look professional. Consider hiring a professional to design the layout for each of these.

Website – Your website should be updated with each collection.

Direct Fixed Cost Per Collection

Season:

Development Cost for Entire Collection

Style #/Name	Cost
Total Development Cost	$

Photography Cost

Photographer	
Model	
Makeup Artist	
Hair Stylist	
Space Rental	
Photoshop	
Prints	
Total Photography Cost	$

Trade show Cost

Show Fee	
Load in/load out	
Display	
Hotel	
Food	
Airfare/Travel	
Car Rental	
Total Trade show Cost	$

Other Collection Costs

Printing	
Print Design & Layout	
Website	
Total Other Collection Costs	$

Total Direct Fixed Cost	$

Case Study: Direct Fixed Cost Per Collection

Season: _Spring 2011_

Development Cost for Entire Collection

Style #/Name	Cost
Baby Doll Dress	$63.55
Cigarette Pants	$301.65
Obi Dress	$62.00
Silk Cover Up	$8.00
Strap Top	$7.55
Swing Dress	$400.30
Urban Knickers	$219.65
Wrap Dress	$306.25
Total Development Cost	$1368.95

Photography Cost

Photographer	$300.00
Model	$0
Makeup Artist	$50.00
Hair Stylist	$50.00
Space Rental	$0
Photoshop	$0
Prints	$50.00
Total Photography Cost	$450.00

Trade show Cost

Show Fee	
Load in/load out	
Display	
Hotel	
Food	
Airfare/Travel	
Car Rental	
Total Trade show Cost	NA – Trade shows starting Fall 2011

Other Collection Costs

Printing	$50.00
Print Design & Layout	$0
Website	$0
Total Other Collection Costs	$50.00

Total Direct Fixed Cost	$1868.95

Chapter 36
Indirect Fixed Expenses

Indirect fixed expenses are everything that it takes to keep your business open each month: rent, website hosting fees, salaries, and the like. These expenses can also be referred to as overhead. These are indirect fixed expenses because they do not directly relate to the number of collections you produce or the revenue you receive.

Below are several indirect fixed expenses typical for a fashion business. These may not exactly match your expenses, but they will help you in determining your own fixed costs. I have broken down the fixed expenses into administrative, marketing & sales and labor.

Administrative

Accounting – The price of accounting services can vary vastly depending on where you live. In larger metropolitan areas, a good accountant can charge about $600 for an annual tax filing. Ask for referrals from friends and colleagues to find a good one. There are accountants who specialize in the apparel business, but any good accountant can do the job. Don't skimp on an accounting service. If you've ever done your own taxes, you know how long it can take. Now that you have your own

Notes:

Notes:

business, your time is valuable and spending those few extra dollars to get your taxes filed properly will free you up from this tedious task and let you focus on other work.

Bookkeeping – The price of a bookkeeper can vary, but a good one will update your books on a monthly basis. You may want to consider hiring a bookkeeper to show you how to do your books yourself. You can invest in a program like QuickBooks if you want to do your bookkeeping yourself, but make sure you have time to learn. If you do your own books you will be able to run reports at any time to track your business progress.

Business License & Renewals – Registration and license renewals are usually fixed costs you must include in your annual budget. Although these may not occur monthly, they are annual recurring expenses that do not vary depending on your revenue.

Bank Charges – Some banks charge a monthly fee for business accounts and may limit the number of transactions you can conduct with the account. Make sure to read the fine print. You may want to consider opening your account with a credit union. They typically have fewer fees and are community based, so even if they do have fees, you know the big corporate executives won't be pocketing those dollars.

Credit Card Merchant Fees – If you will be processing credit cards, which is likely, there are monthly fees linked to these. This is usually a flat monthly rate, plus a percentage of the processed amount. The bank where you opened your checking account most likely has merchant services, so check with them first. Questions to ask yourself when considering credit card services are: 1.Will you be processing orders online? 2. Does your internet service offer online processing? 3. Can you use a virtual terminal, or do you need an actual one? If you will only be taking wholesale orders and selling online, you do not need a terminal. A virtual terminal is a credit card processing service that does not require a physical terminal, but an internet connection.

If you need to process orders at events, street fairs or trunk shows, a virtual terminal will do just fine. You'll record the customers' information manually and run the cards later. This does not guarantee that every sale will go through, due to maxed out cards or incorrectly recorded information.

To help ensure that all your sales will go through, you should take phone numbers and run the sales immediately after you get home. Shoppers sometimes overspend and max out cards at shopping events. Nine times out of ten, if a card doesn't go through and you call, the customer will get back to you.

Equipment Rental – Include equipment rental fees in your budget if you are leasing or paying in installments. This may include a credit card terminal, a copy machine or postage meter.

Insurance – Call the company that insures your home or car and ask if they will cover your business. If not, they may be able to refer you to someone.

Office Supplies – For me, $100 monthly usually covers my office supplies, including the short-lived ink cartridges that my printer

Notes:

Notes:

sucks up. You know your own spending, so budget accordingly.

Postage & Shipping – Account for shipping your products, as well as any office mailings. If you are selling online, you might want to charge the customer a small handling fee to cover your shipping cost and the various related service charges. When shipping merchandise to retailers, it is common practice to charge them for it.

Rent – If you are renting a studio, this would be your main budget item. In some areas, it may only cost you a few hundred dollars for a decent studio space. Don't go for more than what you really need. Because you're not running a store, location isn't as important, so don't overpay for a fabulous location. Try to avoid signing any long term leases; you don't know where your business will go.

Utilities – Figure these for any rented space, as well as your home office if you have one. You will figure the percentage your office takes up in your home and calculate your costs based on it. Utilities include gas, electric, water, telephone and internet. Budget for any designated phone or fax lines for your business, and your cell phone. You can cut costs here by working in the dark (just kidding).

Marketing & Sales
Direct Mail Marketing – This will include any promotional postcards and blind mailings which target retailers or announce your attendance at trade shows.

Email Marketing – Setting up an email marketing campaign can be done by using a monthly fee service. Some services such as

Vertical Response offer a pay per email option. If you have a relatively small list, you might want to consider setting it up as a "pay per email" until you reach a quantity of email signups that makes sense to pay a monthly fee.

Event Fees – Do you plan on participating in street fairs or sample sales? Include all events you plan on selling at. Do not include trade shows in this section.

Online Marketing – Include the fees for selling online through sites such as Etsy.com and Ebay.com. This can also include your budget for blog advertising, Google Adwords and other online marketing efforts.

Print Advertising – You may want to try different advertising approaches including co-op advertising with boutiques. Designer based small print ads from magazines such as Bust and Ready Made are also an option.

Printed Materials – Business cards you usually need to order once or twice a year. Other printed materials include postcards, line sheets and look books.

Public Relations Firm – PR firms may charge a monthly fee of $2000 or more, so you may want to wait until the release of your collection to reach out to a PR firm. You may not see a monetary return immediately, but you will receive press and accolades which can translate to orders when attending trade shows.

Showroom Expenses – If you acquire a showroom, you will need to budget in the fees they may charge you to be included

Notes:

Notes:

in the selection. Commissions could be calculated into this expense.

Travel – Keep track of your business mileage and gas usage. Don't forget your auto insurance. If you really want to cut car costs, and you live in a large metropolitan area, you may be able to use a car share program. You pay a flat hourly fee for the car and your gas and insurance is included. To budget, you will need to know the fee and the number of hours you use your car for business. Check out CityCar Share and Zip Car.

Carpool on fabric buying trips if you can. It's cheaper and more fun. If renting instead of using your own car, you may be able to waive the insurance. What most credit card companies don't tell you is that they insure the car you rent with their card so you don't need to buy additional insurance. Make sure your credit card company offers this before waiving the insurance and renting a car.

Website – You need to include in your budget your hosting service monthly fee, annual domain name renewals, and any other charges associated with maintaining your website.

Now that you have a general idea of what some of your fixed expenses could be, you can start to build your budget for your first year. (Don't forget to multiply monthly costs by 12 for your total annual budget.) In the second and third year, most amounts will increase. On average, with inflation, you can guess that your expenses will grow up to 10% annually.

Labor

Labor expenses are the most important kind of expenses, but are frequently overlooked. As a small business owner, a common misconception is that our salary is our business profits. It sounds realistic enough, but what if we don't see a profit until our third year? How do you plan on supporting yourself? If you are approaching this business as a part-time gig or as a hobby, this may make sense. But for the rest of us, we would like to receive payment for our efforts. Build a salary for yourself into your indirect fixed costs.

Principal Salary – Would you work 80 hours a week for a mere $25,000 a year? I doubt it. Give yourself a salary that reflects the work you do. If you are working on your business 10 hours a week, maybe a $25,000 salary makes sense, but if you are serious about making your business a success, factor in a salary of $40,000 to $50,000 annually.

Assistants – Follow the guidelines we discussed in Chapter 38: Employees and Contractors.

Notes:

Indirect Fixed Costs

	Monthly Estimate
Administrative	
Accounting	
Bank Charges	
Bookkeeping	
Business License Renewals	
Credit Card Merchant Fees	
Equipment Rental	
Insurance	
Office Supplies	
Postage & Shipping	
Rent	
Utilities	
Total Administrative Costs	$
Marketing & Sales	
Direct Mail Marketing	
Email Marketing	
Event Fees	
Online Marketing	
Print Advertising	
Printed Material	
Public Relations Firm	
Showroom Expenses	
Travel	
Vehicle Expenses	
Website	
Total Marketing & Sales Costs	$
Labor	
Principal	
Assistant	
Total Labor Costs	$
Total Indirect Fixed Costs	$

Case Study: Indirect Fixed Costs

	Monthly Estimate
Administrative	
Accounting	$150 Annually
Bank Charges	0
Bookkeeping	I do this myself
Business License Renewals	$55 annually
Credit Card Merchant Fees	0
Equipment Rental	0
Insurance	$300 a year
Office Supplies	$35 a year
Postage & Shipping	$25 a month (other than online sales)
Rent	0
Utilities	0
Total Administrative Costs	$102.06 monthly/ $1225 annually
Marketing & Sales	
Direct Mail Marketing	$20
Email Marketing	$15
Event Fees	$100 – 6 6 times a year
Online Marketing	$45
Print Advertising	0
Printed Material	0
Public Relations Firm	0
Showroom Expenses	0
Travel	0
Vehicle Expenses	0
Website	$5
Total Marketing & Sales Costs	$135 monthly/ $1620 annually
Labor	
Principal	None in first year, $20,000 in 2nd
Assistant	0
Total Labor Costs	$0
Total Indirect Fixed Costs	$237.06 monthly/ $2845 Annual

Chapter 37
Accounting

Accounting is the process of matching "expenses" to the sales you make. This tells you if you are profitable or losing money. Accounting is more than just looking at your cash receipts and cash deposits.

Working with an accountant

I highly recommend that you meet and consult with an accountant before you spend your first dollar. In Chapter 23 we briefly discussed the various business structures that are available to you. That's one decision you should discuss with an accountant. I will discuss how to choose a "good" accountant, as there are a number of considerations impacting that decision.

First, understand that most states allow anyone who can write their name, to call themselves an "accountant." I remember a hand-printed sign hung on a backyard fence that I passed on my way home from school announcing "Income taxes done here!" likely posted by someone who called themselves an accountant. It can be difficult to evaluate the competency and skills of an accountant you meet unless he or she has met certain identifiable standards.

Notes:

Notes:

Your first thought here should be to get a recommendation from another business owner on their accountant. Make sure they have worked with that individual for more than a year. If they haven't worked with an accountant though the tax season (February 1 to April 15), they really don't know how their accountant operates under time commitments. If you cannot get a recommendation that you are comfortable with, look for a Certified Public Accountant (CPA). These are accountants who have passed a national exam on taxation, accounting and business law. They are licensed by the state and are required to adhere to certain ethical standards. They must also satisfy annual continuing education requirements set by the state department of regulation.

What you want your accountant to do is to first advise you on business structures, guide you in setting up your accounting software and to prepare income and payroll tax returns. You should assume that you will be doing the "routine" bookkeeping yourself. What you want to buy from the CPA is his or her expertise on complicated business decisions, not the basic stuff. Finally, I recommend that you look for someone your same age. In that way you and your accountant can plan on working together for a long time. If they are new in their career, they will likely cut you a deal.

I won't go into how you use bookkeeping software; those services do a pretty good job at that. But ask your accountant if you should do anything special to making reporting at year-end easier. You should know that in most cases CPAs and other accountants typically use only one type of software in their office, but that software will accept data files from most of the well-known programs used by businesses. Get confirmation from your accountant that he or she can accept data files from the software that you select, or if you need to print out the files for him.

Business Reports

There are two reports that you should prepare on a monthly basis - a Profit or Loss Statement and a Balance Sheet. These two reports will later allow you to evaluate your overall annual expenditures and how you can improve your income. For convenience, they can be generated through most bookkeeping systems.

If you are doing things the old fashioned way by the way of paper and pencil, you need to calculate the business' total expenses incurred for the month and then calculate the income received. This tracking of income and expenses is compiled in the Profit or Loss Statement (or P&L Statement). It is important to be aware of what you are spending on a monthly basis and on how much of that is actually a profit or loss. You can utilize this report when determining where expenses can be cut or budgets can be increased.

A Balance Sheet shows the business' assets, its liabilities, and your invested capital. In other words, it details the value of the business. It calculates your business's worth by subtracting all the money your business owes from everything it owns. Most balance sheets show some property as being current assets and others as long-term assets.

Current assets are the things you expect to use in the current year to run your business. They include the total cash in the bank, accounts receivable (which is the money owed to you from wholesale purchases) and inventory assets (cost of goods for merchandise on hand which has not sold).

Notes:

Long-term assets are the business properties that will be used over a longer period, such as machinery and delivery trucks. These long-term assets are depreciated each year to reflect their impact on the business' annual expenses. Thus if a truck has a useful life of 3 years, you include in your expenses one-third of the cost of the truck each year as a depreciation expense (your accountant will help you in determining the depreciation). (For the sake of simplicity and keeping the complexities as a minimum, I have not included long-term assets in the forms and have grouped all current assets and long-term assets together.)

The liabilities detail the loan balance, credit cards and accounts payable (accounts billed to you but not yet paid). Capital (also referred to as equity) is basically what you have invested as owners and the net profits that you leave in the business each year. You can calculate your business equity (basically what your business is worth) by using the following calculation:

Equity = Total Assets – Total Liabilities – Net Profits

This statement is named the balance sheet because your Current assets equal your Liabilities and Capital. If you have partners or shareholders, this report is crucial in operations. This report helps place a value the business.

The balance sheet tends to have a lower profile for most small, start-up businesses unless they require a significant investment it equipment and property. If you are operating on a shoe string, than you are frequently better off just paying attention to the cash level of the bank account. But sooner or later, you will need to develop a balance sheet and profit or loss statement just to confirm your profitability.

Profit & Loss Statement

Month: _____   Year: _____

	Amount
Revenue	
Wholesale	
Retail	
Total Revenue	
Variable Cost	
Production Cost	
Direct Fixed Expenses	
Development	
Photography	
Trade show	
Indirect Fixed Expenses	
Administrative	
Marketing & Sales	
Labor	
Amortization of Goodwill	
Depreciation of Equipment	
Interest on Loan	
Total Expenses	
Net Profit/Loss	
Note Payment	-
Net Cash to Operations	

Case Study: Profit & Loss Statement

Month: _January_   Year: _2011_

	Amount
Revenue	
Wholesale	$11,050.00
Retail	$381.83
Total Revenue	**$11,431.83**
Variable Cost	
Production Cost	0
Direct Fixed Expenses	
Development	$376.46
Photography	0
Trade show	0
Indirect Fixed Expenses	
Administrative	$102.08
Marketing & Sales	$135.00
Labor	0
Amortization of Goodwill	$1.25
Depreciation of Equipment	$12.08
Interest on Loan	0
Total Expenses	**$626.87**
Net Profit/Loss	$10,804.96
Note Payment	–0
Net Cash to Operations	**$10,804.96**

Balance Sheet

Month: _____ Year: _____

	Amount
Assets	
Cash/Bank Account	
Fixed Assets	
Accounts Receivable	
Inventory Assets	
Total Assets	
Liabilities & Capital	
Liabilities	
Loan Balance	
Account Payables	
Credit Cards	
Total Liabilities	
Capital	
Equity	
Net Profits	
Total Capital	
Total Liabilities & Capital	

Case Study: Balance Sheet

Month: *January*   Year: *2011*

	Amount
Assets	
Cash/Bank Account	$10,590.99
Fixed Assets	$2175.00
Accounts Receivable	
Inventory Assets	
Total Assets	$12765.99
Liabilities & Capital	
Liabilities	
Loan Balance	0
Account Payables	0
Credit Cards	0
Total Liabilities	0
Capital	
Equity	$1,961.03
Net Profits	$10,804.96
Total Capital	$12,765.99
Total Liabilities & Capital	$12,765.99

Bank account reconciliation

At the end of each month your bookkeeping records need to be reconciled with your bank statements. This is to ensure that you have properly recorded each transaction in your business and that they are included in your Profit & Loss Statements. The two should be in balance once you take into account all checks or deposits in transit. Any difference in the two balances, beyond those in transit, needs to be investigated. Discrepancies can be an early indication that theft may have occurred. Keeping these in balance ensures the likelihood of catching a thief early on.

How long should you keep business records?

We have only scratched the surface on what you need to do to maintain proper business records. Now let's look at how soon you can throw them away. The period that you should keep a business document depends on what the document is and what it is recording. But in general, you must keep your records that support an item of income or deduction on a tax return until the end of the statue-of-limitations.

The term statute-of-limitations refers to the period after which you cannot be prosecuted for a misstatement of your income tax filings. The basic limitation period for an individual filing his or her income tax return, ends three years after the tax return, to which the record relates, is filed. That is, unless the filing contained a significant understatement of your income – generally more than 25% of the gross income you showed on the return—or it was fraudulent, then the statue of limitation extends to 7 years. So just to be sure, 7 years is a target period for most businesses.

Notes:

Internal controls

Before we close out the discussion on accounting, I want to introduce you to something that will be crucial to improving your bottom line. It is establishing appropriate "Internal controls."

Internal controls are created to protect your assets from being misused by employees or customers. They generally start with cash controls, such as reconciling sales to the cash receipts each day. Each individual involved with sales, records all the elements of the sale and you reconcile the cash reported to those sales tying back to the receipts. One obvious control is that the person who does the sales must be different from the individual who reconciles the sales.

 These controls don't need to be an involved complex process; they just need to be set up after you think about the ways various transactions can be misused to your disadvantage. For example, most business owners have all of their banking records come to their home rather than to work. It assures that if anyone other than themselves has access to the checkbook, online bank account or the daily deposits, they know about it directly from the bank.

Controls should also be in place for monitoring the levels of your inventory. You need a way to track and record which items are sold verses what you still have on hand.

The bottom line goal of internal controls is to make sure that your business receives all of its income without any of it being siphoned off by waste, fraud, dishonest employees or just through carelessness. This is an area when your accountant can provide valuable insights on the appropriate controls for your business.

The last is an old accountant's rule: (this one comes directly from my father) – make everyone involved in your business take at least one week off every 6 months or so. A week is generally long enough to detect any scheme to defraud the business. Someone who never takes a vacation is a potential problem!

Measuring Profitability

How can you measure your profitability? Subtract "expenses" and "fees for your services" from your total "sales." Many new businesses measure their "profits" by only subtracting "expenses" from "sales." Individuals may think they are making money as long as they have just enough cash to pay the rent at the end of the month.

If this is the way you think and you only want enough "profit" to keep from starving, then the reality is you have just "bought yourself a job." The job security is nonexistent and has the potential for major liability. How is the rent going to be paid if you are sick for a month or two? How much would you need to pay someone else to do the job of running your business? Try "pricing" every business transaction to give yourself a salary and also a profit. If you always think of both elements, it will become second nature.

Here is an example of buying yourself a job. Let us say you value your time at $25 an hour. A fellow designer asked you to help find a fabric and you know where to acquire it. It would require that you drive 8 hours and some 360 miles to pick up the bolt of material and deliver it. The bolt is going to cost you

Notes:

Notes:

$400, and you know that the designer will pay $800 for the material. Is there a sufficient profit for you to drive to get the material? No. The profit on this is only about $20.

$$\$800 - [(8 \text{ hrs} \times \$25 \text{ for your time} = \$200) + (\text{gas \& wear on the car } \$.50 \text{ a mile} \times 360 = \$180) + \text{the fabric } \$400] = \$20$$

$20 is your profit, although you were paid $200 for your time and $180 for the wear and tear on your car. The profit margin is less than 1% of the sales ($20/$800). Is this an acceptable profit? No. If you need the $220 to pay bills, you might consider doing it, but understand it is not profitable.

Most established businesses set their prices at levels that assure both a profit and the manager's salary by establishing a percentage of sales to cover their salaries and a percentage for profits. If you expect to gross $300,000 in sales, you would want to make at least $75,000 (25-percent of sales) to pay for your earnings and medical insurance, plus a profit. Profit will be discussed in the next chapter when we develop our pricing model.

Inventory Control

Month: _____ Year: _____

Item Number	Item Name	Size	Opening Quantity	Quantity Purchased	Quantity Sold	Quantity Remaining	Reorder Threshold

Chapter 38
Pricing

We are at the point where we need to determine our wholesale price in order to make profits happen. In old school days, keystone pricing was the most common method used in determining a wholesale price. Keystoning is doubling the cost of goods. I strongly disagree with following this practice for many reasons. As a small business we do not produce the quantities to ever create a profit using this method.

Determining your wholesale prices shouldn't be as simple as just doubling your cost. Let me explain why. Have you thought about where the money is coming from to cover your overhead, salary and those direct fixed costs? Yes, I said salary. You must not forget your number one reason for going into business for yourself—to make a living.

If you've started adding up the numbers, you may start to realize you may need to sell well over 5,000 items just to recoup your costs, but let's not get ahead of ourselves.

Wholesale Pricing
Let's start out basic and work out the complicated stuff in a minute. We need to use the information we compiled in the

Notes:

Notes:

chapters on expenses:

Chapter 33: Start-Up Costs & Current Assets

Why might you calculate this into your wholesale price? All expenses need to be considered in determining your pricing. This will ensure that your profits won't be eaten by that ink-sucking printer. A better question to ask is, "How is this calculated?" This bit is a little complicated, but you can take the results and plug them directly into your 5-year projections.

In the finance world, start-up costs are also referred to as a "Goodwill Investment." Even though these expenses occur in the start of your business, the actual expense is usually amortized over 30 years, meaning the expense is spread out equally over 30 years. A similar process occurs with your contributed assets. Your assets are depreciated anywhere from 3 to 15 years. This also means you won't be able to claim it on your taxes in one lump sum. You will need to check with your accountant to determine how to deal with these items. For calculation purposes only, we will use 15 years for depreciation and 30 years for start-up costs. These expenses become part of your indirect fixed expenses.

_____ (Start-up Costs) / 30 years / 12 months = _____ Monthly

_____ (Inventory Assets) / 15 years / 12 months = _____ Monthly

Chapter 34: Variable Costs

You will need your cost of goods calculated for each item in your collection as well as your production estimates. This quantity of production will be used in the next steps.

Chapter 35: Direct Fixed Cost

You need the total direct fixed costs calculated. Make estimations from your research to fill this section out fully. To determine the amount you need to factor into your wholesale price, divide your total direct fixed cost by the quantity planned for production minus the quantity reserved for damages.

___ Direct Costs / (___ Quantity - ___ Damages)

Chapter 36: Indirect Fixed Cost

You will need to make good faith estimates for these expenses as well. Don't forget your salary (I can't stress this enough). Take your total annual indirect fixed expenses and divide them by the quantity minus damages.

(___ Indirect Monthly Cost x 12 Months) / (___ Quantity - ___ Damages)

If you plan to produce more than one collection per year, you can alter this amount to reflect a production cycle, but remember that your first year will be your most expensive, so defaulting to a year as opposed to a production cycle may ensure a little wiggle room for future pricing. It is easy to lower prices after establishing your business, but difficult to raise them. Raising prices can result in lost customers and retailers.

Notes:

Operating Cost per Garment

Direct Fixed Cost
(Based on the collection costs)

Total Direct Fixed Cost	
Divided by Total Quantity (minus damages)	
Total Direct Fixed Cost per Garment	$

Indirect Fixed Cost
(Based on the annual costs)

Indirect Fixed Cost (monthly)	
Amortized Startup Cost (monthly)	
Depreciated Assets (monthly)	
Total Monthly Fixed Cost	
Multiply by 12 for annual	
Divided by Total Quantity (minus damages)	
Total Indirect Fixed Cost per Garment	$

Operating Cost Totals

Total Direct Cost Per Garment	
Total Indirect Fixed Cost Per Garment	
Total Operating Cost Per Garment	$

Case Study: Operating Cost per Garment

Direct Fixed Cost
(Based on the collection costs)

Total Direct Fixed Cost	1868.95
Divided by Total Quantity (minus damages)	559
Total Direct Fixed Cost per Garment	$3.35

Indirect Fixed Cost
(Based on the annual costs)

Indirect Fixed Cost (monthly)	237.06 monthly / 2840 annually
Amortized Startup Cost (monthly)	1.25 monthly / 15 annually
Depreciated Assets (monthly)	12.08 monthly / 145 annually
Total Monthly Fixed Cost	250.39 monthly / 3005 annually
Multiply by 12 for annual	3005
Divided by Total Quantity (minus damages)	559
Total Indirect Fixed Cost per Garment	$5.38

Operating Cost Totals

Total Direct Cost Per Garment	3.35
Total Indirect Fixed Cost Per Garment	5.38
Total Operating Cost Per Garment	$8.73

You have now acquired all the information needed to calculate your wholesale price minus one important factor, profit.

Add your cost of goods to your per piece direct and indirect expenses. Get your total then add your desired profit. A reasonable profit for this industry is 35%, but play around with the percentages to see what profits you can yield. Your final step is to add up each of these totals, resulting in your wholesale price.

$$(\_\_ \text{ Cost of Goods} + \_\_ \text{ Direct Cost} + \_\_ \text{ Indirect Cost}) \times \_\_\% = \text{Profit}$$

$$\_\_ \text{ Profit} + \_\_ \text{ Cost of Goods} + \_\_ \text{ Direct Cost} + \_\_ \text{ Indirect Cost} = \text{Wholesale}$$

Is it safe to say that my dislike for keystoning is valid? Prove me wrong, take your cost of goods and double it. Does that total come close to covering all your expenses? Taking this approach will ensure you make a profit, take a salary and cover all your expenses.

To accurately calculate these formulas, I recommend developing an Excel spreadsheet that will update your amounts automatically or you may use the one I developed. Better yet, the program I developed will do it for you plus so much more. Check out www.fashionunraveled.com for more information on these products.

Retail Pricing

Here's your next wake up call. The retail markup is going to be anywhere from two to three times what the retailer paid for your product wholesale. The retailer needs to ensure they cover all their operating expenses in their markup, as you did your own.

I offer a recommended retail price to my stores at 2.5 times my wholesale price. You can use this amount as a base if you plan on selling your collection directly to the public. It is important to accurately assume a reasonable markup. Your biggest downfall can happen if you undercut your retailers and sell your merchandise online at a lower price. This will discourage stores from re-ordering or purchasing future collections.

Notes:

Pricing Worksheet

Style #	Style Name	Cost of Goods	Operating Cost	Profit ___ %	Wholesale Price	Suggested Retail Price ___ % markup

Case Study: Pricing Worksheet

Style #	Style Name	Cost of Goods	Operating Cost	Profit ____%	Wholesale Price	Suggested Retail Price ____% markup
	Baby Doll Dress	30.80	8.63	13.57	53	106
	Cigarette Pants	43.80	8.63	17.57	70	140
	Obi Dress	20.00	8.63	10.37	39	78
	Silk Cover Up	14.50	8.63	7.87	31	62
	Strap Top	15.80	8.63	8.57	33	66
	Swing Dress	29.80	8.63	13.57	52	104
	Urban Knickers	25.76	8.63	11.61	46	92
	Wrap Dress	48.50	8.63	19.87	77	154

Notes:

Customer and Target Market Checkpoint

Looking back to your original goals when you began reading this book, does your product still fit the price point and customer you defined? If your answer is no, you have some reevaluating to do. Where can you cut your costs? That answer is usually in the fabric and your pattern. If your product has 10 pattern pieces, could you change it to seven pattern pieces without compromising your vision? Your sewing and cutting cost will both be lowered. Hoping you have a great relationship with your pattern maker, ask her for advice on how to cut the costs for production. A good pattern maker will usually have ideas for pattern changes.

If you have re-evaluated your costs, made your changes across the board, and the retail price is still too high for your market or customer, maybe its time to re-evaluate who your customer is. Is it possible that the customer you had planned to target is not the customer you are reaching?

Flexibility in changing your customer is a must, especially if you are not willing to budge on your design. At this point you will need to go back to the beginning, review your target customer and market, and make adjustments. If you do not do this now, you will end up paying severely in time and money in the long run. It could affect the trade show you plan on attending, the stores you plan on selling to, and your entire marketing campaign.

Customer & Market Evaluation

After developing your pricing, has your market changed? Explain.

Has your target customer changed because of your pricing? Explain.

Are your retail prices higher than you expected? Or were they on target?

Where could you adjust your costs to lower your pricing?

What changes do you need to make after evaluating your pricing and all your expenses?

Case Study: Customer & Market Evaluation

After developing your pricing, has your market changed? Explain.

No. My pricing is right on target.

Has your target customer changed because of your pricing? Explain.

No it hasn't.

Are your retail prices higher than you expected? Or were they on target?

No they aren't.

Where could you adjust your costs to lower your pricing?

I could adjust my pricing if I found new sources for my supplies.

What changes do you need to make after evaluating your pricing and all your expenses?

No changes are needed.

Chapter 39
Financial Projections

Overwhelmed yet?

Projecting the financial future of your business is a good faith estimate and you need to be realistic. You need to project your financials for not only your business plan, but for your own business goals. If you are too modest in your projections, no financier will look at you. The same is true if your estimate is unrealistically high. Every dollar amount in your projections needs to be backed up by your plans for the future. If you do not plan any advertising, trade shows, or marketing, and you calculate that you will be doing one million dollars in sales by the third year, you will most likely be wrong.

To do a financial projection, you need to make reasonable assumptions on how many sales you will have, how many stores will carry your merchandise, and how you plan on reaching these goals. Create a timeline of your goals to make them realistic and within reach. Set marketing, advertising and trade show goals. This will help you achieve a visual picture of where your revenue is coming from.

Notes:

Goal Planning

Year: _____

List your goals for the year for each month.

January	February
March	**April**
May	**June**
July	**August**
September	**October**
November	**December**

Case Study: Goal Planning

Year: __2011__

List your goals for the year for each month.

January	February
All inventory ready for spring launch at the store. Send out press release	Launch Party, Etsy push Sell, sell, sell Development for Fall 2011
March	April
Samples for Fall 2011 Prepare for trade show Finalize factory/contractors	Trade show and follow up
May	June
Follow up with orders, fabric suppliers, factory Put in orders for production and fabric	Take a vacation to Disney with the family Quality control of inventory
July	August
Samples for Spring 2012 Start shipping orders	Prepare for trade show for Spring 2012
September	October
Trade show and follow up	Portland fashion week
November	December
Last minute Christmas orders for the store and reorders	Yay! One year down! Vacation with the family

Notes:

One way to determine your projected sales for each year is by planning the expectations of your first collection. Calculate in a percentage of growth for sequential years and relate this directly to your first collection and production costs. This part can get pretty complicated, pretty fast. If you are pretty handy using Excel and math, you shouldn't have a problem figuring this out. But if you are staring blankly at this book right now, I might have a handy tool for you to use.

In a previous career, I worked in computer programming and document automation. I brought these problem solving, analytical, and mathematical skills into creating my own financial projection worksheet in Excel, and into an online program that does it all. I link everything I have discussed in this section into a handy "plug and play" worksheet. If you are interested in acquiring a copy for yourself, see our website FashionUnraveled.com for more details.

Included here are blank financial projection worksheets for one year and for 5 years. Plan on explaining why and how you came to these dollar amounts in your business plan.

One Year Financial Projections

	January	February	March	April	May	June
Revenue						
Wholesale						
Retail						
Total Revenue						
Variable Expenses						
Production						
Direct Fixed Expenses						
Development						
Photography						
Printing						
Print Design & Layout						
Trade show						
Website						
Indirect Fixed Expenses						
Administrative						
Amortization of Goodwill						
Depreciation of Equipment						
Marketing & Sales						
Labor						
Principal Salary						
Assistant						
Total Expenses						
Net Income						

One Year Financial Projections

	July	August	September	October	November	December
Revenue						
Wholesale						
Retail						
Total Revenue						
Variable Expenses						
Production						
Direct Fixed Expenses						
Development						
Photography						
Printing						
Print Design & Layout						
Trade show						
Website						
Indirect Fixed Expenses						
Administrative						
Amortization of Goodwill						
Depreciation of Equipment						
Marketing & Sales						
Labor						
Principal Salary						
Assistant						
Total Expenses						
Net Income						

Case Study: One Year Financial Projections

	January	February	March	April	May	June
Revenue						
Wholesale	11,335.00	11,355.00	561.83	561.83	561.83	561.83
Retail	381.83	381.83	381.83	381.83	381.83	381.83
Total Revenue	11,431.83	11.431.83	943.66	943.66	943.66	943.66
Variable Expenses						
Production				6,579.06	6,579.06	6,579.06
Direct Fixed Expenses						
Development	376.46			376.46	376.46	376.46
Photography		495.00				
Printing						
Print Design & Layout						
Trade show				1,750.00		
Website						
Indirect Fixed Expenses						
Administrative	102.08	102.08	102.08	102.08	102.08	102.08
Amortization of Goodwill	1.25	1.25	1.25	1.25	1.25	1.25
Depreciation of Equipment	12.08	12.08	12.08	12.08	12.08	12.08
Marketing & Sales	135.00	135.00	135.00	135.00	135.00	135.00
Labor						
Principal Salary						
Assistant						
Total Expenses	611.54	732.08	237.08	8,942.60	7,192.60	7,192.60
Net Income	10,804.96	10,686.42	693.25	-8,012.27	-6,262.27	-6,285.98

Case Study: One Year Financial Projections

	July	August	September	October	November	December
Revenue						
Wholesale	14,280.03	14,280.03	674.20	674.20	674.20	674.20
Retail	381.83	840.03	840.03	840.03	840.03	840.03
Total Revenue	14,661.86	14,661.86	1,514.23	1,514.23	1,514.23	1,514.23
Variable Expenses						
Production				6,579.06	6,579.06	6,579.06
Direct Fixed Expenses						
Development	376.46			414.11	414.11	414.11
Photography		495.00				
Printing						
Print Design & Layout						
Trade show			1,925.00			
Website						
Indirect Fixed Expenses						
Administrative	102.08	102.08	102.08	102.08	102.08	102.08
Amortization of Goodwill	1.25	1.25	1.25	1.25	1.25	1.25
Depreciation of Equipment	12.08	12.08	12.08	12.08	12.08	12.08
Marketing & Sales	135.00	135.00	135.00	135.00	135.00	135.00
Labor						
Principal Salary						
Assistant						
Total Expenses	613.54	732.08	2,162.08	7,230.25	7,230.25	7,230.25
Net Income	14,011.28	13,892.74	-684.89	-5,753.06	-5,753.06	-5,753.06

Five Year Financial Projections

	Year 1	Year 2	Year 3	Year 4	Year 5
Revenue					
Wholesale					
Retail					
Total Revenue					
Variable Expenses					
Production					
Direct Fixed Expenses					
Development					
Photography					
Printing					
Print Design & Layout					
Trade show					
Website					
Indirect Fixed Expenses					
Administrative					
Amortization of Goodwill					
Depreciation of Equipment					
Marketing & Sales					
Labor					
Principal Salary					
Assistant					
Total Expenses					
Net Income					

Case Study: Five Year Financial Projections

	2010	2011	2012	2013	2014
Revenue					
Wholesale	22,100.00	53,040.00	63,648.00	76,377.60	91,653.12
Reorders	1,685.49	7,753.29	9,303.96	11,164.77	13,397.73
Retail	1,909.15	10,004.01	12,463.04	14,955.68	17,946.80
Total Revenue	25,694.64	70,797.30	85,415.00	102,498.05	122,997.65
Variable Expenses					
Production	29,605.77	42,106.00	50,527.22	60,632.64	72,802.36
Direct Fixed Expenses					
Development	3,627.72	3,237.58	3,561.34	3,917.46	4,309.22
Photography	945.00	1,039.50	1,143.45	1,257.80	1,383.58
Printing					
Print Design & Layout					
Trade show	1,750.00	3,850.00	4,235.00	4,658.50	5,124.36
Website					
Indirect Fixed Expenses					
Administrative	1,24.96	1,347.48	1,482.24	1,630.44	1,793.52
Amortization of Goodwill	15.00	15.00	15.00	15.00	15.00
Depreciation of Equipment	144.96	144.96	144.96	144.96	144.96
Marketing & Sales	1,620.00	1,782.00	1,960.20	2,156.28	2,371.80
Labor					
Principal Salary	0.00	10,416.65	27,083.31	32,500.00	38,400.00
Assistant					
Total Expenses	3,004.92	13,706.09	30,685.71	36,446.68	42,890.28
Net Income	-13,238.77	6,858.13	-4,737.72	-4,415.03	-3,512.15

Chapter 40
Break Even Point

What is the break even point? It is the point where your sales match your expenses. "Breaking even" does not mean you are making a profit, only that you're not losing any money.

To figure your break even point, calculate how much it costs for you to be in business each month (your direct and indirect fixed costs). Let's just say that amount is $2000. If you think that you need to sell $2000 in merchandise to break even. You are incorrect.

If you make assumptions in this manner, you will go broke faster than a shop-aholic with The Home Shopping Network. You may have forgotten to include your cost of goods (COG) for the merchandise that you sold. To make our lives easy, let's just say your COG for that $2000 of merchandise is $1000. Does it make sense to say that it takes $3000 in sales to break even each month? No.

Calculating your Break Even Point

Instead of spending hours going back and forth with how much you need to sell in order to break even, let's create a mathematical formula to figure it out for us. We need to first

Notes:

Notes:

calculate our Gross Profit Margin (GPM).

Your GPM is the percentage of markup from the Cost of Goods to wholesale. You can only calculate this once you cost your garment and figure out your wholesale pricing. Based on my pricing method, this will vary for each item. To be precise, you can calculate the average of the projected quantities, but that becomes very complicated. I would recommend determining your GPM for each product and use the lowest percentage of the batch to calculate your Break Even Point. This will yield the most conservative numbers.

Divide your Cost of Goods (COG) by your Wholesale Price. Then subtract that percentage from 100% and that number is your Gross Profit Margin.

Example: The COG for a skirt is $12.50 and was marked up to $25 for wholesale.

$12.50 cost of goods/$25 wholesale price = .5 or 50%

100% – 50% = 50% Gross Profit Margin

Let us now calculate the Break Even Point. Take your average direct and indirect fixed cost for one month (which we will say is $2000) and divide it by the GPM (turn the percentage into a decimal point).

Example:
$2000 Fixed Cost / .5 Gross Profit Margin (in decimal form) = $4,000 Break Even Point

Back to a question from earlier. When do you make a profit? When you exceed your Break Even Point. To determine when your business breaks even, add your losses from each month and offset them from your revenues, when you hit zero, your business has broken even. Your actual break even point may not occur until your second year of business or later.

Notes:

Break Even Point

Style #: _____

Cost of Goods	
Wholesale Price	/
Total Cost of Goods Percentage	

	100%
Cost of Goods Percentage	-
Total Gross Profit Margin	

Style #: _____

Cost of Goods	
Wholesale Price	/
Total Cost of Goods Percentage	

	100%
Cost of Goods Percentage	-
Total Gross Profit Margin	

Style #: _____

Cost of Goods	
Wholesale Price	/
Total Cost of Goods Percentage	

	100%
Cost of Goods Percentage	-
Total Gross Profit Margin	

Of the above Gross Profit Margins calculated, use your smallest percentage in the following calculation.

Average Variable Monthly Cost	
Average Fixed Monthly Cost	
Gross Profit Margin (decimal form)	/
Total Break Even Point	

Case Study: Break Even Point

Style #: *Baby Doll Dress*

Cost of Goods	30.80
Wholesale Price	/ 53.00
Total Cost of Goods Percentage	58%

	100%
Cost of Goods Percentage	– 58%
Total Gross Profit Margin	42% or .42

Style #: *Cigarette Pant*

Cost of Goods	43.80
Wholesale Price	/ 70.00
Total Cost of Goods Percentage	63%

	100%
Cost of Goods Percentage	– 63%
Total Gross Profit Margin	37% or .37

Style #: *Obi Dress*

Cost of Goods	20.00
Wholesale Price	/ 39.00
Total Cost of Goods Percentage	51%

	100%
Cost of Goods Percentage	– 51%
Total Gross Profit Margin	49% or .49

Of the above Gross Profit Margins calculated, use your smallest percentage in the following calculation.

Average Variable Monthly Cost	2,467.15
Average Fixed Monthly Cost	777.30
Gross Profit Margin (decimal form)	/ .37
Total Break Even Point	8,768.78

Chapter 41
Exit Strategy

Exit strategies are not there to discourage you, but to help you plan on what you may need to do 2, 5, 10 or 20 years down the road. An exit strategy needs to be in your business plan to show a lender what you plan on doing in the future.

Planning your exit strategy when you are planning your launch might seem a little crazy, but you should really consider who will take over your business when it comes time for you to retire. Do you have plans to build up your business in 3 years then to sell it off? Do you want to sell when you reach a certain sales revenue? Do you want your children to continue a tradition you've build? Investors, partners and financiers are all interested in your plans.

Here are some ways to exit a business endeavor:

- Sell your business
- Pass it on to family
- Take your business public and sell shares
- Dissolve your business.
-

Unfortunately, many design businesses exit via the last option, but I have faith in you that you will break from the pack and choose one of the first three options.

Notes:

Exit Strategy

How do you plan to exit your business?

_____

_____

_____

When do you plan to exit your business?

_____

_____

_____

Who will run your business if you were to get ill? Can everything be placed on hold, or will you have a manager to step in and run things?

_____

_____

_____

_____

_____

What would happen to your business is you or your partner were to become disabled or die? Will the business continue with the remaining partner or would it be passed on to a family member?

_____

_____

_____

_____

_____

State all scenarios that could affect your business closing and how you would handle them.

_____

_____

_____

_____

_____

_____

_____

Case Study: Exit Strategy

How do you plan to exit your business?

Pass it onto my family

When do you plan to exit your business?

In 15 years or so.

Who will run your business if you were to get ill? Can everything be placed on hold, or will you have a manager to step in and run things?

I will need to hire a manager. If at that time I have a support staff, I hope to be able to delegate my way through it.

What would happen to your business is you or your partner were to become disabled or die? Will the business continue with the remaining partner or would it be passed on to a family member?

It it were to happen in the first few years, the business would probably dissolve. In 5 years, I'd hire a manager to take over. In 10 years, I'd hope my son would take over the business.

State all scenarios that could affect your business closing and how you would handle them.

If someone stole my designs, I'd have to reinvent my business.

If a natural disaster were to happen, it would probably take a year or so to rebuild. If it was severe enough, I'd have to sell off my stock and my equipment

BUILDING A BUSINESS PLAN

Chapter 42
Introduction to Your Business Plan

Each form provided in this book will contribute to you building a successful business plan. I've provided a general outline for a business plan in this chapter. In the following chapter I have included the business plan from our case study, A.C. Baker Apparel for your reference. Use these guides and everything else you've learned from this book to write your own business plan.

The included business plan for A.C. Baker Apparel has had some alterations from the original. I removed some personal information, and personal financials and contracts. Other than those changes, this is the plan used by our case study. This is to be used as a reference only. Use your own language to write your business plan. Everything will vary for your own business, so be specific in your descriptions and tailor it to your own line.

A business plan is a crucial part in your business planning, although many design businesses seldom create one. A common misconception is that your business plan is only used when seeking funding. In actuality, your business plan is for you and you alone.

Notes:

In a business plan, you state your company's values, mission statement, your expected growth and your financial projections. Your business plan should be ever changing as your business grows. I advise you to update your business plan every 6 months to incorporate any and all changes you have made in your business growth. The goal of your business plan is to help you plan for your future, budget your expenses and track your growth.

Cover Page

When introducing your business plan, begin with a clear format on your cover page. It is important to be straight to the point and include all the pertinent information. This information should define:

- Business Name
- Business Address
- Business Phone Number
- Logo
- Business owners/partners (name, address and phone of each owner)
- Month and year in which the plan was created
- Name of the preparer

Executive Summary

The first written portion of your business plan should be your executive summary. The executive summary is generally a summary of everything that is discussed in the remainder of the business plan and is generally the last thing written. Another name for the executive summary is the statement of purpose. In this statement, you should include:

- The 4 W's of your company (who, what, where, why)
- The business objectives (why you will be successful)

- Amount of funding you are requesting (including why you need a loan and when you will repay it)

Table of Contents

The table of contents can fall before or after the executive summary. Inclusion of a table of contents is helpful when creating a lengthy plan, but it is not a requirement. Use this page to layout the major topics, references and attachments to your business plan.

Objectives

The objectives section of the business plan describes your business and your goals in detail. Explain your company's history and the expectations of your future plans. Evaluate what your market currently has available and where your product will fit into it.

Use this section to offer your own research including the current size of the market and the future direction you perceive for your market. Include a detailed description of your target customer.

Product

The product section should provide a detailed description for each of your products, the fabrics and the materials used in the production of your line. These details will also include the costs for each of these items including the development costs.

Your pricing model is defined in this area. The pricing model is broken down for each style including the operating expense per piece, the profit percentage and the suggested mark up from wholesale to retail.

Notes:

Marketing

Under the marketing heading, you should describe where you see your target market geographically and what stores you see your products selling in. Listing your competition, your niche market and a detailed strategy is important for your investors. Explain how you plan to advertise your business, what promotion campaigns you foresee and provide your budget for each item. Include answers to these questions:

- How do you expect to sell your products?
- Will you use sales reps or exhibit at trade shows?
- Do you plan to do business online or own your own retail establishment?

Operations

The operation of your business is described here. List the location of your business, showroom and manufacturers.

In this section you can provide an operational timeline for each portion of your business development. Consider answering these questions:

- Where will you manufacture?
- Will you have a production manager?
- What services do you plan to keep in-house and what do you plan to outsource? (patterns, samples, cutting, sewing, grading)
- Will you be hiring additional staff? (state when if you have certain milestones)
- How much and how often will you pay your staff?

Management and Organization

In the organization section of your business plan, you will detail your choice of business entity and why you chose this entity to operate by. List who is on your team. Include a biography of each person involved including his or her level of involvement in your business.

You can include each person's resume as an attached Appendix. Include your staff, consultants and your independent contractors. Create a job description for each: assistants, interns, bookkeepers, graphic designers, web designers, sales reps, pattern makers, etc. Including an organizational chart can be helpful.

Financial Plan

In the financial plan, all the numbers are defined. You should list your major milestones for the first year, including your projected sales for the first year. List your long term growth projections, your expected expenses and sales over the next five years. Detail any plans for your business expansion.

If you are just starting your business, list your start-up costs, your projected balance sheets and income statements for the upcoming year. If you have an existing business and you are revising your business plan, include these statements for the past three years. If you are seeking funding, you may need to include the personal financial statement for each principal owner.

Appendix

The appendix includes attachments of any kind that pertain to the business plan. These might include line sheets, resumes of the owners, copies of past or present orders, press coverage you have received, pictures, brochures, look books, leases, legal documents and letters of reference.

Notes:

Chapter 43
Sample
Business Plan

Business Plan

A.C. Baker Apparel
426 3rd Street
Eureka, California 95501
United States of America
707-834-6911

Owner
Andrea Baker
707-834-6911

Business Plan Created: October 23, 2010
Business Start Date: June 1, 2010

Prepared by Andrea Baker through the Fashion Unraveled Software

A.C. Baker Apparel

Executive Summary

A.C. Baker Apparel, a manufacturer of contemporary women's sportswear apparel, is located in Eureka, CA and is operated as a sole proprietor by Andrea Baker. A.C. Baker Apparel is strategically situated to re-launch its apparel line and expand through its internet and boutique distribution. A.C. Baker Apparel's reputation for developing stylish, comfortable and environmentally friendly clothing will be the cornerstone of future growth for this company.

A.C. Baker Apparel's business plan provides details as to its product development, manufacturing and wholesale/retail distribution efforts. The unique mixture of product materials and manufacturing supports a break even point after year one and a recovery of all production costs by the end of year two. Profit projections are shown at a 20% anticipated growth in production and sales.

A.C. Baker Apparel

Table of Contents

A.C. Baker Apparel

Objectives

Mission Statement

A.C. Baker Apparel values community, great design principles and sustainability. These are the core values that drive a company that has come up in a rural community where everything is interconnected in a very visible way. Catering to community through design and sustainable business practices is what allows A.C. Baker Apparel to bring to bear fearless designs that exemplify people, not trends. A.C. Baker Apparel produces clothing that responds to the marketplace, not media

Target Market

Our moderate price point targets our market to be that of independent designer boutiques and smaller retail chains. Retail prices range from $35 to $200. Studies show that in our target audience, women tend to spend $2,000-$3,000 annually on clothing. They retain use for approximately 3-5 years and are particular about the way things fit.

Market Growth

Women's wear makes up 60% of the apparel industry, the largest segment of the industry according to marketresearch.com. 2009 showed a decline in revenue in the industry, but so far in 2010, revenue has increase by 1.5% and is expected to grow to 11% in the next two years. The average pay for fashion designers employed in the industry is $44,000 annually while the average pay for an entrepreneur is $111,000.

Company History

A.C. Baker Apparel initially began in 2003. After one year of development, marketing and sales, A.C. Baker Apparel readjusted its focus from clothing to that of handbags. For the next 7 years, A.C. Baker Apparel designed and sold a variety of handbags and accessories. In these 7 years, the owner worked in marketing and promotion, began her own development services for the fashion industry and has been raising a family. The past 7 years gave insight as to properly targeting the customer and market, as well as handling the demands of the public and building relationships with manufacturing facilities.

In 2009, Ms. Baker decided to take her knowledge and re-launch her business. She recruited the help of her friend Jennifer Matthews, an instructor, author and business coach. In early 2010, Ms. Matthews and Ms. Baker joined forces to collaborate in re-launching A.C. Baker Apparel and using it as the case study for Ms. Matthew's second book on the fashion business. A.C. Baker officially started her re-launch in June of 2010.

In September 2010, Ms. Baker partnered with an entrepreneur in Eureka to open Origin Design Lab as a place for designers and crafters to launch their businesses. Origin Design Lab will open its doors mid November and will look forward to being successful in establishing a loyal clientele to the A. C. Baker Apparel line.

A.C. Baker Apparel

Company Future

The five year focus for A.C. Baker Apparel is to move into larger markets, observing lean principals that will protect the integrity of the company and its operations. We plan on using our retail establishment success and press support as our major selling points to new retailers outside, enforcing our brand. Our first move to larger markets is scheduled for Spring 2012, but starting in Fall 2011. We will be exhibiting at Focus Tradeshow held in Los Angeles in April 2011 and October 2011. We also plan to showcase our next spring collection at Portland Fashion Week, the premier fashion portal for eco designers.

It is through these concerted efforts that we will grow significantly in the next five years.

A.C. Baker Apparel

Products

A.C. Baker Apparel produces women's sportswear, described as tops, dresses and pants.

Product Cost

The product cost consists of all materials, notions, cutting and sewing. The following products have been developed for the Spring 2011 collection. This collection consists of 8 products and will be released late January. The start ship date is January 15, 2011 and the stop ship date is February 28, 2011. A second collection for 2011 (Fall 2011) is planned for release in July and will include 8-10 pieces.

Name	Style Number	Total Cost	
Baby Doll Dress	10000	$30.80	
Front View		Back View	

Sewing Cost	Cutting Cost	Dying Cost	Printing Cost
$16.00	$2.00	NA	NA
Material	Quantity	Cost	Total Material Cost
Organic Cotton Sateen	1	$12.00	$12.00
Label	1	$0.25	$0.25
Invisible Zipper 8"	1	$0.55	$0.55

A.C. Baker Apparel

Name	Style Number	Total Cost
Cigarette Pants	7000	$43.80
Front View	Back View	

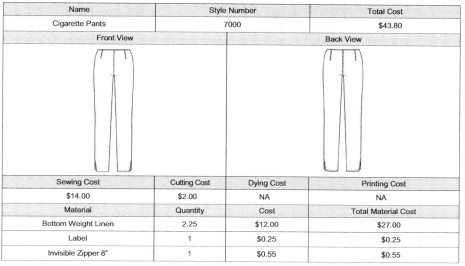

Sewing Cost	Cutting Cost	Dying Cost	Printing Cost
$14.00	$2.00	NA	NA
Material	Quantity	Cost	Total Material Cost
Bottom Weight Linen	2.25	$12.00	$27.00
Label	1	$0.25	$0.25
Invisible Zipper 8"	1	$0.55	$0.55

Name	Style Number	Total Cost
Obi Dress	9000	$20.00
Front View	Back View	

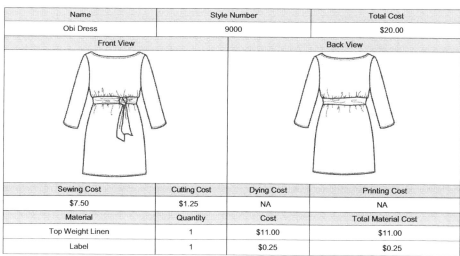

Sewing Cost	Cutting Cost	Dying Cost	Printing Cost
$7.50	$1.25	NA	NA
Material	Quantity	Cost	Total Material Cost
Top Weight Linen	1	$11.00	$11.00
Label	1	$0.25	$0.25

A.C. Baker Apparel

Materials

The materials used in this collection are linen, silk and organic cotton. All of the materials used are 100% blends. The organic cotton sateen is used in select tops and dresses. There are two weights of linen, one used for the pants and the other used for the dresses. The silk organza is used on the wrap and select embellishments on the other garments. Invisible zippers are used for all the zipper closures. Each garment has a sewn in label displaying the A.C Baker Apparel logo.

Item Name	Top Weight Linen	Cost Per Unit	$11.00
Item Number	twlin3	Minimum Order	50
Width	60"	Supplier	Linen Suppliers*
Size		Weight	3 oz
Colors	mushroom, white, orchid	Content	100% Linen
Care Instructions		Item Image	
Wash on Gentle cycle in cold water Tumble dry Hot iron			

Item Name	Bottom Weight Linen	Cost Per Unit	$12.00
Item Number	bwlin7	Minimum Order	50
Width	60"	Supplier	Linen Suppliers*
Size		Weight	7 oz
Colors	mushroom, white, orchid	Content	100% Linen
Care Instructions		Item Image	
Wash on gentle cycle with cold water Tumble dry Hot Iron			

A.C. Baker Apparel

Item Name	Organic Cotton Sateen	Cost Per Unit	$12.00
Item Number	cotsat4	Minimum Order	25
Width	110"	Supplier	Cotton Suppliers*
Size		Weight	4 oz
Colors	mushroom, white, orchid	Content	100% Organic Cotton

Care Instructions	Item Image
Wash with like colors Hang dry or medium heat Hot iron	

Item Name	Silk Organza	Cost Per Unit	$3.00
Item Number	siorg	Minimum Order	25
Width	110"	Supplier	Silk Suppliers*
Size		Weight	3 oz
Colors	45"	Content	100% Silk

Care Instructions	Item Image
Hand wash Hang dry	

Item Name	Invisible Zipper	Cost Per Unit	$12.00
Item Number	IZ	Minimum Order	50
Width		Supplier	Zipper Suppliers*
Size	Various - 4" to 24"	Weight	

Item Name	Label	Cost Per Unit	$0.25
Item Number	labacb	Minimum Order	1000
Width		Supplier	Label Suppliers*
Size	1" x 1/2"	Weight	

Care Instructions	Item Image

A.C. Baker Apparel

Development Cost

The development costs for each product will be allocated to the first season of their release. If a design is re-released in a second season, the pricing will remain the same, despite the lack of development cost for that item. The re-release will yield a higher profit margin because of this. Development costs are broken down per piece by the quantity in production that is expected.

> For example, if my development cost is $1,000 and I expect to produce 5,000 items, my development cost is broken down by 5,000 for a cost of 20 cents a piece.

For the initial collection (Spring 2011), some items were contracted out for development and a set of block patterns were created for future in-house pattern development. It is estimated that development labor will be built into the salary of the owner for future collections, although for financial projections, the development costs have remained as-is with a 10% inflation expense for each year. It is expected that these expenses will diminish over the collections in future years.

These are the development costs for Spring 2011.

Name	Style Number		Total Cost
Baby Doll Dress	10000		$63.55
Pattern Development	Sample Sewing	Pattern Grader	Fitting
NA	NA	$45.00	NA
Material	Quantity	Cost	Total Material Cost
Organic Cotton Sateen	1	$12.00	$12.00
Muslin	6	$1.00	$6.00
Invisible Zipper 14"	1	$0.55	$0.55

Name	Style Number		Total Cost
Cigarette Pant	7000		$301.65
Pattern Development	Sample Sewing	Pattern Grader	Fitting
$75.00	$125.00	$65.00	NA
Material	Quantity	Cost	Total Material Cost
Bottom Weight Linen	2.5	$12.00	$30.00
Muslin	5	$1.00	$5.00
Zipper 8"	3	$1.65	$1.65

A.C. Baker Apparel

Pricing

The wholesale price in the model consists of 6 variables: product cost, indirect fixed costs (an allocation of overhead), direct fixed costs (development, tradeshows and photography which occur for each collection), depreciation of equipment, amortization of goodwill and a profit of 30%. The total operational cost per piece for this collection is $8.63. This is detailed in the Financial Plan.

Our suggested retail pricing is set at 2.5 times the wholesale price. Any merchandise we sell online or direct to consumer will be sold at our suggested retail price.

Suggested Retail Markup		Percentage of Expected Profit		Operating Cost Per Piece	
2.5		30		$8.63	
Style Name	Style Cost	Operating Cost per piece	Profit	Wholesale	Suggested Retail
Baby Doll Dress	$30.80	$8.63	$17.57	$57.00	$143.00
Cigarette Pants	$43.80	$8.63	$22.57	$75.00	$188.00
Obi Dress	$20.00	$8.63	$12.37	$41.00	$103.00
Silk Cover Up	$14.50	$8.63	$10.87	$34.00	$85.00
Strap Top	$15.80	$8.63	$10.57	$35.00	$88.00
Swing Dress	$29.80	$8.63	$16.57	$55.00	$138.00
Urban Knickers	$25.76	$8.63	$14.61	$50.00	$125.00
Wrap Dress	$48.50	$8.63	$24.87	$82.00	$205.00

A.C. Baker Apparel

Marketing

Customer and Market

The target customer is a woman in her late 20s to her late 40s whose income averages $50,000 to $60,000 annually. The customer is environmentally conscious and focuses on the health and well being of herself and family. She spends much of her income on her family and her home. Our customer chooses comfort and fit over luxury name brands. She shops mainly at local boutiques and supports the local arts and the maker community. She is generally married or partnered and lives on the west coast of the US.

Distribution Channels

Direct Sales & Retail

Our merchandise can be located in small shopping districts in suburban neighborhoods. The collection can be classified as a missy contemporary sportswear collection.

The initial launch of A.C. Baker Apparel will be at Origin Design lab, located in Eureka, California. Origin Design Lab is co-founded by Andrea Baker and is the retail showroom for the A.C. Baker Apparel collection and several other clothing lines in Eureka.

Wholesale

Beautiful People Boutique will be the primary wholesale channel for the first collection. The collection will be marketed through tradeshows, sample sales and direct mail for all collections.

A.C. Baker Apparel

Competition

Three national competitors to A.C. Baker Apparel are Stewart and Brown, Marrika Nakk and Isda & Co. The following chart details each company and whether A.C. Baker Apparel shows strength or weakness for each factor.

	Andrea's Business	Strength or Weakness	Stewart and Brown	Marrika Nakk	Isda & Co.
Brief Design Description	Contemporary tailored and romantic wear	S	Contemporary high end casual	Contemporary romantic western wear	Contemporary office clothing
General Observation			Creates several different lines	Business longevity, around since 1980's	Closest competitor, a little dated
Products	Dresses, Pants, Tops and Skirts	S	Sweaters, pant, dresses, knits	Skirts, dresses, jackets, tops	Tops, some skirts and dresses
Fabrics	Hemp silk, silk organza, bamboo fabrics	S	Eco fabrics: hemp, organic cotton	Silk rayon velvet, stretch lace	Silks, cashmeres, linen, high end fabrics
Price	Skirt 60-150, Pant 80-125, Tops and Dresses 85-350	S	Tops, Skirts & Pants 100-150 Dresses 150-300 T-shirts 60-80	Skirts 150 Jackets, 700 Wedding Dresses	Pants, Dresses and Jackets 100-150 Tops 50-150
Quality	High quality	S	High quality	High quality	High quality
Selection and Sizing	Small – 7-10 pieces, 2 colorways	W	Large – 100 pieces, Knits size XS-L, Wovens size 2-10	Moderate - 20 pieces, S/M/L/XL	Moderate to Large – 50 pieces, XS-XL
Fit Reliability	Size 6-8 average size, sample size 8, mothers, hips	S	Narrow fit, not fit for curvy ladies	Better fit, curvy but not for short and petite.	Best fit ever for curvy
Location	N. California,	S	N. California,	S. California,	N. California,
Sales Method	Wholesale, online – etsy	S	Wholesale, Online store	Wholesale, Custom made	Wholesale, Online store
Advertising	Tradeshows, Email list	S	Tradeshows, Blog, Email list	Tradeshows, Print Ads	Tradeshows, Email list, Blog
Press		W	Celebrity placement, lots of press	Editorial press in western magazines	Limited local news

A.C. Baker Apparel

Advertising & Promotion

A.C. Baker Apparel has researched each of these promotional and advertising strategies. The most effective (and least expensive) promotion has been blogging, social media marketing and email marketing. After researching and attending several of the women's sportswear tradeshows, A.C. Baker Apparel is well prepared for exhibiting at these shows.

Marketing or Promotion	Description	Frequency	Projected Cost	Revenue Projected
Facebook Advertising	Maintain business page and advertise to target audience	Ongoing	$50 a month	$100 a month
Sponsored Listings	Marketing based on search key words on adwords, yahoo, bing, ask and youtube	Ongoing	$100 a month	$300 a month
Twitter	Maintain business updates to target customers	Ongoing	Time only - 2 hours a week	$100 a month
Blogging	Pitch to bloggers on current products and promotions. Upkeep a personal designer blog	Quarterly Pitches – ongoing personal	Time only – 2 hours a week	$500 a month
Email Marketing	Email announcements to customers who sign up for mailing list about business happenings, new merchandise and sales	Monthly or on collection releases	$20 a month	$1000 per email sent
Website	Update the website with new merchandise, events, press and awards	Quarterly	Time only – 3 hours a week	NA
Samples Sales	Promote brand awareness, build a customer following, sell samples and seconds.	Quarterly	$200 a quarter – time too	$2000 each sale
Direct Mail Postcard Promotions	Send to retail buyers, follow up with calls	Before Trade Shows	$100 twice a year	Pickup 1-3 stores each mailing
Press Kits	Samples, press releases and marketing material to targeted media to encourage editorial and feature use	Beginning of release of collection	$200 twice a year	$2000 each press coverage
Trade Shows	Exhibit at trade shows in Los Angeles and Las Vegas	2 a year	$3500 twice a year	$40,000 each show

A.C. Baker Apparel

Operations

A.C. Baker Apparel operates as a Sole Proprietorship with its sole owner as Andrea Baker. It is the intention to run this business as a sole proprietorship for the duration of the business. No partners are expected to join the business, although it is expected that family members will take over this business when Andrea Baker ceases to run it. Ms. Baker does not plan to take a salary for the first year and will contribute a portion of her own income to the business during that time.

All business will be operated from the design studio and showroom at Origin Design Lab in Eureka, California. Ms. Baker will manage the business including the books, production and the sales. A sales rep will be hired in the second season.

Samples, Patterns & Grading

Most of the samples and patterns will be created in-house in the design studio by the owner.

For the first collection, a pattern drafter was commissioned to develop the standard blocks for pattern making and select designs. LA Fashion Resource was hired for this work and will be hired to develop any future samples and patterns where assistance is needed. Patterns can be graded through this same resource. Prices for these services vary from $45-$75 depending on task.

The turnaround times are approximately 2 weeks for each sample. All payment arrangements for sample making are COD. For rush projects, there is an additional $100 fee per sample.

Production

The first collection is being created by local contractors in Eureka, CA. For the second collection, a larger quantity will be produced and production will be transferred to a factory in Los Angeles commissioned by LA Fashion Resource. The LA Fashion Resource will handle quality control at the factory on a limited basis.

The turnaround times for finished sewn products in the local arena are 4-6 weeks. All payment arrangements for production are COD. For the production facility in Los Angeles, turnaround time is estimated as 6-8 weeks.

Suppliers

For each material, a different source was required for sourcing.

******* This information has been omitted from this business plan for proprietary reasons.

Inventory

Limited quantities of supplies including fabric and notions will be on-site for sample creation purposes. All supplies for production will be delivered directly to the factory for garment construction.

A.C. Baker Apparel

All inventories will initially be stored on-site for thorough quality control. When production quantity exceeds our capacity for storage, we will obtain a quality control storage facility. At this point, we will keep a reasonable amount on-site for direct to consumer sales and emergency re-orders.

Inventory unsold at the end of each selling season will be sold at either discounted wholesale with no requirements for minimum sales or will be sold at discounted retail prices online or at direct-to-consumer events.

Credit Policies

All wholesale orders with new accounts will be required for COD or credit card payment arrangements. After A.C. Baker Apparel has operated 3 complete seasons, a net 30 credit can be offered to credit worthy clients who have been consistent customers for at least 2 seasons prior.

If credit has been extended and payment is not received after 60 days, the account will be taken into collections with an appropriate collection agency and all orders in play will be frozen until full payment has been received. Further, the account will revert to credit card or COD only for any future orders.

Operational Timeline

	Jun-10	Jul-10	Aug-10	Sep-10	Oct-10	Nov-10	Dec-10	Jan-11	Feb-11	Mar-11	Apr-11	May-11	Jun-11	Jul-11	Aug-11	Sep-11	Oct-11	Nov-11	Dec-11	Jan-12	Feb-12	Mar-12	Apr-12	May-12
Wholesale																								
Reorders																								
Retail																								
Production																								
Development																								
Photography																								
Tradeshow																								

	Jun-12	Jul-12	Aug-12	Sep-12	Oct-12	Nov-12	Dec-12	Jan-13	Feb-13	Mar-13	Apr-13	May-13	Jun-13	Jul-13	Aug-13	Sep-13	Oct-13	Nov-13	Dec-13	Jan-14	Feb-14	Mar-14	Apr-14	May-14
Wholesale																								
Reorders																								
Retail																								
Production																								
Development																								
Photography																								
Tradeshow																								

	Jun-14	Jul-14	Aug-14	Sep-14	Oct-14	Nov-14	Dec-14	Jan-15	Feb-15	Mar-15	Apr-15	May-15
Wholesale												
Reorders												
Retail												
Production												
Development												
Photography												
Tradeshow												

A.C. Baker Apparel

Management and Organization

Andrea Baker, Owner & Designer

Andrea Baker is the sole proprietor of A.C. Baker Apparel. Her responsibilities include day to day bookkeeping and record keeping. Marketing efforts will be planned by Ms. Baker and carried out through personal efforts and select independent contractors. Design development will be managed by Ms. Baker, as will sample development including fit, color, and custom orders. Sales will be tracked through bookkeeping software and quality control will be handled in-house.

Professional and Advisory Support

Jennifer Matthews, Consultant for Business Development

Jennifer Matthews is the author of Fashion Unraveled, a business planning book and software. Ms. Matthews works as a business consultant for A.C. Baker Apparel and will assist in the procurement of a factory in Los Angeles. Ms. Matthews is an instructor at the Fashion Institute of Design and Merchandising in Los Angeles and also helps in the pattern and sample development for A.C. Baker Apparel.

A.C. Baker Apparel

Financial Plan

Production Costs

The expected production costs for Spring 2011 total $16,447.66. These are based on orders of 40-75 per style. These numbers were created based on the market research and the response to the individual styles. Additional quantities are being ordered for damages, direct sales and reorders. Damages are an additional 5%. Direct sales are an additional 10% and Reorders are an additional 15%.

Allowance for Damaged Goods	Allowance for Direct Sales		Allowance for Reorders		Total Production Cost	
5%	10%		15%		$16,447.66	
Style Name	Style Cost	Quantity Ordered	Damages	Direct Sales	Reorders	Total Cost
Baby Doll Dress	$30.80	40	2	4	6	$1,601.60
Cigarette Pants	$43.80	40	2	4	6	$2,277.60
Obi Dress	$20.00	50	3	5	8	$1,320.00
Silk Cover Up	$14.50	50	3	5	8	$957.00
Strap Top	$15.80	75	4	8	11	$1,548.40
Swing Dress	$29.80	75	4	8	11	$2,920.40
Urban Knickers	$25.76	50	3	5	8	$1,700.16
Wrap Dress	$48.50	65	3	7	10	$4,122.50

A.C. Baker Apparel

Direct Fixed Cost

The direct fixed costs for Spring 2011 are as follows. These include the development and photography expenses for this collection.

Development Costs	
Style	Cost
Baby Doll Dress	$63.55
Cigarette Pants	$301.65
Obi Dress	$62.00
Silk Cover Up	$8.00
Strap Top	$7.55
Swing Dress	$400.30
Urban Knickers	$219.65
Wrap Dress	$306.25
Total	$1,368.95

Photography Cost			
Name of Shoot	Location	Shoot Date	Total Cost
October Photo Shoot	James' Studio	October 2010	$450.00
Photographer Cost	Model Cost	Model Cost	Makeup Artist Cost
$300			$50
Location Cost	Photoshop Cost	Printing Cost	Hair Stylist Cost
		$50	$50

The direct fixed cost for Fall 2011 will include a development and photography cost, as well as a tradeshow. A tradeshow is not planned for Spring 2011.

Trade Show Cost			
Name of Show	Location	Show Date	Total Cost
Focus Trade Show	Los Angeles	April 2011	$1750.00
Trade Show Fee	Load In Cost	Load Out Cost	Display Expenses
$900	$75	$75	$200
Airfare	Car Rental	Food	Hotel
$300		$200	

A.C. Baker Apparel

Indirect Fixed Cost

The indirect fixed costs are the monthly operational expenses for the business. These include all administrative, marketing and labor expenses. The owner is choosing not to take an income until 2012 in order to build the business. In 2012, the owner plans to take a base salary of 25,000. If the business growth is more than the estimated 20% growth planned, the owner will take an annual end of the year bonus based on the percentage of profit obtained.

Administrative Cost	Monthly	Annually
Accounting	$12.50	$150.00
Business License Renewals	$4.58	$55.00
Insurance	$25.00	$300.00
Office Supplies	$35.00	$420.00
Postage & Shipping	$25.00	$300.00
Total Administrative	$102.08	$1,225.00

Marketing & Sales	Monthly	Annually
Direct Mail Marketing	$20.00	$240.00
Email Marketing	$15.00	$180.00
Events	$50.00	$600.00
Online Marketing	$50.00	$600.00
Total Marketing & Sales	$135.00	$1,620.00

A.C. Baker Apparel

Start Up Costs

These start up costs are expenses that happened during my initial business launch in 2002.

Start Up Costs	Estimate
Business Entity	$50.00
Licenses & Permits	
Business license	$50.00
Legal Fees	$150.00
Technology & Computer Software	
Accounting Software	$200.00
Total Start Up Costs	$450.00

Start up costs are amortized over 30 years and equipment is depreciated over 15 years. This breakdown is factored into the pricing as well as into the Profit & Loss Statement and Financial Projections.

	Monthly	Annually
Amortization of Goodwill	$1.25	$15.00
Depreciation of Equipment	$12.08	$145.00

A.C. Baker Apparel

Contributed Capital

The owner has contributed $20,000 of her own to the business re-launch. A.C. Baker Apparel does not plan to take out a loan to infuse the business assets. Equipment has been contributed to this business. The total contributed capital to this business is $22,175 as of June 2010. The owner plans to infuse this capital with her own income when needed.

Cash Contribution	$20,000.00
Fixed Assets	$2,175.00
Total Assets	$22,175.00

Fixed Assets

Steamer	$75.00
Hangers	$50.00
Rolling Rack	$75.00
Mannequin	$50.00
Industrial Straight Sewing Machine	$250.00
Industrial Overlock Machine	$600.00
Serger	$50.00
Home Machine	$25.00
Computer	$1,000.00
Total Fixed Assets	$2,175.00

A.C. Baker Apparel

Five Year Profit and Loss Projection

The business start date for these projections is June 1, 2010. This profit and loss projection assumes a 10% increase for inflation and 20% growth of the company. Due to the nature of this industry, sales and revenue are received up to nine months after the initial expenses have occurred.

Summary

	2010	2011	2012	2013	2014
Income from sales					
Wholesale	$23,610.00	$56,664.00	$65,822.40	$81,596.16	$97,915.40
Reorders	$1,800.99	$8,284.59	$9,941.52	$11,929.86	$14,315.79
Retail	$2,555.00	$13,387.20	$16,679.04	$20,014.88	$23,134.84
Gross Revenue	$27,965.99	$78,335.79	$92,442.96	$113,540.90	$135,366.03
Variable Cost of Production					
Production Costs	$29,605.77	$42,106.00	$50,527.22	$60,632.64	$72,802.36
Total Variable Cost	$29,605.77	$42,106.00	$50,527.22	$60,632.64	$72,802.36
Direct Fixed Cost					
Development Costs	$3,627.72	$3,237.58	$3,561.34	$3,917.46	$4,309.22
Photography Costs	$945.00	$1,039.50	$1,143.45	$1,257.80	$1,383.58
Tradeshow Costs	$1,750.00	$3,850.00	$4,235.00	$4,658.50	$5,124.36
Total Fixed Costs	$6,322.72	$8,127.08	$8,939.79	$9,833.76	$10,817.16
Income from Production	($10,233.85)	$20,564.22	$25,947.99	$32,031.65	$39,378.13
Indirect Fixed Cost					
Administrative	$1,224.96	$1,347.48	$1,482.24	$1,630.44	$1,793.52
Amortization of Goodwill	$15.00	$15.00	$15.00	$15.00	$180.00
Depreciation of	$144.96	$144.96	$144.96	$144.96	$144.96
Marketing & Sales	$1,620.00	$1,782.00	$1,960.20	$2,156.28	$2,371.80
Administrative Labor	$0.00	$10,416.65	$27,083.31	$32,500.00	$38,400.00
Total Fixed Costs	$3,004.92	$13,706.09	$30,685.71	$36,446.68	$42,890.28
Net Profit	($10,967.42)	$14,396.62	$2,290.24	$6,627.82	$8,856.23
Note Payment	$0.00	$0.00	$0.00	$0.00	$0.00
Break Even Analysis	($72,631.11)	$83,132.35	$172,506.05	$246,046.01	$369,104.06

A.C. Baker Apparel

Detail

	10-Jun	10-Jul	10-Aug	10-Sep	10-Oct	10-Nov	10-Dec	11-Jan	11-Feb	11-Mar	11-Apr	11-May
Income from sales												
Wholesale	0	0	0	0	0	0	0	$11,805.00	$11,805.00	0	0	0
Reorders	0	0	0	0	0	0	0	0	0	$600.33	$600.33	$600.33
Retail	0	0	0	0	0	0	0	$511.00	$511.00	$511.00	$511.00	$511.00
Gross Revenue	0	0	0	0	0	0	0	$12,316.00	$12,316.00	$1,111.33	$1,111.33	$1,111.33
Variable Cost of Production												
Production Costs	0	0	0	0	$5,482.55	$5,482.55	$5,482.55		0	0	$6,579.06	$6,579.06
Total Variable Cost	0	0	0	0	$5,482.55	$5,482.55	$5,482.55	0	0	0	$6,579.06	$6,579.06
Direct Fixed Cost												
Development Costs	$684.48	$684.48	0	0	$376.46	$376.46	$376.46	$376.46	0	0	$376.46	$376.46
Photography Costs		0	0	0	$450.00	0	0	0	$495.00	0	0	
Tradeshow Costs	0	0	0	0	0	0	0	0	0	0	$1,750.00	0
Total Fixed Costs	$684.48	$684.48	$0.00	$0.00	$826.46	$376.46	$376.46	$376.46	$495.00	$0.00	$2,126.46	$376.46
Income from Production	($684.48)	($684.48)	$0.00	$0.00	($6,309.01)	($5,859.01)	($5,859.01)	$11,939.54	$11,821.00	$1,111.33	($7,594.19)	($5,844.19)
Indirect Fixed Cost												
Administrative	$102.08	$102.08	$102.08	$102.08	$102.08	$102.08	$102.08	$102.08	$102.08	$102.08	$102.08	$102.08
Amortization of Goodwill	$1.25	$1.25	$1.25	$1.25	$1.25	$1.25	$1.25	$1.25	$1.25	$1.25	$1.25	$1.25
Depreciation of Equipment	$12.08	$12.08	$12.08	$12.08	$12.08	$12.08	$12.08	$12.08	$12.08	$12.08	$12.08	$12.08
Marketing & Sales	$135.00	$135.00	$135.00	$135.00	$135.00	$135.00	$135.00	$135.00	$135.00	$135.00	$135.00	$135.00
Administrative Labor	$0.00	$0.00	$0.00	$0.00	$0.00	$0.00	$0.00	$0.00	$0.00	$0.00	$0.00	$0.00
Total Fixed Costs	$250.41	$250.41	$250.41	$250.41	$250.41	$250.41	$250.41	$250.41	$250.41	$250.41	$250.41	$250.41
Net Profit	($934.89)	($934.89)	($250.41)	($250.41)	($6,559.42)	($6,109.42)	($6,109.42)	$11,689.13	$11,570.59	$860.92	($7,844.60)	($6,094.60)
Note Payment	0	0	0	0	0	0	0	0	0	0	0	0
Break Even Analysis	($934.89)	($1,869.78)	($2,120.19)	($2,370.60)	($8,930.02)	($15,039.44)	($21,148.86)	($9,459.73)	$2,110.86	$2,971.78	($4,872.82)	($10,967.42)

A.C. Baker Apparel

	11-Jun	11-Jul	11-Aug	11-Sep	11-Oct	11-Nov	11-Dec	12-Jan	12-Feb	12-Mar	12-Apr	12-May
Income from sales												
Wholesale	0	$14,166.00	$14,166.00	0	0	0	0	$14,166.00	$14,166.00	0	0	0
Reorders	$600.33	$600.33	$600.33	$720.40	$720.40	$720.40	$720.40	$720.40	$720.40	$720.40	$720.40	$720.40
Retail	$511.00	$1,124.20	$1,124.20	$1,123.20	$1,124.20	$1,124.20	$1,124.20	$1,226.40	$1,226.40	$1,226.40	$1,226.40	$1,226.40
Gross Revenue	$1,111.33	$15,890.53	$15,890.53	$1,843.60	$1,844.60	$1,844.60	$1,844.60	$16,112.80	$16,112.80	$1,946.80	$1,946.80	$1,946.80
Variable Cost of Production												
Production Costs	$6,579.06	0	0	0	$6,579.06	$6,579.06	$6,579.06	0	0	0	$7,894.88	$7,894.88
Total Variable Cost	$6,579.06	0	0	0	$6,579.06	$6,579.06	$6,579.06	0	0	0	$7,894.88	$7,894.88
Direct Fixed Cost												
Development Costs	$376.46	$376.46	0	0	$414.11	$414.11	$414.11	$414.11	0	0	$414.11	$414.11
Photography Costs	0	0	$495.00	0	0	0	0	0	$544.50	0	0	0
Tradeshow Costs	0	0	0	$1,925.00	0	0	0	0	0	$1,925.00	0	0
Total Fixed Costs	$376.46	$376.46	$495.00	$1,925.00	$414.11	$414.11	$414.11	$414.11	$544.50	$1,925.00	$414.11	$414.11
Income from Production	($5,844.19)	$15,514.07	$15,395.53	($81.40)	($5,148.57)	($5,148.57)	($5,148.57)	$15,698.69	$15,568.30	$21.80	($6,362.19)	($6,362.19)
Indirect Fixed Cost												
Administrative	$112.29	$112.29	$112.29	$112.29	$112.29	$112.29	$112.29	$112.29	$112.29	$112.29	$112.29	$112.29
Amortization of Goodwill	$1.25	$1.25	$1.25	$1.25	$1.25	$1.25	$1.25	$1.25	$1.25	$1.25	$1.25	$1.25
Depreciation of Equipment	$12.08	$12.08	$12.08	$12.08	$12.08	$12.08	$12.08	$12.08	$12.08	$12.08	$12.08	$12.08
Marketing & Sales	$148.50	$148.50	$148.50	$148.50	$148.50	$148.50	$148.50	$148.50	$148.50	$148.50	$148.50	$148.50
Administrative Labor	$0.00	$0.00	$0.00	$0.00	$0.00	$0.00	$0.00	$2,083.33	$2,083.33	$2,083.33	$2,083.33	$2,083.33
Total Fixed Costs	$274.12	$274.12	$274.12	$274.12	$274.12	$274.12	$274.12	$2,357.45	$2,357.45	$2,357.45	$2,357.45	$2,357.45
Net Profit	($6,118.31)	$15,239.95	$15,121.41	($355.52)	($5,422.69)	($5,422.69)	($5,422.69)	$13,341.24	$13,210.85	($2,335.65)	($8,719.64)	($6,719.64)
Note Payment	0	0	0	0	0	0	0	0	0	0	0	0
Break Even Analysis	($17,085.73)	($1,845.78)	$13,275.63	$12,920.11	$7,497.42	$2,074.73	($3,347.96)	$9,993.28	$23,204.13	$20,868.48	$12,148.84	$3,429.20

A.C. Baker Apparel

	12-Jun	12-Jul	12-Aug	12-Sep	12-Oct	12-Nov	12-Dec	13-Jan	13-Feb	13-Mar	13-Apr	13-May
Income from sales												
Wholesale	0	$16,999.20	$16,999.20	0	0	0	0	$15,912.00	$15,912.00	0	0	0
Reorders	$720.40	$720.40	$720.40	$864.48	$864.48	$864.48	$864.48	$864.48	$864.48	$864.48	$864.48	$864.48
Retail	$1,226.40	$1,349.04	$1,349.04	$1,349.04	$1,349.04	$1,349.04	$1,349.04	$1,471.68	$1,471.68	$1,471.68	$1,471.68	$1,471.68
Gross Revenue	$1,946.80	$19,068.64	$19,068.64	$2,213.52	$2,213.52	$2,213.52	$2,213.52	$18,248.16	$18,248.16	$2,336.16	$2,336.16	$2,336.16
Variable Cost of Production												
Production Costs	$7,894.88	0	0	0	$7,894.88	$7,894.88	$7,894.88	0	0	0	$9,473.85	$9,473.85
Total Variable Cost	$7,894.88	0	0	0	$7,894.88	$7,894.88	$7,894.88	0	0	0	$9,473.85	$9,473.85
Direct Fixed Cost												
Development Costs	$414.11	$414.11	0	0	$455.52	$455.52	$455.52	$455.52	0	0	$455.52	$455.52
Photography Costs	0	0	$544.50	0	0	0	0	0	$598.95	0	0	0
Tradeshow Costs	0	0	0	$2,117.50	0	0	0	0	0	$2,117.50	0	0
Total Fixed Costs	$414.11	$414.11	$544.50	$2,117.50	$455.52	$455.52	$455.52	$455.52	$598.95	$2,117.50	$455.52	$455.52
Income from Production	($6,362.19)	$18,654.53	$18,524.14	$96.02	($6,136.88)	($6,136.88)	($6,136.88)	$17,792.64	$17,649.21	$218.66	($7,593.21)	($7,593.21)
Indirect Fixed Cost												
Administrative	$123.52	$123.52	$123.52	$123.52	$123.52	$123.52	$123.52	$123.52	$123.52	$123.52	$123.52	$123.52
Amortization of Goodwill	$1.25	$1.25	$1.25	$1.25	$1.25	$1.25	$1.25	$1.25	$1.25	$1.25	$1.25	$1.25
Depreciation of Equipment	$12.08	$12.08	$12.08	$12.08	$12.08	$12.08	$12.08	$12.08	$12.08	$12.08	$12.08	$12.08
Marketing & Sales	$163.35	$163.35	$163.35	$163.35	$163.35	$163.35	$163.35	$163.35	$163.35	$163.35	$163.35	$163.35
Administrative Labor	$2,083.33	$2,083.33	$2,083.33	$2,083.33	$2,083.33	$2,083.33	$2,083.33	$2,500.00	$2,500.00	$2,500.00	$2,500.00	$2,500.00
Total Fixed Costs	$2,383.53	$2,383.53	$2,383.53	$2,383.53	$2,383.53	$2,383.53	$2,383.53	$2,800.20	$2,800.20	$2,800.20	$2,800.20	$2,800.20
Net Profit	($8,745.72)	$16,271.00	$16,140.61	($2,287.51)	($8,520.41)	($8,520.41)	($8,520.41)	$14,992.44	$14,849.01	($2,581.54)	($10,393.41)	($10,393.41)
Note Payment	0	0	0	0	0	0	0	0	0	0	0	0
Break Even Analysis	($5,316.52)	$10,954.48	$27,095.09	$24,607.58	$16,287.17	$7,766.76	($753.65)	$14,238.79	$29,087.80	$26,506.26	$16,112.85	$5,719.44

A.C. Baker Apparel

	13-Jun	13-Jul	13-Aug	13-Sep	13-Oct	13-Nov	13-Dec	14-Jan	14-Feb	14-Mar	14-Apr	14-May
Income from sales												
Wholesale	0	$20,399.04	$20,399.04	0	0	0	0	$20,399.04	$20,399.04	0	0	0
Reorders	$864.48	$864.48	$864.48	$1,037.38	$1,037.38	$1,037.38	$1,037.38	$1,037.38	$1,037.38	$1,037.38	$1,037.38	$1,037.38
Retail	$1,471.68	$1,618.85	$1,618.85	$1,618.85	$1,618.85	$1,618.85	$1,618.85	$1,766.02	$1,766.02	$1,766.02	$1,766.02	$1,766.02
Gross Revenue	$2,336.16	$22,882.37	$22,882.37	$2,656.23	$2,656.23	$2,656.23	$2,656.23	$23,202.44	$23,202.44	$2,803.40	$2,803.40	$2,803.40
Variable Cost of Production												
Production Costs	$9,473.85	0	0	0	$9,473.85	$9,473.85	$9,473.85	0	0	0	$11,368.62	$11,368.62
Total Variable Cost	$9,473.85	0	0	0	$9,473.85	$9,473.85	$9,473.85	0	0	0	$11,368.62	$11,368.62
Direct Fixed Cost												
Development Costs	$455.52	$455.52	0	0	$501.07	$501.07	$501.07	$501.07	0	0	$501.07	$501.07
Photography Costs	0	0	$598.95	0	0	0	0	0	$658.85	0	0	0
Tradeshow Costs	0	0	0	$2,329.25	0	0	0	0	0	$2,329.25	0	0
Total Fixed Costs	$455.52	$455.52	$598.95	$2,329.25	$501.07	$501.07	$501.07	$501.07	$658.85	$2,329.25	$501.07	$501.07
Income from Production	($7,593.21)	$22,426.85	$22,283.42	$326.98	($7,318.69)	($7,318.69)	($7,318.69)	$22,701.37	$22,543.59	$474.15	($9,066.29)	($9,066.29)
Indirect Fixed Cost												
Administrative	$135.87	$135.87	$135.87	$135.87	$135.87	$135.87	$135.87	$135.87	$135.87	$135.87	$135.87	$135.87
Amortization of Goodwill	$1.25	$1.25	$1.25	$1.25	$1.25	$1.25	$1.25	$1.25	$1.25	$1.25	$1.25	$1.25
Depreciation of Equipment	$12.08	$12.08	$12.08	$12.08	$12.08	$12.08	$12.08	$12.08	$12.08	$12.08	$12.08	$12.08
Marketing & Sales	$179.69	$179.69	$179.69	$179.69	$179.69	$179.69	$179.69	$179.69	$179.69	$179.69	$179.69	$179.69
Administrative Labor	$2,500.00	$2,500.00	$2,500.00	$2,500.00	$2,500.00	$2,500.00	$2,500.00	$3,000.00	$3,000.00	$3,000.00	$3,000.00	$3,000.00
Total Fixed Costs	$2,828.89	$2,828.89	$2,828.89	$2,828.89	$2,828.89	$2,828.89	$2,828.89	$3,328.89	$3,328.89	$3,328.89	$3,328.89	$3,328.89
Net Profit	($10,422.10)	$19,597.96	$19,454.53	($2,501.91)	($10,147.58)	($10,147.58)	($10,147.58)	$19,372.48	$19,214.70	($2,854.74)	($12,395.18)	($12,395.18)
Note Payment	0	0	0	0	0	0	0	0	0	0	0	0
Break Even Analysis	($4,702.66)	$14,895.30	$34,349.83	$31,847.92	$21,700.34	$11,552.76	$1,405.18	$20,777.66	$39,992.36	$37,137.62	$24,742.44	$12,347.26

A.C. Baker Apparel

	14-Jun	14-Jul	14-Aug	14-Sep	14-Oct	14-Nov	14-Dec	15-Jan	15-Feb	15-Mar	15-Apr	15-May
Income from sales												
Wholesale	0	$24,478.85	$24,478.85	0	0	0	0	$24,478.85	$24,478.85	0	0	0
Reorders	$1,037.38	$1,037.38	$1,037.38	$1,244.85	$1,244.85	$1,244.85	$1,244.85	$1,244.85	$1,244.85	$1,244.85	$1,244.85	$1,244.85
Retail	$1,766.02	$1,942.62	$1,942.62	$1,942.62	$1,942.62	$1,942.62	$1,942.62	$1,942.62	$1,942.62	$1,942.62	$1,942.62	$1,942.62
Gross Revenue	$2,803.40	$27,458.85	$27,458.85	$3,187.47	$3,187.47	$3,187.47	$3,187.47	$27,666.32	$27,666.32	$3,187.47	$3,187.47	$3,187.47
Variable Cost of Production												
Production Costs	$11,368.62	0	0	0	$11,368.62	$11,368.62	$11,368.62	0	0	0	$13,663.94	$13,663.94
Total Variable Cost	$11,368.62	0	0	0	$11,368.62	$11,368.62	$11,368.62	0	0	0	$13,663.94	$13,663.94
Direct Fixed Cost												
Development Costs	$501.07	$501.07	0	0	$551.18	$551.18	$551.18	$551.18	0	0	$551.18	$551.18
Photography Costs	0	0	$658.85	0	0	0	0	0	$724.73	0	0	0
Tradeshow Costs	0	0	0	$2,562.18	0	0	0	0	0	$2,562.18	0	0
Total Fixed Costs	$501.07	$501.07	$658.85	$2,562.18	$551.18	$551.18	$551.18	$551.18	$724.73	$2,562.18	$551.18	$551.18
Income from Production	($9,066.29)	$26,957.78	$26,800.00	$625.29	($8,732.33)	($8,732.33)	($8,732.33)	$27,115.14	$26,941.59	$625.29	($11,027.65)	($11,027.65)
Indirect Fixed Cost												
Administrative	$149.46	$149.46	$149.46	$149.46	$149.46	$149.46	$149.46	$149.46	$149.46	$149.46	$149.46	$149.46
Amortization of Goodwill	$15.00	$15.00	$15.00	$15.00	$15.00	$15.00	$15.00	$15.00	$15.00	$15.00	$15.00	$15.00
Depreciation of Equipment	$12.08	$12.08	$12.08	$12.08	$12.08	$12.08	$12.08	$12.08	$12.08	$12.08	$12.08	$12.08
Marketing & Sales	$197.65	$197.65	$197.65	$197.65	$197.65	$197.65	$197.65	$197.65	$197.65	$197.65	$197.65	$197.65
Administrative Labor	$3,000.00	$3,000.00	$3,000.00	$3,000.00	$3,000.00	$3,000.00	$3,000.00	$3,000.00	$3,600.00	$3,600.00	$3,600.00	$3,600.00
Total Fixed Costs	$3,374.19	$3,374.19	$3,374.19	$3,374.19	$3,374.19	$3,374.19	$3,374.19	$3,374.19	$3,974.19	$3,974.19	$3,974.19	$3,974.19
Net Profit	($12,440.48)	$23,583.59	$23,425.81	($2,748.90)	($12,106.52)	($12,106.52)	($12,106.52)	$23,740.95	$22,967.40	($3,348.90)	($15,001.84)	($15,001.84)
Note Payment	0	0	0	0	0	0	0	0	0	0	0	0
Break Even Analysis	($93.22)	$23,490.37	$46,916.18	$44,167.28	$32,060.76	$19,954.24	$7,847.72	$31,588.67	$54,556.07	$51,207.17	$36,205.33	$21,203.49

A.C. Baker Apparel

Five Year Balance Sheet Projection

This profit and loss projection assumes a 10% increase for inflation and 20% growth of the company. Due to the nature of this industry, sales and revenue are received up to nine months after the initial expenses have occurred.

Summary

	2010	2011	2012	2013	2014
Current Assets					
Cash/Bank Account	($213.97)	$17,586.93	$20,181.24	$22,340.07	$28,782.61
Fixed Assets	$2,175.00	$2,175.00	$2,175.00	$2,175.00	$2,175.00
Total assets	$1,961.03	$19,761.93	$22,356.24	$24,515.07	$30,957.61
Liabilities & Capital					
Liabilities					
Loan Balance	0	0	0	0	0
Credit Cards	0	0	0	0	0
Total Liabilities	$0	$0	$0	$0	$0
Capital					
Equity	$8,070.45	$25,184.62	$30,876.65	$34,662.65	$43,064.13
Net profits	($21,148.86)	$17,800.90	$2,594.31	$2,158.83	$6,442.54
Total Capital	($13,078.41)	$42,985.52	$33,470.96	$36,821.48	$49,506.67
Total Liabilities & Capital	($13,078.41)	$42,985.52	$33,470.96	$36,821.48	$49,506.67

A.C. Baker Apparel

Detail

	10-Jun	10-Jul	10-Aug	10-Sep	10-Oct	10-Nov	10-Dec	11-Jan	11-Feb	11-Mar	11-Apr	11-May
Assets												
Cash/Bank Account	$20,000.00	$19,065.11	$18,814.70	$18,564.29	$12,004.87	$5,895.45	($213.97)	$11,475.16	$23,045.75	$23,906.67	$16,062.07	$9,967.47
Fixed Assets	$2,175.00	$2,175.00	$2,175.00	$2,175.00	$2,175.00	$2,175.00	$2,175.00	$2,175.00	$2,175.00	$2,175.00	$2,175.00	$2,175.00
Total assets	$22,175.00	$21,240.11	$20,989.70	$20,739.29	$14,179.87	$8,070.45	$1,961.03	$13,650.16	$25,220.75	$26,081.67	$18,237.07	$12,142.47
Liabilities & Capital												
Liabilities												
Loan Balance	0	0	0	0	0	0	0	0	0	0	0	0
Credit Cards	0	0	0	0	0	0	0	0	0	0	0	0
Total Liabilities	$0	$0	$0	$0	$0	$0	$0	$0	$0	$0	$0	$0
Capital												
Equity	$23,109.89	$22,175.00	$21,240.11	$20,989.70	$20,739.29	$14,179.87	$8,070.45	$1,961.03	$13,650.16	$25,220.75	$26,081.67	$18,237.07
Net Profit	($934.89)	($934.89)	($250.41)	($250.41)	($6,559.42)	($6,109.42)	($6,109.42)	$11,689.13	$11,570.59	$860.92	($7,844.60)	($6,094.60)
Total Capital	$22,175.00	$21,240.11	$20,989.70	$20,739.29	$14,179.87	$8,070.45	$1,961.03	$13,650.16	$25,220.75	$26,081.67	$18,237.07	$12,142.47
Total Liabilities & Capital	$22,175.00	$21,240.11	$20,989.70	$20,739.29	$14,179.87	$8,070.45	$1,961.03	$13,650.16	$25,220.75	$26,081.67	$18,237.07	$12,142.47

A.C. Baker Apparel

	11-Jun	11-Jul	11-Aug	11-Sep	11-Oct	11-Nov	11-Dec	12-Jan	12-Feb	12-Mar	12-Apr	12-May
Assets												
Cash/Bank Account	$3,849.16	$19,089.11	$34,210.52	$33,855.00	$28,432.31	$23,009.62	$17,586.93	$30,928.17	$44,139.02	$41,803.37	$33,083.73	$24,364.09
Fixed Assets	$2,175.00	$2,175.00	$2,175.00	$2,175.00	$2,175.00	$2,175.00	$2,175.00	$2,175.00	$2,175.00	$2,175.00	$2,175.00	$2,175.00
Total assets	$6,024.16	$21,264.11	$36,385.52	$36,030.00	$30,607.31	$25,184.62	$19,761.93	$33,103.17	$46,314.02	$43,978.37	$35,258.73	$26,539.09
Liabilities & Capital												
Liabilities												
Loan Balance	0	0	0	0	0	0	0	0	0	0	0	0
Credit Cards	0	0	0	0	0	0	0	0	0	0	0	0
Total Liabilities	$0	$0	$0	$0	$0	$0	$0	$0	$0	$0	$0	$0
Capital												
Equity	$12,142.47	$6,024.16	$21,264.11	$36,385.52	$36,030.00	$30,607.31	$25,184.62	$19,761.93	$33,103.17	$46,314.02	$43,978.37	$35,258.73
Net Profit	($6,118.31)	$15,239.95	$15,121.41	($355.52)	($5,422.69)	($5,422.69)	($5,422.69)	$13,341.24	$13,210.85	($2,335.65)	($8,719.64)	($8,719.64)
Total Capital	$6,024.16	$21,264.11	$36,385.52	$36,030.00	$30,607.31	$25,184.62	$19,761.93	$33,103.17	$46,314.02	$43,978.37	$35,258.73	$26,539.09
Total Liabilities & Capital	$6,024.16	$21,264.11	$36,385.52	$36,030.00	$30,607.31	$25,184.62	$19,761.93	$33,103.17	$46,314.02	$43,978.37	$35,258.73	$26,539.09

A.C. Baker Apparel

	12-Jun	12-Jul	12-Aug	12-Sep	12-Oct	12-Nov	12-Dec	13-Jan	13-Feb	13-Mar	13-Apr	13-May
Assets												
Cash/Bank Account	$15,618.37	$31,889.37	$48,029.98	$45,742.47	$37,222.06	$28,701.65	$20,181.24	$35,173.68	$50,022.69	$47,441.15	$37,047.74	$26,654.33
Fixed Assets	$2,175.00	$2,175.00	$2,175.00	$2,175.00	$2,175.00	$2,175.00	$2,175.00	$2,175.00	$2,175.00	$2,175.00	$2,175.00	$2,175.00
Total assets	$17,793.37	$34,064.37	$50,204.98	$47,917.47	$39,397.06	$30,876.65	$22,356.24	$37,348.68	$52,197.69	$49,616.15	$39,222.74	$28,829.33
Liabilities & Capital												
Liabilities												
Loan Balance	0	0	0	0	0	0	0	0	0	0	0	0
Credit Cards	0	0	0	0	0	0	0	0	0	0	0	0
Total Liabilities	$0	$0	$0	$0	$0	$0	$0	$0	$0	$0	$0	$0
Capital												
Equity	$26,539.09	$17,793.37	$34,064.37	$50,204.98	$47,917.47	$39,397.06	$30,876.65	$22,356.24	$37,348.68	$52,197.69	$49,616.15	$39,222.74
Net Profit	($8,745.72)	$16,271.00	$16,140.61	($2,287.51)	($8,520.41)	($8,520.41)	($8,520.41)	$14,992.44	$14,849.01	($2,581.54)	($10,393.41)	($10,393.41)
Total Capital	$17,793.37	$34,064.37	$50,204.98	$47,917.47	$39,397.06	$30,876.65	$22,356.24	$37,348.68	$52,197.69	$49,616.15	$39,222.74	$28,829.33
Total Liabilities & Capital	$17,793.37	$34,064.37	$50,204.98	$47,917.47	$39,397.06	$30,876.65	$22,356.24	$37,348.68	$52,197.69	$49,616.15	$39,222.74	$28,829.33

A.C. Baker Apparel

	13-Jun	13-Jul	13-Aug	13-Sep	13-Oct	13-Nov	13-Dec	14-Jan	14-Feb	14-Mar	14-Apr	14-May
Assets												
Cash/Bank Account	$16,232.23	$35,830.19	$55,284.72	$52,782.81	$42,635.23	$32,487.65	$22,340.07	$41,712.55	$60,927.25	$58,072.51	$45,677.33	$33,282.15
Fixed Assets	$2,175.00	$2,175.00	$2,175.00	$2,175.00	$2,175.00	$2,175.00	$2,175.00	$2,175.00	$2,175.00	$2,175.00	$2,175.00	$2,175.00
Total assets	$18,407.23	$38,005.19	$57,459.72	$54,957.81	$44,810.23	$34,662.65	$24,515.07	$43,887.55	$63,102.25	$60,247.51	$47,852.33	$35,457.15
Liabilities & Capital												
Liabilities												
Loan Balance	0	0	0	0	0	0	0	0	0	0	0	0
Credit Cards	0	0	0	0	0	0	0	0	0	0	0	0
Total Liabilities	$0	$0	$0	$0	$0	$0	$0	$0	$0	$0	$0	$0
Capital												
Equity	$28,829.33	$18,407.23	$38,005.19	$57,459.72	$54,957.81	$44,810.23	$34,662.65	$24,515.07	$43,887.55	$63,102.25	$60,247.51	$47,852.33
Net Profit	($10,422.10)	$19,597.96	$19,454.53	($2,501.91)	($10,147.58)	($10,147.58)	($10,147.58)	$19,372.48	$19,214.70	($2,854.74)	($12,395.18)	($12,395.18)
Total Capital	$18,407.23	$38,005.19	$57,459.72	$54,957.81	$44,810.23	$34,662.65	$24,515.07	$43,887.55	$63,102.25	$60,247.51	$47,852.33	$35,457.15
Total Liabilities & Capital	$18,407.23	$38,005.19	$57,459.72	$54,957.81	$44,810.23	$34,662.65	$24,515.07	$43,887.55	$63,102.25	$60,247.51	$47,852.33	$35,457.15

A.C. Baker Apparel

	14-Jun	14-Jul	14-Aug	14-Sep	14-Oct	14-Nov	14-Dec	15-Jan	15-Feb	15-Mar	15-Apr	15-May
Assets												
Cash/Bank Account	$20,841.67	$44,425.26	$67,851.07	$65,102.17	$52,995.65	$40,889.13	$28,782.61	$52,523.56	$75,490.96	$72,142.06	$57,140.22	$42,138.38
Fixed Assets	$2,175.00	$2,175.00	$2,175.00	$2,175.00	$2,175.00	$2,175.00	$2,175.00	$2,175.00	$2,175.00	$2,175.00	$2,175.00	$2,175.00
Total assets	$23,016.67	$46,600.26	$70,026.07	$67,277.17	$55,170.65	$43,064.13	$30,957.61	$54,698.56	$77,665.96	$74,317.06	$59,315.22	$44,313.38
Liabilities & Capital												
Liabilities												
Loan Balance	0	0	0	0	0	0	0	0	0	0	0	0
Credit Cards	0	0	0	0	0	0	0	0	0	0	0	0
Total Liabilities	$0	$0	$0	$0	$0	$0	$0	$0	$0	$0	$0	$0
Capital												
Equity	$35,457.15	$23,016.67	$46,600.26	$70,026.07	$67,277.17	$55,170.65	$43,064.13	$30,957.61	$54,698.56	$77,665.96	$74,317.06	$59,315.22
Net Profit	($12,440.48)	$23,583.59	$23,425.81	($2,748.90)	($12,106.52)	($12,106.52)	($12,106.52)	$23,740.95	$22,967.40	($3,348.90)	($15,001.84)	($15,001.84)
Total Capital	$23,016.67	$46,600.26	$70,026.07	$67,277.17	$55,170.65	$43,064.13	$30,957.61	$54,698.56	$77,665.96	$74,317.06	$59,315.22	$44,313.38
Total Liabilities & Capital	$23,016.67	$46,600.26	$70,026.07	$67,277.17	$55,170.65	$43,064.13	$30,957.61	$54,698.56	$77,665.96	$74,317.06	$59,315.22	$44,313.38

Good Luck

I would like to take this opportunity to say good luck in your endeavors with your new business. I hope this book has been of assistance to you in organizing your thoughts and getting your business off the ground or to the next level. I would love to hear from you and how this book has helped out. I will be updating this book regularly and am open to your feedback.

I plan to update this book every 2-3 years and will be featuring a new case study for each book. If you are planning the launch of your business and you wish to be one of my case studies, please contact me. If you are chosen as one of my case studies, you will receive complimentary business coaching and assistance in your development.

You may send your commends by email to jennifer@lafashionresource.com.

About the Author

Jennifer Lynne Matthews attended Fashion Institute of Technology in New York City and graduated in 1999 with a specialization in intimate apparel. After working in the industry as a stylist and freelance designer, she launched her business, Porcelynne Lingerie in 2002. Jennifer has been consulting with small business startups for several years and is presently teaching pattern drafting, draping and sewing at the Fashion Institute of Design and Merchandising in Los Angeles.

Jennifer serves on the Advisory Board for the Innovative Fashion Council of San Francisco, the first incubator program in the Bay Area sponsored by the Mayor Office. Jennifer is an active member in the Los Angeles design community through many outlets, from sponsoring events, education and promotion of new talent.

Prior to opening East Bay Fashion Resource (now known as Los Angeles Fashion Resource) in 2007, Jennifer owned and operated an independent designer co-op in San Francisco's Mission District for 2 years. In early 2008, Jennifer closed the doors to Porcelynne Designer Collective to concentrate on her role as an educator.

Los Angeles Fashion Resource

The Los Angeles Fashion Resource (LAFR) is an independent resource structured to educate entrepreneurs on the business of fashion. Offering many services, from product development to business implementation, LAFR is now focusing on educational books for the fashion industry.

Originally founded in 2007 as the East Bay Fashion Resource, Jennifer Lynne Matthews and accessory designer Misty Rose wanted to provide a centralized resource for the San Francisco bay area design community. LAFR now offers business seminars to give designers, hobbyists or just an individual with an idea, an in depth look at design, finance and the legal aspects of running a fashion design business.

In 2009, the East Bay Fashion Resource relocated their offices to Los Angeles, CA and became Los Angeles Fashion Resource, although a presence in the San Francisco bay area remains constant. LAFR's focus is on their educational resources, books and business planning software. Although product development is still available, it is not their main focus.

Made in the USA
Lexington, KY
19 February 2013